Diversity and Equality

LAW AND SOCIETY

Law and Society Series
W. Wesley Pue, General Editor

The Law and Society Series explores law as a socially embedded phenomenon. It is premised on the understanding that the conventional division
of law from society creates false dichotomies in thinking, scholarship,
educational practice, and social life. Books in the series treat law and
society as mutually constitutive and seek to bridge scholarship emerging
from interdisciplinary engagement of law with disciplines such as politics,
social theory, history, political economy, and gender studies.

A list of the titles in this series appears at the end of this book.

Edited by Avigail Eisenberg

Diversity and Equality: The Changing Framework of Freedom in Canada

UBCPress · Vancouver · Toronto

15 14 13 12 11 10 09 08 07 06   5 4 3 2 1

Printed in Canada on ancient-forest-free paper (100% post-consumer recycled) that
is processed chlorine- and acid-free, with vegetable-based inks.

Library and Archives Canada Cataloguing in Publication

   Diversity and equality : the changing framework of freedom in Canada /
edited by Avigail Eisenberg.

(Law and society series, ISSN 1496-4953)
Includes bibliographical references and index.
ISBN-13: 978-0-7748-1239-9 (bound); 978-0-7748-1240-5 (pbk.)
ISBN-10: 0-7748-1239-7 (bound); 0-7748-1240-0 (pbk.)

   1. Minorities – Civil rights – Canada. 2. Minorities – Legal status, laws, etc. –
Canada. 3. Civil rights – Canada. I. Eisenberg, Avigail. II. Series

JC599.C3D59 2006   323.1'71   C2005-907853-7

Canadä

UBC Press gratefully acknowledges the financial support for our publishing
program of the Government of Canada through the Book Publishing Industry
Development Program (BPIDP), and of the Canada Council for the Arts, and
the British Columbia Arts Council.

The volume editor and publisher gratefully acknowledge the financial assistance
of the University of Victoria in support of publication.

UBC Press
The University of British Columbia
2029 West Mall
Vancouver, BC V6T 1Z2
604-822-5959 / Fax: 604-822-6083
www.ubcpress.ca

Contents

Acknowledgments / vii

Introduction: New Approaches to Freedom in Canada / 1
Avigail Eisenberg

1 Reconciling Struggles over the Recognition of Minorities:
Towards a Dialogical Approach / 15
James Tully

2 Reasoning about Identity: Canada's Distinctive Culture Test / 34
Avigail Eisenberg

3 The Imperative of "Culture" in a Colonial and *de facto* Polity / 54
Shauna McRanor

4 Culture as a Basic Human Right / 78
Cindy Holder

5 The Misuse of "Culture" by the Supreme Court of Canada / 97
Neil Vallance

6 Gender, Difference, and Anti-Essentialism: Towards a Feminist Response
to Cultural Claims in Law / 114
Maneesha Deckha

7 Interpreting the Identity Claims of Young Children / 134
Colin Macleod

8 Protecting Confessions of Faith and Securing Equality of Treatment
for Religious Minorities in Education / 153
John McLaren

9 The Irreducibly Religious Content of Freedom of Religion / 178
Jeremy Webber

Contributors / 201

Index / 203

Acknowledgments

I embarked on this project at the invitation of Conrad Brunk, the director of the Centre for Religion and Society at the University of Victoria, when I was fortunate enough to hold a fellowship at the centre in 2003. The project began as a conversation among colleagues and students who share similar research interests. My secret hope was that I could encourage each of them to think about the research question that I was working on at the time. They were, as ever, cooperative and enthusiastic. Eventually the centre organized a symposium on the topic of diversity and equality, which was a great success. I am grateful to Conrad Brunk and the centre for their encouragement and for providing me with a wonderful term away from my home department. I hope they will consider doing it again.

The University of Victoria was unfailingly supportive of this research project as well. My thanks to the Department of Political Science, the faculties of Social Sciences, Law, and Humanities, and the offices of the Vice President Academic and the VP Research for their contributions to this project.

The Social Sciences and Humanities Research Council of Canada (SSHRC) funded a research grant of which this book is a partial product. SSHRC also funded the work of many of the contributors to this collection through their own individual grants. My thanks to the council for this support.

I am also grateful to Cara McGregor for her excellent research assistance, which was crucial to bringing the different parts of this collection together.

Emily Andrew at UBC Press was supportive of my proposal to publish this collection from the start. I am grateful for her enthusiasm and for all the good things she is doing at UBC Press.

My greatest debt is to my colleagues at UVic, who were willing to contribute some of their best work to this collection and who continue to participate in colloquia and symposia and, generally, in creating an intellectually stimulating environment at the university.

Diversity and Equality

Introduction: New Approaches to Freedom in Canada

Avigail Eisenberg

When Thomas Berger published *Fragile Freedoms* in 1981, the *Canadian Charter of Rights and Freedoms* had yet to be passed into constitutional law, multiculturalism was mentioned in a celebratory sentence in a document that focused on bilingualism and biculturalism, and rights stood for treasured ideals meant to protect individual dissent from both the state and the thick political and religious norms of Canadian society. Berger contributed (and still contributes) to a progressive tradition of Canadian scholars and activists who saw Canada's small-c conservative politics in high tension with the liberal and social democratic values that shaped Anglo-American political and legal thought. Even without the Charter, the Aboriginal rights in section 35, or more robust multicultural principles to contend with, the themes and problems that Berger's book touched upon were the subjects of ongoing debates in Canadian society about minority rights. His chapter headings read like a survey of Canadian history: "Louis Riel and the New Nation"; "Mackenzie King and the Japanese Canadians"; "Jehovah's Witnesses: Church, State and Religious Dissent"; "Democracy and Terror: October, 1970"; "The Nishga Indians and Aboriginal Rights." Yet, perhaps surprisingly, the problems Berger explored twenty-five years ago are still the subject of debates about minority rights in Canada today – and, in some cases, involve exactly the same groups. For instance, Métis rights remain in a nascent state, urged on only slightly by a Supreme Court of Canada case in 2003 (*R. v. Powley*); redress is again used, and is still controversial, as a means to respond to past wrongs, including colonial policies that led to the abuse of Aboriginal children in residential schools; freedom and security are balanced according to the calibrated threat of terrorism, perhaps more today than ever before; and the rights of First Nations to self-determination have yet to be adequately defined or recognized within Canada and internationally.

While many of the key issues about minority rights in Canada remain the same, two important changes have occurred in the last twenty-five years.

First, the public engagement with rights discourse is broader and more active than it was twenty-five years ago, and this brings with it both benefits and burdens for guaranteeing minority rights or securing autonomy for national minorities and Aboriginal peoples. Second, the instruments by which rights are secured have changed, the most important change being the entrenchment of the Charter and of Aboriginal rights in 1982. But equally important are new conceptual tools and frameworks with which minority rights and autonomy are debated and discussed in the public sphere.

The changing needs and demands of immigrants, Aboriginal peoples, French and English linguistic minorities, and the Québécois have helped to reveal that, despite universalistic pretensions, rights assume a specific and particular shape within any historical or social context. These changes have had an enormous impact on the institutional context of and scholarly debates about rights, diversity, equality, autonomy, and self-determination. They are worth exploring further in order to gain a better sense of the questions and arguments addressed in this book, which examine the changing framework of freedom and diversity in democratic societies like Canada.

Public Engagement and Deliberation about Minorities

Even though the chapters in this book go well beyond Charter politics and jurisprudence, in most discussions in Canada about the rights of minorities, including national minorities and indigenous peoples, the Charter is an important starting place. This is because the entrenchment of the Charter in 1982 created a sea-change in Canadian politics, partly by introducing Canadians to their constitution and cultivating in them a proprietary attitude to it. Alan Cairns (1990) described this phenomenon as "constitutional minoritarianism" and showed, along with other scholars, who amended and challenged his views (see Abu-Laban and Nieguth 2000; Dobrowlosky 1999; James 2004; Trimble 1998), that the link between Canadian citizens and their constitution was not forged merely by civic pride in having entrenched a strong bill of rights, but was also the product of extensive political lobbying in the years preceding entrenchment. This lobbying turned out to be crucial to shaping a kind of citizen engagement with rights. The architects of the *Constitution Act, 1982*, including Pierre Elliot Trudeau, lobbied particular communities to "buy in" to the deal as a way to stymie provincial government opposition to it. Aboriginal peoples, feminist organizations, and cultural minorities were particular targets of this lobbying. In the end, these communities and networks could claim a role in shaping sections of the new *Constitution Act* in ways that, in some cases, strengthened the protection of rights for Aboriginal peoples, women, and ethnic minorities.

The activated and engaged citizenry that, at least outside Quebec, rallied around Trudeau's project, proved hostile to elite-driven attempts in 1987 to change the constitution to include the Meech Lake Accord. It also rejected the Charlottetown Accord amendments in 1992, and this time the reasons had less to do with the process, which, after all, included a nationwide referendum, than with substance. In Quebec, opponents argued that the Charlottetown Accord did not offer enough autonomy to their provincial government, while in the rest of Canada the concern was that the accord weakened individual Charter rights because it went too far in enhancing the autonomy and status of Quebec and Aboriginal peoples. One concern, which had considerable sway in the referendum campaign (see Johnston et al. 1996, 66 and 88), was that stronger and more comprehensive guarantees for minority autonomy and self-government would mean weaker and more vulnerable guarantees for individual rights and equality within those communities. This is a classic example of the purported tension between diversity and individual rights that informs many of the chapters in this book. It was also one of the first attempts by the Canadian public to think about rights in terms of the tension between diversity and equality.

What has become of this engaged citizenry, nurtured on Charter values and post-Charter constitutionalism, since the early 1990s? The answers to this question, so far, take us in two different directions. On one hand, this public has, unsurprisingly, organized itself into groups to advance particular interests using the rights available through the Charter and other legal instruments (Brodie 2002; Seidle 1993). Interest-group advocacy using the Charter has steadily increased since the 1980s, partly because many groups see the opportunity to advance their interests using the courts and the Charter rather than by engaging in political lobbying. Some critics have gone so far as to suggest that the Charter has spawned a network of activists and advocates – including liberals, feminists, gays and lesbians, ethnic minorities – within and outside public institutions, who together advance a somewhat coordinated agenda to define Canada's governing values according to their interests (see Knopf and Morton 2000). Other critics argue, to the contrary, that the Charter is deeply hostile to progressive politics and that the values it entrenches do more to secure property rights and ensure the domination of a corporate elite than to improve substantive equality or the quality of freedom that all Canadians ought to enjoy (see Anderson 2004; Bakan 1997; Petter 1987).

More generally, the Charter has, ironically, inspired concern that citizens' engagement with rights is steadily impoverishing Canadian democratic life as the real decisions about how the country is governed are taken to the courts and away from accountable democratic institutions. The evidence for this trend is mixed. Though participation rates in federal and provincial elections have declined since the 1980s, and more attention is devoted by news media to court decisions, it is nearly impossible to link Canada's new rights consciousness to a demise in electoral participation.

Lax participation in electoral politics is more likely related to the lacklustre nature of political parties and current leaders and their failure to attract young voters; to a change in political culture sometimes described as the "decline of deference" (Nevitte 1996); or to the growing crisis in civic literacy (Milner 2002). And in any given case, the interaction between the legislative and judicial spheres over rights-based policy decisions is highly complex at best (Hiebert 2002). As the controversy over same-sex marriage legislation in some Canadian provinces and the United States continues to illustrate, even court decisions that are widely viewed as protecting fundamental rights may not withstand direct and sustained opposition from a hostile legislative majority. For these reasons, it appears to be more likely that the Charter's role in discouraging electoral participation is minor.

On the other hand, in the last twenty-five years Canadians have seen the growth and development of a deliberative culture largely primed by the Charter's entrenchment, though engaged by issues that go well beyond Charter concerns. The Canadian public, or different "publics," are more involved now in shaping the basic principles of democratic governance and coexistence than ever before. Deliberative forums and assemblies have convened to propose fundamental reforms to democratic institutions. For example, in British Columbia, the Citizen's Assembly on Electoral Reform met to consider and suggest changes to the voting system for provincial elections. Deliberative models were used to reassess the role of religious values in public education in Quebec (see Quebec 1999), to shape complex and seemingly expert-intensive policy decisions on such issues as nuclear waste management (see Johnson 2005) or the use of genetic modification on animals and crops, and to work out the terms of coexistence between Aboriginal peoples and settler society through treaty negotiations (see Woolford 2005). What makes these forums deliberative rather than merely participatory is that instead of providing a setting in which people merely express their opinions, they are structured to encourage an exchange of reasons and perspectives and to foster learning among participants, which can become the basis of mutual understanding and ongoing dialogue.[1]

One could argue that a deliberative revolution of sorts has touched political theory and public institutions. Increasingly, all kinds of public institutions are assessed with a view to how well or poorly they facilitate deliberative values and deliberative solutions to conflicts, including those involving minorities. Some scholars have argued that even deep cultural conflicts are best addressed through deliberative forums and interaction rather than through institutions, such as courts, that apply legal rules and liberal principles from on high (see Deveaux 2003; Tully, this volume). In Chapter 1 of this book, James Tully explains why "struggles over recognition" are, by their nature, deliberative as they define and redefine ongoing relations among peoples.

In debates about deliberation in ethnically divided societies, the focal question is to what degree deliberative forums should be structured and supplemented by guarantees for individual rights – such as the right to sexual equality or to participate as an equal in decision making (see Deveaux 2005; Spinner-Halev 2001) – that may limit the terms on which dialogue proceeds or the sort of resolutions that may be reached regardless of what participants decide. In other debates, the focus is on what counts as a deliberative principle or forum in the first place. Even seemingly nondeliberative institutions, such as courts, engage in forms of dialogue that take place either within the institution (e.g., through judicial engagement with evidence, claimants, other judges, or other courts) or between institutions, especially between courts and parliament (see Hogg and Thornton 1999; Petter forthcoming).

The Terms and Tools to Discuss Diversity

The Charter, the equality rights in section 15, the rights of Aboriginal people in section 35, the *Multiculturalism Act,* the *Official Languages Act,* the Nisga'a Agreement, the *Declaration on the Rights of Indigenous Peoples,* Article 27 of the *International Covenant on Civil and Political Rights,* ILO Convention No. 169 ... These are just some of the many legal and political instruments invoked in debates about minority rights in Canada. The scholarship examining these legal instruments is vast, too vast to itemize here. Some of the chapters in this book contribute to this literature by looking at important changes in how the law protects diversity, equality, minority rights, and autonomy. For example, in Chapter 2, I examine the distinctive culture test developed by the Supreme Court of Canada; Cindy Holder, in Chapter 4, looks at the right to culture in international human rights documents; in Chapter 5, Neil Vallance shows how culture is now invoked by Canadian courts in relation to language and Aboriginal rights; and John McLaren traces substantive changes to freedom of religion in Canada in Chapter 8.

Equally profound are the changes within the last twenty-five years to the theoretical frameworks used in public debates about protecting minorities and recognizing self-determination. Two related conceptual frameworks, which both emerged in the late 1980s, established new ways of understanding relations among different peoples in diverse societies such as Canada. The first framework, developed in the work of Charles Taylor, framed struggles among peoples in terms of a "politics of recognition." According to Taylor (1992), a politics of recognition involves a dialogue and struggle with others over the terms on which we understand each other and thereby understand ourselves. Through recognition we form our identities in relation to others, while misrecognition, either by close others or public institutions, can distort and confine our conception of ourselves. The second framework, developed by Will Kymlicka, frames group relations in terms of a normative approach to multiculturalism. The aim of "multicultural citizenship" is to ensure that each individual has equal access to a secure cultural context and that possessing a minority cultural identity is viewed as conventional and fully accepted within mainstream society (Kymlicka 1995). With the guidance of these two frameworks, scholars, activists, and policy makers began to reassess the relations between minorities and majorities, between national groups, and between individuals and their communities in nearly every area of social, political, and economic life in Canada.

One of the first dimensions highlighted by these new frameworks was that different kinds of groups – e.g., minority nations, immigrant communities, religious communities, linguistic minorities, indigenous peoples – have different kinds of political needs and interests that affect the terms of recognition they seek or the kinds of cultural resources to which their access is impeded, with damaging consequences. In this sense, attention to "difference" rather than sameness, and a "politics of difference" rather than homogeneity, arose as an important way to approach the fair treatment of different peoples (Tully 1995; Young 1990). Taylor's work was particularly successful in pointing out the tension that exists between individualist and communitarian values that groups seek to protect, whereas Kymlicka's work highlighted the sense in which postwar approaches to liberal theory and rights were far too influenced by American political thought. Postwar liberalism was largely shaped by American experiences, especially the distinctive experience of slavery, discrimination, and exclusion suffered by African-Americans. American liberalism provided a poor set of resources for other minorities to draw on, especially immigrant communities, national minorities, and indigenous peoples, each of whom had different experiences of disadvantage and oppression.

A second dimension highlighted by the new frameworks was a tension between individualist and collectivist values. In the early Charter scholarship it was believed that, for good or ill, the Charter entrenched both individualist and collectivist values. Fundamental individual freedoms, such as freedom of speech, religion, association, and equality, had to be reconciled and balanced with rights that protected communities, such as Aboriginal people and linguistic minorities, and the multicultural nature of Canadian society. Some people believed that the tension between these two types of rights gave rise to a healthy and quintessentially Canadian understanding of liberal values. In traditional rights scholarship, this understanding had been expressed in terms of the balance between "dissent" and "social harmony" (see Borovoy 1988). Others argued that the coexistence of individual and collective rights was destructive to Canada's commitment to uphold liberal principles and placed our courts in the unacceptable position of making what amounted to political choices between irreconcilable values (Morton 1985).

But in relation to the rights of cultural, linguistic, and national minorities, the tensions between individual and collective values have given rise to a new and rich set of debates about diversity and equality. The main question that motivates the discussion in this book arises from these debates: How can measures to respect group membership, including autonomy, be reconciled with protections for other fundamental rights? This question gets to the core of what minority rights substantively amount to within any society or jurisdiction, even though it is only recently that questions about minority rights have been framed in this way. The extent to which minorities are protected can be gauged in terms of how public institutions weigh the claims of minorities against other values, like individual rights, children's rights, women's equality, and so forth. In fact, it is not clear that we can understand what any of these fundamental freedoms substantively amount to unless we understand how they are reconciled, in each place and each case of conflict, with the values of minority communities and the values of the broader community. For instance, the meaning of the right to freedom of religion in Canada can only be substantively understood by looking at how this right has been limited by public institutions (e.g., in relation to public property, in forums of public debate, in public schools), how it is accommodated (e.g., in relation to workplace safety, animal slaughter, gender discrimination in employment), and, as Jeremy Webber shows in Chapter 9, how the presumptions about freedom underpin the right.

The tension between diversity and equality has advanced scholarship perhaps most profoundly in the areas of gender equality and children's rights. This is partly because, in relation to gender equality, feminist thought focuses on addressing oppression, not simply ensuring that women are treated the same as men. This means that feminists have to find ways, some of which are discussed by Maneesha Deckha in Chapter 6, of responding to both the oppression of patriarchy as it is upheld by women's cultural, national, or religious communities, and the oppression that women experience as a result of racism, imperialism, and discrimination against their communities by mainstream society. In the case of children, as Colin Macleod shows in Chapter 7, the presence of individual autonomy and the individual's capacity (and right) to consent, which are central assumptions in liberal theories of cultural accommodation, are thrown into question when thinking about children's rights. Children do not choose their religious or ethnic communities, nor can they leave communities that oppress them, so liberalism's usual methods for sorting out how to protect individuals from oppressive communities are not available to children, and this leads to the question of how children's identities ought to be understood.

Finally, the tension between diversity and equality has attracted critical attention to the frameworks that Taylor and Kymlicka helped develop. Much of this criticism has followed from the explosion of theoretical research that draws on legal cases and political case studies in which diversity and equality, or cultural autonomy and individual rights, are seen to conflict. A key criticism made against the "politics of recognition" is that it works at cross-purposes with a politics of redistribution in the sense that political resources and activism devoted to enhancing recognition sap efforts to amend the unfair distribution of resources (see Fraser 1995). According to these critics, material inequality – including poverty, lack of education and employment opportunities, and inadequate health care and social benefits (which putatively don't count as matters of recognition) – has a more profound impact on the well-being of minorities than denials of recognition. A key criticism made against liberal multiculturalism is that cultural accommodation is insufficiently radical to deal with the aftermath of colonialism and with the kind of oppression that many ethnic groups and indigenous peoples face. These critics, including Shauna McRanor in Chapter 3, argue that multiculturalism facilitates state power because its main project is to set out the terms by which the state can manage ethnic minorities and indigenous peoples without diminishing its authority or power (also see Day 2002; Dhamoon 2005; Kernerman 2005). They also argue, as do many of the contributors to this book, that the interpretation and understanding of culture are central components for sorting out conflicts among peoples using the frameworks of multiculturalism. Yet culture is also a notoriously ambiguous concept, and most attempts by public institutions, like courts, to define or assess cultures are destined to be controversial.

The tension between cultural autonomy and individual rights is an aspect of many legal cases and political controversies that involve minorities. No one thinks that a single resolution to this tension exists. The relationship between diversity and equality is, in this sense, a good example of why the terms on which people interact and deliberate with each other in diverse societies is the subject of ongoing dialogue and inevitable change. Yet amid this discussion and change, citizens demand that public institutions apply nonarbitrary and fair methods to resolve conflicts between protecting minorities and protecting individual rights and equality. Debates about the meaning and interpretation of culture, what it protects, how pluralistic it is, and its relation to individual autonomy, identity, recognition, and freedom are central components of the project to devise methods of inquiry that treat minorities fairly. The new legal instruments and conceptual frameworks examined in this book are some of the tools with which this sort of exploration takes place.

Themes and Approaches
The particular meaning of any right is bound to the social and political debates, negotiations, and commitments that inform the history of the country.

To understand our rights tradition in any other way is to understand it un-hinged from the particular groups and precise protections, including the limits and gaps in these protections, that have been either the subject of intense debate (such as the rights of racial minorities) or, until recently, the subject of little debate at all (such as the rights of gays and lesbians). The meaning of rights in Canada, and the character of the freedom minorities enjoy relative to majorities, is bound to this history and to the needs and demands of the particular groups that have been active participants in this history.

This is another way of saying that rights traditions do not exist apart from the cultural and historical debates, negotiations, and commitments among particular peoples. All rights traditions are informed by concrete attempts to accommodate individuals, minorities, and majorities. This does not mean that all peoples in Canada have been accommodated fairly. To the contrary, the meaning of rights in Canada is also informed by the gaps in rights protection. For instance, approaches that only guarantee rights to each individual are now generally viewed as naïve or neglectful of commu-nities whose central values or fragile status require communal rights for protection. The meaning of rights is also informed by the particular groups that have been treated unfairly. For example, the meaning of freedom of religion was historically shaped by relations between Catholics and Protes-tants, and failed to comprehend the sort of disadvantages faced by Jehovah's Witnesses in the 1950s, by Sikhs in the 1990s, or by Muslims today. And finally, the meaning of rights was in part shaped by the attempts made to balance the protection of minority communities with the fair treatment of women and children within these communities. To understand what free-dom of religion or cultural rights mean in Canada involves understanding how these kinds of conflicts have been dealt with historically. All rights traditions are tied to the particular character of the debates in which they have been historically implicated. And the history to which they are tied is messy, full of different ideas and ideals of accommodation and autonomy, some of which, today, are viewed as unjust and biased, and others of which addressed one problem but created many others.

This book does not aim to survey this history, although several contribu-tors provide useful historical accounts that help to explain why new ap-proaches are needed. The main aim is to explore new approaches to address the goals and problems associated with the accommodation of cultural, religious, and national minorities in Canada. The volume brings together nine scholars from philosophy, law, politics, and anthropology whose work critically examines accommodation strategies and means of mutual recog-nition. Taken together, four themes inform their contributions and repre-sent four areas in which the accommodation or autonomy of minorities is the subject of particularly intense debate in Canada.

The first theme is the tension between, on the one hand, recognizing the self-determination of Aboriginal people and, on the other hand, guaranteeing rights that carry with them homogenizing effects that Aboriginal peoples rightly resist. James Tully provides a leading account of the nature of different kinds of struggles over recognition that have arisen in the last forty years. He shows that these struggles engage the norms of recognition themselves and are dialogical, enduring, and imperfect. His chapter provides the most compelling account to date of why institutions must be designed to facilitate rather than impede struggles over recognition, which requires them to understand and facilitate "dialogical civic freedom."

As one of the few theorists writing today who defends the assessment of minority identities by public institution like courts, I argue, in Chapter 2, that assessing the claims groups advance about their identity is a conventional part of democratic politics and one that often cannot be avoided in diverse communities. Rather than trying to excise identity from democratic politics, public institutions must develop fair and transparent criteria to guide their assessments of identity. In this context, I critically examine the distinctive culture test developed by the Supreme Court of Canada to see how it fares as such a guide.

In Chapter 3, Shauna McRanor provides one of the most powerful accounts of why cultural accommodation strategies are unjust to Aboriginal peoples. What McRanor calls "liberal culturalism" depoliticizes culture as a means to accommodate it. She argues that culture is irrevocably political in nature, and cultural accommodation is thereby irrevocably tied to the distribution of power. Accommodation strategies end up being a means to undermine rather than enhance or protect the freedom of indigenous peoples.

The second theme focuses more acutely on the tensions between protecting culture and protecting rights. Cindy Holder, in Chapter 4, takes the debate to the international level and shows that the concept of cultural rights, although invoked throughout international legal debates, is neither used nor understood uniformly. Holder's analysis cuts through these muddy waters and proposes that culture be interpreted as an activity to which all people ought to have access and thereby a basic right. The most difficult problems that plague "cultural rights theory" cease to be so confounding using this innovative solution.

Neil Vallance provides, in Chapter 5, one of the strongest arguments against the concept of culture being used by the courts and in legal cases. With the eye of an anthropologist and a lawyer, Vallance compares cases involving different minorities that show the Supreme Court applies the term "culture" inconsistently and in a manner that potentially restricts the rights of Aboriginal peoples. Vallance argues that the court's inconsistency and lack of critical awareness render discussion of culture ill-suited to the reification of legal processes and decisions.

The third theme is the conflict between the accommodation of minorities and protection of the rights of vulnerable members within minority communities. In Chapter 6, Maneesha Deckha offers the most comprehensive survey to date of ethical feminism's resources for addressing problems of cultural and sexual justice. Deckha argues that, of the many approaches, a "differentiated" approach to culture is able to avoid the unjust subordination of minorities and women while also ensuring that discrimination and repression of dissent are not the prices paid by some for the cultural protection enjoyed by others.

Colin Macleod's scholarship on children's rights focuses, in Chapter 7, on the tensions between adults' interests in securing cultural and religious accommodation, and children's interests in developing and protecting their own identities, as well as in securing protection for their basic welfare interests including access to resources and opportunities. Macleod's work goes further than any other scholarship in political philosophy to develop a framework that provides a means to understanding the distinctive interests of adults and children in relation to cultural accommodation.

For the fourth theme, two chapters explore and shape the direction of new approaches to protecting religious minorities in Canada. John McLaren's authoritative account in Chapter 8 traces the history, character, and uneven protection of freedom of religion in Canada. He argues for a new approach to this right, in which judges would deal head-on and openly with the faith-based reasons religious communities wish to follow the practices they do. This kind of open and respectful dialogue, though seemingly bold, is already evident, though inconsistently so, in the approach to religious freedom adopted by Canadian courts.

In Chapter 9, Jeremy Webber also explores how freedom of religion has been interpreted in Canadian jurisprudence, and argues, in what is certainly the most thoughtful reflection written on the philosophical underpinnings of this right in Canada, that religious freedom has an irreducible religious content. The right to freedom of religion is not neutral between religious and secular beliefs, but is founded on a distinctive valuing of religious belief. Freedom of religion therefore involves a richer set of moral choices than approaches to this right have thus far supposed, and these choices have implications for how the freedom is interpreted and, more broadly, for how religious diversity is accommodated in public life.

Readers will note that much ground is covered in this rich collection of work. But the philosophical approach here holds that all conversations are local and all are anchored in a specific set of examples, debates, and problems. This collection is no exception. Rather than pretend that the authors here cover the gamut and represent the whole state of scholarship on minorities and Aboriginal rights in Canada, I would point out just the opposite. This book does not reflect, nor does it aim to reflect, the state of the debates about minorities or indigenous peoples in Canada. A collection that did engage in such an ambitious project would be plagued by what in my mind are insurmountable problems related to what is included and excluded, what is marginalized and what is represented as central. Too often in scholarship that strives for this level of generality, the reader is offered a product that either surveys the landscape in terms of regional problems (a common Canadian approach that only serves to underline the implicit fact that Toronto, Montreal, and Vancouver dominate popular concerns about minorities) or offers an ideological survey of sorts (thus tipping the metaphorical hat to the liberal values that implicitly set the standard from which all discussions deviate).

The enthusiasm for this book is founded largely in its partiality and local roots. The perspectives and preoccupations of the authors are both broad and narrow. The concerns of these scholars tend to be focused on questions that engage religious freedom and indigenous rights, feminism, children's rights, and the problems of racism. Each of these themes not only describes the contribution of each author but also informs the pieces implicitly. It is with an eye on the same sorts of problems, and on gaps with respect to others, that the perspectives of these authors come alive. This is not to suggest that the gaps are not true gaps or that their absence doesn't skew the conversation. These are certainly relevant concerns. But they are the sort of concerns that we should have about all conversations, whether they are in Nanaimo or Toronto. They are local and incomplete.

Note

1 The political theory and empirical research on deliberative democracy is extensive. Some of the best studies include Ackerman and Fishkin (2004); Bohman (1996); Chambers (2001); Deveaux (2003); Tully (1995); and Warren (2004).

References

Books, Articles, and Public Documents

Abu-Laban, Yasmeen, and Tim Nieguth. 2000. Reconsidering the Constitution, Minorities and Politics in Canada. *Canadian Journal of Political Science* 33(3):465-98.

Ackerman, Bruce, and James S. Fishkin. 2004. *Deliberation Day.* New Haven, CT, and London: Yale University Press.

Anderson, Gavin. 2004. Social Democracy and the Limits of Rights Constitutionalism. *Canadian Journal of Law and Jurisprudence* 27(1):31-59.

Bakan, Joel. 1997. *Just Words: Constitutional Rights and Social Wrongs.* Toronto: University of Toronto Press.

Berger, Thomas R. 1981. *Fragile Freedoms: Human Rights and Dissent in Canada.* Toronto and Vancouver: Clarke, Irwin and Co.

Bohman, James. 1996. *Public Deliberation: Pluralism, Complexity, and Democracy.* Cambridge, MA: MIT Press.

Borovoy, A. Alan. 1988. *When Freedoms Collide.* Toronto: Lester and Orpen Dennys.

Brodie, Ian. 2002. *Friends of the Court.* Albany, NY: SUNY Press.

Cairns, Alan C. 1990. Constitutional Minoritarianism in Canada. In *Canada: The State of the Federation,* ed. Ronald L. Watts and Douglas M. Brown, 71-96. Kingston, ON: Institute of Intergovernmental Relations.

Canadian Charter of Rights and Freedoms, Part I of the *Constitution Act, 1982,* being Schedule B to the *Canada Act 1982* (U.K.), 1982, c. 11.

Chambers, Simone. 2001. Constitutional Referendum and Democratic Deliberation. In *Referendum Democracy: Citizens, Elites and Deliberation in Referendum Campaigns,* ed. Matthew Mendelsohn and Andrew Parkin, 220-33. London, UK: Palgrave Macmillan.

Day, Richard F. 2002. *Multiculturalism and the History of Canadian Diversity.* Toronto: University of Toronto Press.

Deveaux, Monique. 2003. A Deliberative Approach to Conflicts of Culture. *Political Theory* 31(6):780-807.

–. 2005. A Deliberative Approach to Conflicts of Culture: The Litmus Test of Gender. In *Minorities Within Minorities: Diversity, Rights and Equality,* ed. Avigail Eisenberg and Jeff Spinner-Halev, 340-62. Cambridge: Cambridge University Press.

Dhamoon, Rita. 2005. Rethinking Culture and Cultural: The Politics of Meaning-Making. PhD diss., University of British Columbia.

Dobrowolsky, Alexandra. 1999. *The Politics of Pragmatism: Women, Representation and Constitutionalism in Canada.* Don Mills, ON: Oxford University Press.

Fraser, Nancy. 1995. From Redistribution to Recognition? Dilemmas of Justice in a "Postsocialist" Age. *New Left Review* 212:68-93.

Hiebert, Janet. 2002. *Charter Conflicts: What Is Parliament's Role?* Kingston and Montreal: McGill-Queen's University Press.

Hogg, Peter W., and Allison A. Thornton. 1999. The Charter Dialogue Between Courts and Legislatures. *Policy Options* (April):19-22.

James, Matt. 2004. The Politics of Honourable Constitutional Inclusion and the Citizens' Constitution Theory. In *Insiders and Outsiders: Alan Cairns and the Reshaping of Canadian Citizenship,* ed. Gerald Kernerman and Philip Resnick, 132-47. Vancouver: UBC Press.

Johnson, Genevieve. 2005. The Discourse of Dèmocracy: The Democratic Evolution of Canadian Nuclear Waste Management Policy. Unpublished manuscript.

Johnston, Richard, André Blais, Elisabeth Gidengil, and Neil Nevitte. 1996. *The Challenge of Direct Democracy: The 1992 Canadian Referendum.* Kingston and Montreal: McGill-Queen's University Press.

Kernerman, Gerald. 2005. *Multicultural Nationalism: Civilizing Difference, Constituting Community.* Vancouver: UBC Press.

Knopf, Rainer, and F.L. Morton. 2000. *The Charter Revolution and the Court Party.* Peterborough, ON: Broadview Press.

Kymlicka, Will. 1995. *Multicultural Citizenship.* Oxford: Oxford University Press.

Milner, Henry. 2002. *Civic Literacy: How Informed Citizens Make Democracy Work.* Vancouver: UBC Press.

Morton, F.L. 1985. Group Rights Versus Individual Rights in the Charter: The Special Cases of Natives and the Québécois. In *Minorities and the Canadian State,* ed. Neil Nevitte and Allan Kornberg, 71-84. Oakville, ON: Mosaic Press.

Nevitte, Neil. 1996. *The Decline of Deference.* Peterborough, ON: Broadview Press.

Petter, Andrew. 1987. Immaculate Deception: The Charter's Hidden Agenda. *The Advocate* 45:857-68.

–. Forthcoming. Looks Who's Talking Now: Dialogue Theory and the Return to Democracy. In *The Role of Legislatures in the Constitutional State,* ed. Richard Bauman and Tsvi Kahana. New York: Cambridge University Press.

Quebec. 1999. *Religion in Secular Schools: A New Perspective for Quebec – Report of the Task Force on the Place of Religion in Schools in Quebec.* Québec: Ministère de l'Éducation.

Seidle, F. Leslie. 1993. *Equity and Community: The Charter, Interest Group Advocacy, and Representation.* Kingston and Montreal: McGill-Queen's University Press.

Spinner-Halev, Jeff. 2001. Feminism, Multiculturalism, Oppression and the State. *Ethics* 112(1):84-113.

Taylor, Charles. 1992. The Politics of Recognition. In *Multiculturalism and the "Politics of Recognition,"* ed. Amy Gutmann, 25-73. Princeton, NJ: Princeton University Press.

Trimble, Linda. 1998. Good Enough Citizens: Canadian Women and Representation in Constitutional Deliberations. *International Journal of Canadian Studies* 17:131-56.

Tully, James. 1995. *Strange Multiplicity: Constitutionalism in an Age of Diversity.* Cambridge: Cambridge University Press.

Warren, Mark E. 2004. What Can Democratic Participation Mean Today? In *Representation and Democratic Theory,* ed. David Laycock, 197-219. Vancouver: UBC Press.

Woolford, Andrew. 2005. *Between Justice and Certainty: Treaty Making in British Columbia.* Vancouver: UBC Press.

Young, Iris Marion. 1990. *Justice and the Politics of Difference.* Princeton, NJ: Princeton University Press.

Case

R. v. Powley, [2003] 2 S.C.R. 207.

1

Reconciling Struggles over the Recognition of Minorities: Towards a Dialogical Approach

James Tully

The contributors to this volume were asked to respond to the following question:

How can measures to protect the freedom of cultural, linguistic, national, and religious minorities be reconciled with measures to protect other fundamental rights when conflicts between the two arise? This question has been historically important in many nations and in the context of developing doctrines of religious freedom, multiculturalism, federalism, and Aboriginal self-determination and self-government. The need to develop a method of resolving such conflicts will continue to grow as many nations become more diverse through immigration, and more committed to decolonization and to recognizing distinctive aspirations of cultural groups.

Over the last forty years, the volatile conflicts among individuals, minorities, and majorities over these diverse concerns have been characterized as "struggles over recognition." Various solutions for reconciling these struggles have been presented by the individuals and groups involved and by decolonization and anti-imperialism spokespersons, indigenous peoples, policy communities, nongovernmental organizations, courts, parliaments, states, international organizations, and legal and political theorists. This chapter is not another solution in the form of the definitive theory of recognition of individuals and groups or the definitive theory of dispute reconciliation procedures. Rather, it is a reflection on aspects of the field of both struggles for and against recognition of various kinds in practice and in the theoretical literature that has developed in response to these local and global conflicts over the last forty years.

If we stand back and reflect on the recent history of the practice and theory of struggles over recognition, we can see a certain trend. It is not the only trend nor the dominant one, but it is significant. It can be seen as a learning process undergone to some extent by the agents involved – by citizens engaged in the conflicts on the ground, policy communities in various orders of government, nongovernmental organizations, state and international courts, and legal and political theorists. The aim of this chapter is not only to describe the trend but also to characterize it in such a way that we can learn from it. This historical and critical reflection on the recent successes and failures in the recognition of minorities can teach us a new orientation to reconcile clashes over recognition in the future, an orientation that promises to bring peace rather than conflict to the twenty-first century. This is an orientation towards what I will call the *dialogical civic freedom* of citizens engaged in and affected by struggles over recognition.

This chapter explores the learning process in five steps. The first sets out the defining features of struggles over recognition. The second summarizes the dominant way in which these conflicts have been approached in practice and theory – the monological and finality orientation – and the problems with this approach. The third step introduces the dialogical approach and the reasons for it. The transition from the ideal of reaching a final consensus to the reality of irreducible reasonable disagreement is examined in the fourth step, while the fifth gathers these trends together in defence of an orientation grounded in dialogical civic freedom to reconcile struggles over recognition. This orientation consists in a turn to studying the activities of struggling for and against a norm of recognition, rather than focusing on the final resolution of these struggles, as the site of civic freedom and citizen identity-formation. For if the five steps in this trend are significant and enduring, it is unlikely that there will be definitive reconciliations of struggles over recognition. The struggles are likely to be enduring features of culturally diverse political and legal associations. The central questions then become, first, how do we develop institutions that are always open to the partners in practices of governance to call into question and renegotiate freely the always less-than-perfect norms of mutual recognition to which they are subject, with a minimum of exclusion and assimilation, and to be able to negotiate reasonably fairly without recourse to force, violence, and war? Yet, second, how do we ensure that participation in these open institutions of negotiation (institutions whose norms of recognition must also be open to negotiation) helps generate a sense of attachment to the system of governance under dispute, even among those who do not always achieve the recognition they seek? A short discussion of the reciprocal relationship between academic research and struggles on the ground that follows from this approach rounds off the chapter.[1]

What Are Struggles over Recognition?

The wide variety of conflicts over the appropriate forms of the recognition of minorities vis-à-vis individuals (outside as well as inside the minority in question) and other minorities and majorities have come to be characterized as "struggles over recognition." The first reason for this characterization is that such conflicts are *not* seen as the struggle of one minority for recognition in relation to other actors who are independent of, unaffected by, and neutral with respect to the form of recognition that the minority seeks. Rather, a struggle for recognition of a "minority" always calls into question and (if successful) modifies, often in complex ways, the existing forms of recognition of the other members of the system of government of which the minority is a member. No members (including parliaments, courts, and states) transcend the field of struggle. The second reason is that the number of other members affected is almost always more than one, so these struggles cannot, except in the most simplified cases, be conceptualized as two-member struggles between self and other, minority and majority, minority and the state, or individual and collective, as an older tradition of reflection on struggles over recognition, from Kant and Hegel to Sartre and Fanon, tended to assume. That is, struggles over recognition are relational and mutual rather than independent, and they are multiple rather than dyadic. In short, they are struggles "over" recognition, not simply "for" recognition.

The most perspicuous way to conceptualize these first two features is to say that struggles over recognition are struggles over the intersubjective "norms" (laws, rules, conventions, or customs) under which the members of any system of government recognize each other *as* members and coordinate their interaction. Hence, struggles over recognition are, in Habermas' helpful phrase, struggles over the prevailing "intersubjective norms of mutual recognition" through which the members (individuals and groups under various descriptions) of any system of action coordination (or practice of governance) are recognized and governed (1998, 203-38). Let us call these "norms of mutual recognition" and draw out those features that are relevant for the argument at hand.

Norms of mutual recognition are a constitutive feature of any system of rule-governed cooperation, not just of formal political systems such as municipalities, First Nations, provinces, states, supranational political associations, and the United Nations. Classrooms, schools, voluntary organizations, corporations, markets, international human rights regimes, and other systems of action coordination have norms or rules by which the partners recognize each other and cooperate. Acting in accordance with the norms under which the members (individuals and groups) recognize each other, and to which they are subject in their cooperative activities, gives the members their characteristic forms of relational subjectivity or "identity" *as* members, for example, as "subjects" of such and such a government. There are three main axes of the forms of subjectivity of members (as members): (1) members' characteristic discursive forms of self-awareness or self-consciousness, (2) their characteristic nondiscursive forms of conduct in the cooperative system, and (3) their access to resources through the rights and entitlements attached to the identity under which they are recognized. Norms always normalize or subjectify to varying degrees, as Weber and Foucault have famously shown. Due to the normalizing and relational character of the norms, a conflict that modifies the way one member is recognized necessarily alters the forms of recognition, types of subjectivity, modes of cooperation, and access to resources of all other members in the system of cooperation to some extent.

Further, there are several norms of mutual recognition to which we are subject as members of various associations. While the system of legal rules is the most obvious example, norms can also be cultural, religious, familial, educational, class, medical, corporate, customary, covert, and so on. Individuals are usually subject to many and overlapping norms of mutual recognition and corresponding identities: landed immigrant, individual, male, female, transsexual, family member, member of this or that religion or culture, Vancouver Islander, British Columbian, westerner, indigenous or non-indigenous, union member, retiree, gay or heterosexual, Canadian, and so on. They can be imposed and enforced by a wide variety of informal and formal institutions in an equally wide variety of ways. In self-governing associations, the members impose and modify the norms themselves or through their representatives. In other forms of association, norms are imposed nondemocratically, behind the backs of the members, as in markets and other complex functional systems, or covertly, as in deeply sedimented racist and sexist customary norms. Some norms of mutual recognition are egalitarian, at least in theory, such as individual citizenship; others hierarchical, such as the elaborate ranks in educational systems, bureaucracies, corporations, or the recognition of linguistic groups; some are fixed and relatively immovable systems of domination; others more flexible and open to modification by those subject to them.

A struggle over recognition erupts whenever a prevailing norm of mutual recognition is experienced as intolerable by (some of) the individual or collective agents subject to it. They challenge it and it becomes the site of contestation and struggle. This is the second quality of norms. Although acting in accord with a norm subjectifies or normalizes the actors, it is also possible for those individuals and groups subject to a set of norms to turn against them, to call a norm into question, to challenge its validity, and to struggle to negotiate its modification (in various ways) with the other members who hold it in place, except in extreme cases of total domination. Accordingly, norms are said to have a dual quality: they are both normalizing and normative.[2]

The reasons for a challenge, as we shall see, can be various: because, for example, the prevailing norm fails to recognize individuals or groups at all (exclusion), or it misrecognizes them (as, say, a band rather than a people, a

minority rather than a nation, a religious minority rather than a civilization), or it is imposed undemocratically, or, more recently, it recognizes
them and induces them to perform and affirm their identity, yet in an assimilative, folkloric, or manipulative way (as in government and corporate
strategies to market diversity). Finally, a "struggle" can also take a variety of
forms: the alteration of customary understanding of interrelated selves and
others through the open-ended narrativity of everyday dialogue (for example, the way we recognize each other changes over the course of interaction); a relatively voluntary negotiation and amendment of the contested
norm of mutual recognition by the partners subject to it, in the best of
circumstances; overt compliance with an imposed and oppressive norm,
coupled with covert thoughts and acts of minute resistance, as in residential schools and other total institutions; major legal, political, and constitutional negotiations through legislatures, courts, and referenda; campaigns
of civil disobedience; and more violent forms of armed struggle, such as
civil wars, anti-imperialist wars of decolonization and self-determination,
and the wide variety of intermediate ethnic, cultural, and civilizational conflicts today.

Let this stand as a compressed introduction to the idea of struggles over
recognition as struggles over the existing intersubjective norms of mutual
recognition in a system of governance; that is, as struggles over the relationships of communication and power through which we are governed. Other
features will be introduced in the following sections. I hope to show that
this intersubjective and relational way of approaching conflicts over the
recognition and accommodation of individuals and groups enables us to
see more clearly the trends and learning processes that the field has undergone over the last several decades.

The Monological and Finality Orientation

I will begin by describing the predominant early orientation to struggles
over the recognition of multicultural minorities, nations within existing
constitutional states (multinationalism), and indigenous peoples. In this
approach, theorists, courts, and policy makers looked for a definitive and
final solution to these struggles. They did this by trying to work out the
theory, legal rules, or policy of the just norms of mutual recognition for
these kinds of groups vis-à-vis the recognition; of individuals as free and
equal. In the first phase this often involved simply reasserting the two dominant forms of legal and political recognition; that is, difference-blind liberalism or uniform nationalism. But since many of the struggles over
multicultural, multinational, and indigenous recognition are precisely
against the assimilative injustices of these policies of recognition and governance, the result was to increase rather than resolve the conflicts.

In response to the failure of attempts to deny or subordinate the recognition of minorities relative to recognizing individual equality (understood as treating each individual identically) and the uniformity of the nation, many theorists, courts, and policy makers within this orientation accepted the legitimacy of minority recognition and, therefore, the need to reconcile it with the freedom and equality of individuals. They tried to do this by working out theories and policies of the just norms for the mutual recognition of types of minorities and individuals; that is, theories and policies of minority rights. Despite the benefits of this second phase of liberal and nationalist approaches to minority recognition, these attempts generated further problems in theory and practice. The most powerful and vocal minorities gained public recognition at the expense of the least powerful and most oppressed; the rights tended to freeze the minority in a specific configuration of recognition; they failed to protect minorities within the groups who gained recognition; and they did little to develop a sense of attachment to the larger cooperative association among the members of minorities, occasionally increasing fragmentation and secession (the problem they were supposed to solve). The response to these problems, in turn, has been a kind of unresolved oscillation in theory and practice between the two phases.[3]

In retrospect, we can now see that there are two problematic features of this early orientation in both its phases. First, the solutions are handed down to the members from on high, from theorists, courts, or policy makers, rather than passed through the democratic will-formation of those who are subject to them. They are thus experienced as imposed rather than self-imposed. The second problem is the assumption that there are definitive and final solutions to struggles over recognition in theory and practice. The norms of mutual recognition handed down are thus experienced as a "straight jacket."[4] Let's call these the monological and finality presumptions respectively and take up each in turn.

From Monologue to Dialogue

The first step in transforming the way we think about conflicts over recognition is to move from the presumption that there can be monological solutions, handed down by a theorist, court, or policy community, to the approach that any resolution has to be worked out as far as possible by means of dialogues among those who are subject to the contested norm of mutual recognition. Reconciliation should be dialogical. This important step is expressed in the widespread turn to varieties of deliberative democracy in theory and policy and in the astonishing proliferation of democratic procedures of dispute resolution in all areas of contemporary societies, from the resolution of local conflicts over recognition in equity policies through to global conflicts over the recognition of suppressed minorities, nations, and international human rights, and on to the United Nations' commitment to reconciling civilizational conflicts through global dialogue.

What are the main reasons for this first step, for the hypothesis that an acceptable norm of mutual recognition should be worked out as far as possible by those who are subject to it through some form of the exchange of reasons in negotiation, deliberation, bargaining, and other forms of dialogue? I think there are four main considerations that have moved many theorists, courts, policy makers, and citizens to take this dialogical turn.

First, in recent decades there has been a deepening commitment to democracy in both theory and practice, not in the institutionalized, representative majority rule sense, but in the more direct sense of popular sovereignty, civic participation, and people "having a say" over the norms to which they are subject. The old principle of *quod omnes tangit* (What touches all must be approved by all) has reappeared in dialogical form, as, for example, in Habermas' proposed formulation D: "Only those norms can claim to be valid that meet (or could meet) with the approval of all affected in their capacity as participants in a practical discourse" (1995, 93). This direct democratic principle is now said to be equal in status to the liberal principle of the rule of law. If the rule of law is imposed without passing through a practical discourse of those affected by it, it is now commonly said to be illegitimate in virtue of a democratic deficit. A legitimate rule or norm of law must also be a rule "of and by the people." Even liberalism and constitutionalism, which used to be thought of in terms of a set of basic principles (rules) that limit democracy from the outside, have been reconceived around the ideal of the exchange of public reasons among free and equal citizens who work up the principles themselves.[5]

The second consideration is a condition of the acceptability of a norm of mutual recognition. The identities under which individuals and groups are reciprocally recognized in any form of cooperation actually count as *their* identities only if they can accept them from a first-person perspective; that is, if they can acknowledge them as their own. If an elite determines them, they are experienced as imposed and alien. It follows that the persons who bear the identities need to have some sort of say over their formulation, or over the selection of trusted representatives who negotiate for them, if they are not to be alienated from the outcome. Due to the relational character of recognition, this consideration holds not only for the members of the minority seeking recognition but also for the other affected members of the system of governance. Thus, to ensure that a new norm of mutual recognition is acceptable by all, it needs to pass through an inclusive dialogue or what we should call a "multilogue." If all affected are not in on the exchange of reasons, they will not understand why the agreement was reached, what were the reasons for the demands of others that helped shape the agreement, why their own negotiators seemed to moderate their demands, and so on. The agreed-upon norm of mutual recognition would thus seem like a sell-out or an unnecessary compromise, and would therefore be seen or felt as imposed and unacceptable.

The third reason relates to an important characteristic of the identities recognized under any norm. Identities, and thus acceptable forms of recognition and modes of cooperation with others, are partly dependent on, and constituted by, the dialogical exchange of reasons over them. This is the power of the exchange of reasons. The forms of recognition that individuals and groups struggle for are articulated, discussed, altered, reinterpreted, and renegotiated in the course of the struggle. They do not pre-exist their articulation and negotiation in some unmediated or ascriptive pre-dialogue realm. For example, the self-understanding of men and women, Muslim and Christian, French and English, and indigenous and non-indigenous has changed enormously over the last decades of conflict, negotiation, and discussion because engagement in the give-and-take of reasons for and against different proposed norms of mutual recognition from the different perspectives of the participants changes (and often transforms) the self-understanding of the interlocutors by breaking down the unexamined group prejudices, stereotypes, and blind spots that they bring to the dialogue.

Thus, our understanding of who we are, of the partners with whom we are constrained to cooperate, and hence of the acceptable norms of mutual recognition change in the course of the dialogue. Accordingly, the members need to be in on the webs of interlocution of the struggle in order to go through these changes in self-understanding and other-understanding or they will literally not be able to identify with the norm of recognition that others, who have gone through the negotiations, find acceptable (Young 1997, 38-74; 2000, 52-120).

A fourth, pragmatic consideration is that the only fairly reliable and effective way to work up a norm of mutual recognition that does justice to the diversity and changeability of the members of contemporary political associations is to ensure that all affected have an open and effective say in the deliberations and formulations. A lone theorist, an elite court, or a distant ministry are, in contrast, probably least able to meet this requirement and more likely to universalize their own partial perspective or to work with unexamined stereotypes.

For example, struggles over recognition were initially simply taken to be conflicts between particular cultural, religious, linguistic, indigenous, and other forms of "minority diversity" and the impartial and universal "equality" of individuals. But this was based on a lack of understanding of many of the claims classified under "diversity." Many of the claims that indigenous peoples are actually making around the world are not claims for minority status, nor are they primarily based on culture or diversity. They are claims to be recognized as "peoples" with the "universal" right of self-determination, based on prior occupancy and sovereignty, and thus to be recognized as "equal" in status to other "peoples" under international law. As a result, the monological orientation, with its preset categories of recognition, misconstrued the nature of the demands.[6]

Another example is the demand for recognition of a minority language, culture, or religion. Often the demand is not for the recognition of some kind of particular diversity that conflicts with impartial equality, but for another kind of equality. In Canada, for example, the prevailing norm of mutual recognition of languages and cultures is neither impartial nor evenhanded, but enormously unequal: French and English are publicly supported and enforced as the languages of integration. Speakers of minority languages are not asking for special treatment, but rather for some kind of equality of respect in this situation of inequality.

If we listen to what people are trying to say in actual cases, the demands of minorities are often made in the face of a majority having the power to suppress or misrecognize minorities, to assimilate them to the majority's cultural norms, and to present this as if it were universal. These cases are not conflicts between "diversity" and "equality," but conflicts among groups with tremendous inequalities in power and resources (in virtue of the three axes of the prevailing norms of mutual recognition), and corresponding inequalities in the power to construct the identities of others through the day-to-day exercise of the prevailing norms of governance and cooperation (Benhabib 2002; Laden 2001, 131-85).

The actual struggles are often about these sorts of underlying inequalities, not some hypothetical conflict between diversity or special treatment on one side and the defenders of the universal equality of the status quo on the other, as the monological approach tends to structure the debate.[7] Therefore, the point is not to start with some general thesis about diversity *versus* equality, or any other framework, but to examine actual cases to see what the conflict is about. This entails listening to the people engaged in the struggles over the prevailing norms of recognition, and thus taking the dialogical step.[8] As a result of this learning experience, the maxim *audi alteram partem* (Always listen to the other side) has come to be a widespread convention of reconciliation procedures.

Considerations such as these four have called into question the top-down, monological approaches and have moved many participants, policy makers, courts, and theorists to turn to inclusive dialogical approaches to resolve recognition conflicts.

From Consensus to Reasonable Disagreement and Non-Finality

Recall the second problem with the early orientation: the finality presumption. When citizens struggling over norms of mutual recognition, policy makers, courts, and theorists turned to dialogue, they initially brought a version of this presumption with them. They presumed that, under the best of circumstances, a consensus among the participants could be reached and thus that consensus ought to function as the regulative ideal of actual negotiations. There could still be a just, definitive, and final resolution, only now the people affected, rather than the theorist or policy maker, would reach agreement on it, or approximate it, through some form of dialogue. Partly for theoretical reasons and partly from experience in diverse dispute-resolution situations, this presumption has given way to the contrary hypothesis (and critical ideal) that no matter what procedures for the exchange of reasons are applied to the dialogue about proposed norms of mutual recognition, in either theory or practice, an element of "reasonable disagreement" or "reasonable dissent" will usually remain. That is, an agreement on a norm reached through dialogue can be reasonable (with good but not decisive reasons for accepting it), even though some interlocutors will have good but not decisive reasons for not accepting it.

There are several reasons for this step from consensus to accepting that even in ideal theory practical reasoning of this general and complex kind is inherently indeterminate and disagreement ineliminable, thus leaving a plurality of contestable conceptions of the just norms of mutual recognition in any case.[9] In practice, this may seem an obvious point to anyone familiar with negotiations.

First, there are always asymmetries in power, knowledge, influence, and argumentative skills that block the most oppressed from getting to negotiations in the first place and then structure the negotiations if they do. Time is always limited; a decision has to be made before all affected have had their say, so usually the powerful have an inordinate say; future generations have no say, yet are often the most affected; limitations in the agreement are often exposed only after it is implemented and experimented with; and so on. Second, as we have seen, the identities of those involved in the multilogue are modified in the course of the negotiations in complex and unpredictable ways. Given these features, nonconsensus and reasonable disagreement seem inevitable. Third, there is always a certain room to manoeuvre – to appear to agree, yet to think and act differently – in interpreting and acting in accord with a norm of mutual recognition (whether it is a norm of argumentation in the dialogue or a norm of mutual recognition that has been implemented in practice after negotiations). Even in the most routine instance of acting in accord with a norm of mutual recognition, the members of an association subtly alter it through interpretation, application, and negotiation (Taylor 1995, 165-80). In other cases, overt agreement, or a manufactured consensus, can mask the vast terrain of hidden scripts and arts of resistance by which subjects act out their reasonable disagreement to oppressive norms in day-to-day life (De Certeau 1988; J. Scott 1990).

Considerations of this kind in theory and in reflection on dispute resolution in practice have led many to lower the threshold of expectations in struggles over recognition from the finality-through-consensus presumption to the working hypothesis that a reasonable agreement will be faced with reasonable disagreement. Reasonable "dissent is inevitable," as the Supreme Court of Canada nicely puts it (*Reference re Secession of Quebec,* para. 68).[10]

Nevertheless, many theorists and practitioners who took this step retained the finality presumption in one crucial area. They argued that even though agreements would always be subject to reasonable dissent, there could still be a consensus on a definitive theory of the just procedures of dialogue. This could be worked up in theory and employed as a transcendental standard to judge any existing negotiation and to specify what counts as a reasonable or unreasonable claim.[11]

However, there is no reason why the considerations of "reasonable disagreement" should not apply to the procedures of negotiation and thus to the concept of a "reasonable" claim as well. It is the most common thing in both the ideal world of theoretical debate and the real world of negotiation for theorists and negotiators to move backwards to challenge the procedural rules with which they began. So we now have the view that the procedures of negotiation must be open to question in the course of negotiations, reasonable disagreement over them will persist, and there will be an indeterminate plurality of reasonable procedures. This should be unsurprising, for procedures of negotiation are themselves norms of mutual recognition. Consequently, the modes of acceptable argumentation have expanded from the initial ideal of consensus on what counts as a "public reason," "claim of validity," or "procedure of argumentation," to the view that criteria and procedures of argumentation are plural and open to question in the course of the negotiations.

In practice this has led to a whole new field of alternative dispute-resolution methods, and in theory has led to approaches that highlight different types of dialogue: deliberative democracy, communicative democracy, deliberative liberalism, agonistic democracy, and so on.[12] It is not just that there are different models of dialogical negotiations. In addition, there are various aspects to the complex activity of negotiation under any model that need to be exposed and analyzed with different approaches. Most importantly, if we are to understand dialogical interaction in all its variations and complexity, we need to study more than some abstract and limited model of "conversation" or "deliberation." Rather, we must study the full range of strategic, communicative, deliberative, and decision-making phases, from Intifada-like strategic bargaining by recourse to armed struggle at one end through to the idealized calm and nonstrategic exchange of an agreed-upon range of public reasons on which political philosophers tend to focus.[13]

Two conclusions follow from these reflections on theory and practice. First, in the early phases of research in this field, the finality presumption was strengthened by the complementary assumption that struggles over recognition could be confined to a narrow and clearly demarcated range of issues of "cultural" and "identity-related" conflicts. This has been shown to be false in two different yet related ways. Once these conflicts are seen as struggles over prevailing norms of mutual recognition, they can be seen to be an aspect of any kind of struggle. For example, struggles classified as conflicts over distribution, where workers fight for a say in the workplace and environmentalists negotiate for a say over the way their employer's production affects the environment, are also contests to alter the way they are recognized as members. That is, they move from not having a right to a say to having such a right as part of their identity as workers or employees. Next, as our examples have shown, these struggles are always struggles over the third axis of forms of recognition (the access to resources) to some extent and thus cannot be neatly separated from struggles over distribution and redistribution. To use a familiar example, the struggle of the Iraqi people, or of a Kurdish minority within Iraq, to be recognized as a free and self-determining people is also a struggle over the control of their oil reserves, just as the struggle by the United Kingdom and the United States to have Iraq recognized as an open, free-trade, and free-market society is a struggle to ensure that their oil reserves are controlled by the wealthy and powerful.[14]

Second, for the reasons we have surveyed, neither the isolated theorist, court, or policy maker, nor the members engaged in the struggles and democratic dialogues, nor some ideal set of procedures can be expected to provide the final and definitive resolution to what counts as the just norms of mutual recognition. None has the final word. Any agreement will be less than perfect. It will rest to some extent on unjust exclusion and assimilation and thus be confronted with reasonable disagreement (overt or covert) that cannot be eliminated. A norm of mutual recognition is thus never final, but questionable. It follows that in a free and open society, existing norms of mutual recognition should be open to public questioning so these reasons can be heard and considered. They should be open to review and potential renegotiation. Reconciliation is thus not a final end-state but an activity that inevitably will be reactivated from time to time.

In summary, negotiations to reconcile conflicts over recognition should be dialogical in form, potentially ongoing in practice, general in range, and inseparable from other types of conflict.

Civic Freedom and Practices of "Citizenization"

What implications follow from the learning process we have surveyed and the transformation it brings about in understanding the reconciliation of conflicts over the recognition of minorities?

First, if the route to resolving conflicts over norms of mutual recognition is to turn to inclusive and dialogical practices of negotiation and if, in the best of circumstances, there will be reasonable disagreement over the imperfect procedures and particular resolution, it follows that the primary orientation of reconciliation should not be the Platonic search for definitive and final procedures and solutions, but, rather, the institutionalization and protection of a specific kind of democratic freedom. The primary aim will be to ensure that those subject to and affected by any system of governance are always free to call its prevailing norms of recognition and action coordination into question; to present reasons for and against modifying it; to enter into dialogue with those who govern and who have a duty to listen and respond; to be able to challenge the prevailing procedures of negotiation in the course of the discussions; to reach or fail to reach an imperfect agreement to amend (or overthrow) the norm in question; to implement the amendment; and then to ensure that this agreement is open to review and possible renegotiation in the future. This is the fundamental democratic or civic freedom of citizens – having an effective say in a dialogue with their governors over the norms through which they are governed.

Let us call this fundamental freedom "dialogical civic freedom." It is not only the right or freedom to speak out against oppressive, exclusionary, or assimilative norms of mutual recognition, as important as freedom of speech is. For it to be effective, it also needs to be correlated with a duty on the part of the powerful to listen to these voices and to respond with their reasons for the status quo; that is, to enter into an open dialogue governed by *audi alteram partem*. If the duty to listen and respond is ignored and dialogue suppressed, then civic freedom takes the many forms of civic dissent (discussed above) to bring the powerful to the table. As the Supreme Court explains, this dialogical civic freedom (formulated as the right to challenge a prevailing norm and the duty to negotiate if the challenge is well-supported) underlies and provides the basic test of legitimacy of any legal or constitutional norm in Canada, including the *Charter of Rights and Freedoms (Reference re Secession of Quebec* paras. 68-69). And we have seen that this basic freedom is a formulation of the normative quality of norms. Those members who are subject to norms are free in the sense that there is a field of possible responses available to members in which they can test the acceptability of norms. We can thus see yet another, democratic, reason for rejecting the monological and finality orientation. If a norm is presented and imposed as final, as this orientation presents all norms, it *eo ipso* violates this fundamental freedom and renders the norm illegitimate.

The second implication is that the experience of direct or indirect participation in these kinds of dialogical struggles helps to generate a new kind of second-order citizen identity appropriate to free and open, culturally diverse political associations. One comes to acquire an identity *as* a citizen through participation in the practices and institutions of one's society, through having a say in them and in the ways one is governed. In complex contemporary political and legal associations, one of the fundamental ways that this process of becoming a citizen occurs is through participation in the very activities in which the norms of mutual recognition in any subsystem are discussed, negotiated, modified, reviewed, and questioned again.[15]

The partners involved, while struggling for recognition of their group, nevertheless come to develop an attachment to the larger association, precisely because it allows them to engage in this second-order free and democratic activity from time to time. These activities of struggling over recognition also allow citizens to dispel *ressentiment* that might otherwise be discharged in violent forms of protest and terrorism if this openness were suppressed and a norm of mutual recognition were imposed unilaterally. The turn to violence and terrorism increases as the openness to democratic dissent and effective dialogue decreases.

Even those who do not win the latest struggle have good reasons to develop a sense of belonging to a political association that is free and open in this contestatory sense. Because they were in on the discussions, they learned that there were good reasons on the other side and vice versa; they probably gained some degree of recognition in the compromise agreement; and, given reasonable disagreement, they can continue to believe that their cause is reasonable and worth fighting for again. Most importantly, they know that they have the freedom to challenge the latest hegemonic norm of mutual recognition in the future if they can generate the reasons to support such a challenge. And, in fact, this kind of identification is a common feature of most contestatory games: the players competing in them generate a form of identification with the game itself above their team loyalties and their particular victories and losses. So perhaps the Greek term for contest, *agonistics,* which is now widely used to characterize these struggles, is appropriate.

The dialogical approach thus provides a genuinely democratic solution to the problem of generating a sense of solidarity (and thus peace) in culturally diverse societies. As we saw, the monological and finality orientation fails on this count, either by denying or limiting recognition from the outside in the first phase (thereby fuelling the conflicts) or by handing down recognition rights from on high in the second phase (thereby fuelling separateness). In the dialogical and non-finality orientation, the citizens work out the limits of mutual recognition themselves (as they learn the limits of their own and others' demands through dialogue) and thus identify with them; they acquire a sense of attachment to, and respect for, their culturally diverse fellow citizens and institutions through the dialogical experience. If this analysis is correct, the path to global peace runs through practices of civic freedom and dialogical reconciliation.[16]

The third implication is cautionary and deflationary. It is important not to elevate civic dialogue to the status of the new solution to all problems of recognition. It too is defeasible. First, the theorists, courts, and policy makers have an important yet nonsovereign counterbalancing role to play in this new approach. Although they have been dethroned from their position of legislating the just solution or procedures prior to dialogue with their fellow citizens, their proposals for a just resolution remain crucial to the process. As we have seen, while they do not have the final word, neither do the citizens engaged in the dialogue nor any particular institutional set of procedures. Contrary to the consensual, majoritarian, and procedural interpretations of the dialogical approach, the deliberations of citizens in specific institutions cannot become the indubitable source and standard of justice, because they too are always fraught with imperfections, injustices, and irreducible disagreements.[17] Rather, the role of theorists, policy makers, and courts, as well as other concerned groups, is to broaden and enter indirectly into the dialogue on a par with others: to present their theories, guidelines, and proposals to those engaged in the negotiations; to help clarify the claims of justice and injustice, equality and inequality put forth by the members involved in the direct negotiations; to criticize the procedures and outcomes; and to respond to questions and challenges in turn. In general, the deliberations will be better informed if they are open to the wider context of reciprocal criticism and scrutiny from other public actors, institutions, and epistemic communities.

Second, while dialogue is essential for all the reasons that have been given, it is necessary to distinguish it from decision making. The asymmetries in recognition and power that are the underlying cause of a struggle over recognition carry over into the forms of negotiation. The ability of the members' exchange of reasons to unsettle the prejudices and alter the outlooks of the most powerful groups is limited. In these circumstances a majority decision-making rule (such as a referendum) leaves an oppressed minority hostage to the majority at the end of the discussions (and the foreknowledge of this often drains the dialogue of its capacity to alter the prejudices of the majority). Therefore, minorities need to be able to appeal to other decision-making institutions at the end of the dialogue, such as courts, parliaments, international human rights regimes, nonpartisan adjudicators or mediators, global transnational networks, and so on. These too are imperfect and need to be open to challenge in turn, but they provide indispensable checks and balances on the powers of the dominant groups to manipulate the dialogue and manufacture agreement.

These three implications illustrate a central feature of the dialogical approach. In the monological and finality approach, justice and the rule of norms are given priority over the democratic freedom of citizens. As we have seen, the dialogical orientation does not reverse this ordering in an unlimited celebration of unbounded contestation or the will of the majority. Rather, in each step it seeks to place the claims of justice and the rule of norms in an equal and reciprocal relationship with the right of citizens to test the acceptability of claims and rules through dialogical civic freedom.[18]

Conclusion

If the trend outlined above is significant and worthy of further study, then the type of research that is able to throw critical light on conflicts over recognition will also be different from the model of research associated with the monological and finality orientation. The aim will not be to retreat to an abstract normative point of view and elaborate standards for norms of mutual recognition and procedures of negotiation. Normative studies, as we have seen, will continue to play an important yet less lofty role. However, these studies will form part of a broader range of academic research in a relationship of reciprocal and ongoing elucidation with the parties engaged in struggles over recognition, where research throws critical light on the limitations and possibilities in practice, and practice tests the relevance of theory. This more practice-oriented research has developed over the last decades in concert with the trends outlined above and is now well-established. There are two main lines of this kind of critical research on struggles over intersubjective norms of mutual recognition oriented towards civic freedom and peace through dialogue.

The first is to study the multiplicity of ways in which individuals and groups are excluded from calling into question the imposed norms through which they are recognized, governed, and blocked from entering into a dialogue over their legitimacy, thereby rendering assimilation, silent oppression, or the recourse to nonviolent and violent resistance the only alternatives. This kind of research aids in making specific systems of norms of recognition and governance more inclusive and dialogical, open to the ongoing negotiation of those subject to them.

The second and more recent line of research takes the global trends to inclusivity, dialogue, and the negotiated character of identities in practice and theory as its starting point and reflects critically on them. While it takes a positive attitude towards these three trends, it is like the third, cautionary implication of the previous section. It does not celebrate inclusivity, dialogue, and negotiated identities unconditionally and complacently, as a kind of "just so" story. Rather, it takes these trends as a new form of emerging national and global governance that induces individuals, groups, communities, regions, and minority nations to perform their identity-related differences and to enter into dialogues and negotiations over their norms of action coordination themselves in downloaded and quasi-autonomous regimes of self-rule.[19] Thus, this kind of research studies who sets the agenda in the negotiations, what techniques of assimilation and domestication are at work in specific types of negotiation (such as treaty negotiations with First Nations), which norms of mutual recognition in a structure of negotiation are insulated from challenge, to what extent recognition is detached from changes in the unequal access to resources (the third axis of analysis), and to what extent are seemingly free and open procedures of negotiations governed at a distance by national governments, global corporations, international regulatory regimes, and military imperialism. In short, it asks to what extent civic freedom is subtly encouraged, manipulated, and governed within these new regimes of inclusive and negotiable norms of mutual recognition in order to make the world "safe for difference."[20]

This new partnership between academic research and struggles over the recognition of minorities thus continues the perennial task of testing the limits imposed on our civic freedom by means of our critical freedom.

Notes

1 For more detailed arguments and cases in support of the approach advanced in this chapter see Gagnon and Tully (2001). I would also like to thank Jakeet Singh for many helpful discussions of this chapter.

2 For a groundbreaking survey of the dual quality of norms see the forthcoming paper by Weiner.

3 For examples of these two phases see Barry (2000), Cairns (2000), and Kymlicka (1995a and 1995b). The limitations of the monological and finality orientation in both phases are analyzed in detail in Kelly (2002). Kymlicka has moved somewhat closer to a dialogical approach in his more recent work. See Coulthard (2003) and McRanor (this volume) for objections to his recent work from the perspective set out here.

4 "Straight jacket" is the phrase used by the Supreme Court of Canada to characterize and criticize the finality presumption. See *Reference re Secession of Quebec*, para. 150.

5 See Laden (2001) and Rawls (1996) for this dialogical reformulation of liberalism.

6 See Ivison, Patton, and Sanders (2000) and Venne (1998).

7 For example see Cairns (2000).

8 An excellent example of the turn to actual cases is Carens (2000).

9 See Rawls (1996, 54-58) and the deepening of Rawls' argument for reasonable disagreement in Waldron (1999).

10 For an analysis of this case see Tully (2001).

11 This is the approach of Habermas and his followers. The classical statement of his consensus view is Habermas 1995.

12 For a critical survey of these different approaches see Dryzek (2000).

13 For a recent survey of the complexity of constitutional deliberations regarding recognition claims in Canada and the various approaches to them see Noël (2003).

14 For a discussion of the relations between recognition and redistribution see Emcke, Markell, and Tully (2000).

15 For a defence of these first two implications see McKinnon and Hampsher-Monk (2000, 1-12) and Maclure (2003a and 2003b).

16 Alan Cairns (2000, 2003) sees this problem of solidarity as the central problem facing culturally diverse societies. The monological and finality solution that he proposes in Cairns 2000 has, I believe, the defects that I outline in the adjoining paragraph.

17 For example, Habermas (1996) and Waldron (1999) tend to equate just agreements with the de facto outcomes of existing representative democratic procedures and majority rule institutions respectively.
18 I would like to thank Oliver Schmidtke for pointing out that I failed to address this point in the conference version of this chapter. For the co-equal status of justice and freedom see Tully (2002).
19 The pioneering study in this second line of analysis is Rose (1999).
20 For critical studies in these two lines of practice-oriented research see Abu-Laban and Gabriel (2002), Alfred (2001), Coulthard (2003), Day (2000), and Strong-Boag et al. (1998). I am indebted to David Scott for pointing out the tendency to complacency in the dialogical literature and the critical need for the second line of research (see D. Scott 2003).

References

Books and Articles

Abu-Laban, Yasmeen, and Christina Gabriel, ed. 2002. *Selling Diversity: Immigration, Multiculturalism, Employment Equity, and Globalization*. Peterborough, ON: Broadview Press.

Alfred, Taiaiake. 2001. Deconstructing the British Columbia Treaty Process. *Bayali: Culture, Law and Colonialism* 3:37-66.

Barry, Brian. 2000. *Culture and Equality*. Cambridge, UK: Polity Press.

Benhabib, Seyla. 2002. *The Claims of Culture: Equality and Diversity in a Global Era*. Princeton, NJ: Princeton University Press.

Cairns, Alan C. 2000. *Citizens Plus: Aboriginal Peoples and the Canadian State*. Vancouver: UBC Press.

–. 2003. Post-Banff Reflections on the Diversity of Diversity. In *Limits to Diversity?* ed. Robert Higham, 219-22. Ottawa: University of Ottawa Press.

Carens, Joseph. 2000. *Culture, Citizenship, and Community: A Contextual Exploration of Justice as Even-Handedness*. Oxford: Oxford University Press.

Coulthard, Glen. 2003. Dene Nationalism and the Politics of Cultural Recognition. MA thesis, Indigenous Governance Program, University of Victoria.

Day, Richard. 2000. *Multiculturalism and the History of Canadian Diversity*. Toronto: University of Toronto Press.

De Certeau, Michel. 1988. *The Practice of Everyday Life*. Trans. Steven Rendall. Berkeley: University of California Press.

Dryzek, John. 2000. *Deliberative Democracy and Beyond: Liberals, Critics and Contestations*. Oxford: Oxford University Press.

Emcke, Carolin, Patchen Markell, and James Tully. 2000. Recognition Redux. *Constellations* 7(4):469-506.

Gagnon, Alain, and James Tully, ed. 2001. *Multinational Democracies*. Cambridge: Cambridge University Press.

Habermas, Jurgen. 1995. *Moral Consciousness and Communicative Action*. Trans. Christian Lenhardt and Shierry Weber Nicholsen. Cambridge, MA: MIT Press.

–. 1996. *Between Facts and Norms: Contributions to a Discourse Theory of Law and Democracy*. Trans. William Rehg. Cambridge, MA: MIT Press.

–. 1998. *The Inclusion of the Other*. Trans. C. Cronin and Pablo De Greiff. Cambridge, MA: MIT Press.

Ivison, Duncan, Paul Patton, and Will Sanders, ed. 2000. *Political Theory and the Rights of Indigenous Peoples*. Melbourne: Cambridge University Press.

Kelly, Paul, ed. 2002. *Multiculturalism Reconsidered*. Cambridge, UK: Polity Press.

Kymlicka, Will. 1995a. *Multicultural Citizenship*. Oxford: Oxford University Press.

–, ed. 1995b. *The Rights of Minority Cultures*. Oxford: Oxford University Press.

Laden, Anthony. 2001. *Reasonably Radical: Deliberative Liberalism and the Politics of Identity*. Ithaca, NY: Cornell University Press.

Maclure, Jocelyn. 2003a. Disenchantment and Democracy: Public Reason under Conditions of Pluralism. PhD diss., University of Southampton.

–. 2003b. *Quebec Identity: The Challenge of Pluralism*. Trans. Peter Feldstein. Montreal and Kingston: McGill-Queens University Press.

McKinnon, Catriona, and Ian Hampsher-Monk, ed. 2000. *The Demands of Citizenship*. London, UK: Continuum.

Noël, Alain. 2003. Democratic Deliberation in a Multinational Federation. Paper presented at the annual conference of the Canadian Political Science Association, Halifax.

Rawls, John. 1996. *Political Liberalism*. New York: Columbia University Press.

Rose, Paul. 1999. *The Powers of Freedom*. Cambridge: Cambridge University Press.

Scott, David. 2003. Culture and Political Theory. *Political Theory* 31(1):93-116.

Scott, James. 1990. *Domination and the Arts of Resistance*. New Haven, CT: Yale University Press.

Strong-Boag, Veronica, Sherrill Grace, Avigail Eisenberg, and Joan Anderson, ed. 1998. *Painting the Maple: Essays on Race, Gender, and the Construction of Canada*. Vancouver: UBC Press.

Taylor, Charles. 1995. *Philosophical Arguments*. Cambridge, MA: Harvard University Press.

Tully, James. 2001. *The Unattained Yet Attainable Democracy: Canada and Quebec Face the New Century*. Montreal: Programmes d'études sur le Québec.

–. 2002. The Unfreedom of the Moderns in Relation to Their Ideals of Constitutionalism and Democracy. *Modern Law Review* 65(2):204-28.

Venne, Sharon Helen. 1998. *Our Elders Understand Our Rights: Evolving International Law Regarding Indigenous Peoples*. Penticton, BC: Theytus Books.

Waldron, Jeremy. 1999. *Law and Disagreement*. Cambridge: Cambridge University Press.

Weiner, Antje. Forthcoming. The Dual Quality of Norms: Stability and Flexibility. *Critical Review of International Social and Political Philosophy* 6.

Young, Iris Marion. 1997. *Intersecting Voices: Dilemmas of Gender, Political Philosophy and Policy*. Princeton, NJ: Princeton University Press.

–. 2000. *Inclusion and Democracy*. Oxford: Oxford University Press.

Case

Reference re Secession of Quebec, [1998] 2 S.C.R. 217. Reprinted in David Schneiderman, ed. 1999. *The Quebec Decision: Perspectives on the Supreme Court Ruling on Secession*. Toronto: Lorimer.

2
Reasoning about Identity: Canada's Distinctive Culture Test
Avigail Eisenberg

Debates about "identity" are the favoured terrain of much abstract theorizing, but the problems and conflicts underlying these debates are far from abstract and often involve difficult concrete political choices. That's why so many scholars who study identity and cultural politics take into account both theoretical and practical dimensions of the issues. While abstract theories provide different ways of conceptualizing conflicts, practice-focused analysis, including case studies, addresses the particular choices people confront and the specific reasons they adopt the political strategies they do. This chapter focuses on the interplay between theory and practice in the area of identity politics in order to determine what the protection of identities can require of the state. The analysis will draw lessons from recent attempts by Canadian courts to assess the claims of minorities and indigenous peoples.

I begin by distinguishing different types of cases – some involving Aboriginal peoples, others involving cultural, linguistic, and religious minorities – that have given rise to "identity claims." Of special interest here is the "distinctive culture test," which has been developed by the courts to respond to Aboriginal claims in Canada and which promises to provide a method for resolving controversies involving identity claims. I then survey three key objections often made against the assessment of identity claims by public institutions such as courts. These objections raise important problems of evidence, essentialism, and social conflict. But they also exaggerate and mischaracterize the problems associated with framing conflicts in terms of identity-based interests.

The point of departure here is the observation that the assessment of identity claims occurs frequently within public institutions and is unavoidable in some cases. Moreover, the public assessment of identity claims is not always undesirable in that it can foster mutual understanding and is often the site of what James Tully calls "struggles over recognition" (see Chapter 1, this volume). Yet, despite its ubiquity, the assessment of identity by public institutions is fraught with difficulty. In this chapter I examine some of the difficulties of developing transparent and fair criteria with a view to developing a normative guide to the assessment of the identity claims of different groups. A successful guide has to grapple with three problems. First, it has to specify what sort of evidence can be presented about the nature and importance of an identity claim and how that evidence should be interpreted. Second, it has to provide a way of assessing and protecting identity without essentializing group identities. And third, it has to assess identity without heightening social conflict. The examination of Canada's distinctive culture test is instructive in this context. Although, as I explain in the final section, the test does not provide a satisfactory way of reasoning about identity, it does provide some insights into how a successful guide to the assessment of such claims might be developed.

Some Cases

Consider, to start, the case of *R. v. Van der Peet*. In this case, a member of the Sto:lo First Nation claimed an exemption from regulations that restrict individual fishers from selling salmon without a licence. Van der Peet argued that her right to trade in salmon could be derived from her membership in the Sto:lo nation, whose cultural identity, she claimed, is intimately tied to salmon fishing and thereby protected by section 35 of Canada's *Constitution Act, 1982*.[1] After applying what is called the "distinctive culture test" to assess her claim, the majority on the Supreme Court of Canada found against Van der Peet. The distinctive culture test requires, first, that claimants show that a disputed practice is jeopardized by state regulation and, second, that the practice is integral to the "precontact" indigenous culture of their community. Only practices that were central to the community before Aboriginal-European contact are eligible for protection. On the basis of these criteria, the court argued that Sto:lo trade in salmon (as opposed to fishing and consuming salmon) was not central to precontact Sto:lo identity and therefore could not count as a protected Aboriginal right.

Van der Peet's claim was an identity claim in the sense that she argued that the disputed practice of trading salmon is important to her due in part to its connection to the way of life of the Aboriginal community in which she is a member and with which she identifies. *Van der Peet* is one of a trilogy of cases in which the Supreme Court has applied the distinctive culture test to assess the identity claims advanced on behalf of indigenous communities.[2] But the basic project it entails – setting out a method for the public assessment of the identity of a group – is reflected in a large set of cases heard by courts in Western democracies in which religious, linguistic, national, or cultural minorities advance claims for protection for their community or for exemption from laws directly on the basis that the practice, rule, or tradition they defend is important to their identity.

Such cases are also heard internationally, where the venues available to minorities and indigenous peoples for framing their claims against states in terms of identity have multiplied in the last decade. These cases are often associated with an older provision of international law found in Article 27 of the United Nation's 1966 *International Covenant on Civil and Political Rights* (UN General Assembly 1966).[3] Article 27 cases frequently require the UN Human Rights Committee to assess evidence about whether disputed practices are central to group identity and to determine the extent to which central practices are jeopardized by state regulation. International cases brought by many indigenous peoples involving land claims and property use are framed, using Article 27, in terms of how the central practices of, for example, the Sami in Finland *(Länsman v. Finland)*, the Lubicon in Canada *(Ominayak v. Canada)*, or the Hopu in Tahiti *(Hopu v. France)*[4] are jeopardized by state-sanctioned land development and resource extraction. Linguistic groups have also used Article 27 to make identity-based arguments to restrict (or not to restrict) the language used on commercial signs in Quebec *(McIntyre v. Canada)* or to include Breton on signs in France *(Guesdon v. France)*. Other international venues have also heard such claims. For instance, in light of recent controversies surrounding artificial growth hormones in animals and raw milk cheeses, the World Trade Organization has come under pressure to modify its criteria for assessing food-related disputes to include considerations not just of food safety but also of identity (Brom 2004). So numerous are the cases in which claims are presented in terms of their role in the identity of a group that international institutions have begun to develop a set of criteria for assessing these claims. Though not as formal as Canada's distinctive culture test, these criteria include, for instance, the requirement that practices essential to the cultural survival of groups, including economic activities, be protected and that states consult groups whose central practices are affected by regulation (Scheinin 2000).

Many political theorists consider it a bad idea for public institutions to assess people's identity, especially the identity of minority groups. Liberal theorists worry that identity is inscrutable because claims made about identity are likely to be based on obscure, controversial, and highly subjective evidence. Minority rights advocates are also skeptical. Two of their concerns are that public institutions will apply ethnocentric criteria in assessing minority identity claims and that the dynamic nature of cultural identities will be jeopardized when institutions such as courts choose particular practices to exempt from state law by deeming these practices central and integral to a particular culture at a particular time, while designating other practices to be contingent and marginal. Following from this is the more general problem of outsiders such as courts assuming the role of shaping the identities of minorities and indigenous peoples. Edward Said's work on "orientalism" is instructive in this context in explaining how mainstream and majority groups often possess a cultural identity that relies on characterizing, understanding, and interpreting the identities of minorities and indigenous peoples in submissive and ultimately oppressive ways. Feminists bring a similar message to this debate through studies that point to the plethora of cultural and religious practices that oppress women, children, and dissenters.[5] And, finally, those who advocate solutions to improve democratic relations between minorities and majorities worry that if legal and political institutions are sympathetic to identity claims, groups will frame as many interests as they can in terms of their identity, which will result in an "unproductive cacophonic war of words" (Brom 2004, 426), if not violent confrontations among ethnic or national groups whose relations are already strained (also see Dryzek 2005, 219-20).

From all of these different points of view, identity is considered to be an unhelpful and perhaps dangerous way of framing and assessing political and legal disputes that involve minorities. The *Van der Peet* case seems to confirm this general conclusion. The distinctive culture test has been criticized for placing at risk the well-being of Aboriginal communities for several reasons. It freezes Aboriginal rights in a precontact era (Borrows 1997-98). It is ethnocentric. It lacks reciprocity. And it further aggravates the unjust relations between Canada and Aboriginal peoples by facilitating the court's authority to decide on the nature and meaning of central aspects of Aboriginal identities (Barsh and Henderson 1997, 1002).

Although the critics are right to alert us to hazards of assessing identity, there is no denying that many groups, including many indigenous groups, frame their claims for autonomy, protection, or accommodation, both domestically and internationally, in terms of identity. Perhaps this is generally a bad idea and perhaps it reflects (as it surely does in the case of national minorities and Aboriginal peoples) the absence of better ways to argue for autonomy. But the discussion of identity claims takes place in relation to all sorts of groups (religious, linguistic, cultural minorities, gays and lesbians) and could, at least in theory, be used outside frameworks of domination. So before dismissing the framework *in toto*, it's worth taking a closer look at three of the most challenging objections raised mainly in political theory to the assessment of identity claims by public institutions: (1) the inscrutability problem, (2) the essentialism problem, and (3) the social conflict problem. Each of these problems is analyzed here in an institutional context, by which I mean a context where we imagine public institutions or forums framing conflicts in terms of identity-based considerations and assessing conflicting claims in terms of the strengths and weaknesses of their relation to the identity of a group or individual. By situating this discussion in this context, I do not mean to suggest that public institutions should frame all disputes in terms of identity. Rather, the question is whether any dispute is best framed in terms of identity, and, if so, what sort of dispute and what sort of public standards can be used for assessment. After assessing the three objections, I return to the case of *Van der Peet* and the distinctive problems raised by this particular case.

Are Identity Claims Inscrutable?

In most theoretical discussions, identity is defined in terms of self-understanding and is related to an individual's authentic understanding of his or her "self." What often follows, according to some critics, is the worry that claims framed in terms of, for example, "X ought to be protected because it is important to my/our identity" are by their nature opaque and deeply personal, have an all-or-nothing quality, and cannot be shown to be false. Overall, these characteristics make identity an unsuitable and inappropriate subject for public reasoning. From the perspective of public institutions, identity is thereby normatively inscrutable.

Jeremy Waldron raises this objection by stating that "*authenticity* connotes the idea that each of us should live in a way that is true to himself, not conforming to a way of life simply because it is accepted by others" (2000, 157). If identity is, by its nature, tied to authenticity, then individual identity is "interpersonally and socially non-negotiable" in the sense that it is informed by beliefs and practices whose authenticity rests with the rationales they have for those individuals who follow or practise them, and not with how they might be justified to external political or legal institutions (158). To explain one's attachment to a particular tradition "because it is important to my identity" is to offer an inauthentic explanation of what are often personal and religious reasons for following the tradition. I *really* follow the traditions I do "because I believe that God commands me to" (or, even more authentically, "*because* God commands me to"), or because, "according to my holy book, this is a way of being closer to God." To turn these reasons into subjects of public assessment is potentially to assault the very integrity of the person who holds them. So an approach to conflict resolution that focuses on publicly assessing identity claims will either undermine the authenticity of such claims by treating them as positions that individuals can publicly negotiate or, if it treats them authentically, will implicate the core of an individual's self in social conflicts and thereby raise the stakes in public deliberation and exacerbate conflict (also see Weinstock 2001).

Put in slightly different terms, the objection is that defending identity claims implicates minorities in the impossible task of trying to convince the public or other groups of the "correctness" or desirability of particular practices. This is what makes identity claims inscrutable in Waldron's account. He explains the point using a hypothetical example: a disagreement between coexisting communities over whether the polygynous practices of one community ought to be tolerated by the other community, which disapproves of polygyny. Individuals who practise polygyny, he suggests, would "presumably be expected to try to explain to [their] fellow citizens why polygyny is not only not wrong ... *but in fact positively desirable*" (2000, 163; emphasis added).

The objection that Waldron advances is distinct from a less normatively charged evidentiary objection which holds that people cannot prove that X is *important* to their authentic identity using reliable and public evidence because whatever it is that is important to their identity is just too personal, subjective, and cannot be shown to be false. This objection holds that identity claims cannot be assessed via ordinary evidentiary standards. As I just described it, this objection seems to be clearly false. It directly contradicts what occurs in many public forums in diverse societies all the time. Individuals and groups often bring before courts evidence that is designed to establish that a crucial aspect of their cultural or religious identity is threatened by a law or policy. In many cases, courts and legislatures are asked to decide, on the basis of historical records, demographic statistics, or various kinds of "expert" evidence from within and outside the community making the claim, whether the claim that a practice is important to a group's cultural or religious identity is valid. This process of justification may be objectionable for other reasons, but usually the problem is not that identity claims cannot be verified. Aboriginal people have successfully defended the sanctity of particular places, the centrality of practices and traditions, and the continuity or unjust discontinuity of particular ways of living by framing arguments about the importance of such things – historically, spiritually, culturally, and politically – in terms of their identities. Religious minorities, such as Jews and Muslims, have used evidence to defend the right to slaughter animals according to religious laws. Sikhs have done the same in relation to the wearing of turbans and the kirpan, as have Catholics in relation to employing gays and lesbians. Some Christian sects have argued that they ought to be allowed to discipline their children by beating them with a rod, to take them out of school when they are young, or to deny them blood transfusions because their interpretation of the Bible says they should do so. The list goes on and on. All of these claims involve groups and individuals explaining the role of particular practices, places, or traditions in their cultural or religious identities, and often there is no shortage of evidence in relation to such claims.

But the normative objection that Waldron is making is unlike the evidentiary objection because it suggests that groups and individuals who defend their identity publicly have to convince others not merely of the importance of a practice to their identity but of its correctness or desirability; that it is "not only not wrong ... but in fact positively desirable" (2000, 163). This normative objection also seems to be mistaken, or at least it speaks to a problem that is highly atypical of cases involving identity claims about controversial practices. To take the example Waldron mentions first, groups that view polygamy as central to their religious identity, such as the fundamentalist Mormon community of Bountiful near Creston, British Columbia, are unlikely to argue their case by trying to convince Canadians that polygamy is good. Rather, they will, if they are prosecuted, defend their right to practise polygamy by arguing that it is important to their religious beliefs and therefore to their community's identity. Similarly, those who have defended their right to spank their children or deny their children blood transfusions because the Bible tells them to do not attempt to justify these claims publicly on the basis of the veracity of their religious doctrines or the desirability of their practices. In some cases, what might be reasonably required is that they show their practices do not harm others or that any risk of harm is easily addressed through precautionary measures (and many religious practices fail to meet this test). A higher standard might require that groups explain why their practices are important to them so as to generate a public understanding of their importance.[6] But showing that practices are (1) unharmful or that (2) they are important to a group's identity, and showing that (3) they are desirable, entails three entirely different standards. We might even adopt as a standard the requirement of mutual understanding, which is similar to (2) above and would require that people be able to recognize the importance of practices that are not their own. But Waldron's normative objection goes beyond even this high standard. It goes beyond what is necessary to resolve disputes between different peoples in a fair manner or otherwise to ensure just conditions of coexistence.[7]

The objection that identity claims are inscrutable suggests that when an identity claim is made by one group, especially a vulnerable minority, it has to be accepted at face value by others because no legitimate basis exists to deny what one group says is important to its identity. Put in these terms, the inscrutability problem rests on the mistake of supposing that we respect others by treating their claims as though they were empirically mysterious. But in most cases the problem is not that identity claims are so mysterious and impenetrable that no method exists by which others outside the group can adequately understand their importance. There are many means for validating the claim that a practice is important to the identity of a group, including historical records, community testimonies, and scholarly studies of all sorts. More often the problem is that the methods of investigation used to verify claims are themselves viewed as biased and imperfect.[8] These controversies over methods of gathering and substantiating evidence are complex and difficult. But they are not a sign that intercultural understanding is futile. Rather, they are the site at which such understanding is built. There is no better sign of mutual respect than when peoples work together to design methods by which to settle their disputes. The question of what counts as good evidence involves exactly the kinds of deliberative interactions that are important to successful interactions among different peoples. This is not to deny that many cases are complex. But as complex as they are, the projects of explaining and understanding the spiritual, economic, sociological, historical, political, or psychological place of practices within a culture or religion, and of designing mutually fair methods of assessing evidence, do not involve the more obscure demand that we need to uncover the "authentic self I think I am and am striving to be" (Waldron 2000, 157).

Can Identity Be Legally Protected without Being Essentialized?

A second general objection to the public assessment of identity is that legal and public policy decisions will tend to freeze what is in fact a fluid and malleable phenomenon when they protect a practice because it is central to a group's identity. The objection is that culture is constantly being made and remade through human interactions. It is fluid and ever-changing, and these characteristics pose significant challenges not only to examining cultural claims in a public and fair manner (see Benhabib 2002 and Scott 2003) but also to legally and politically reifying these claims (see McRanor, this volume; Scott 2003). The concern is that giving legal standing to a particular practice because it seems to be "central and integral" to a group's identity ends up artificially freezing a culture in time to that practice; this thereby imposes a "historical essentialist picture" of it that interrupts the ebb and flow of cultural change and isolates culture from the means by which cultural practices are reshaped (Narayan 1997).

Two aspects of the problem of essentialism are worth distinguishing. The first aspect is usually called "historical essentialism." Because cultures are inherently fluid, relational, and revisable, it is wrong, or at least highly problematic, for public institutions to tie them to particular practices through laws that recognize practices to be central and integral to these cultures for all time. The second aspect is the problem of essentializing the individual. Here the concern is that, because the importance of a practice within a culture is often contested and the subject of political struggle within communities, public institutions should avoid protecting practices, even if they are central to cultures, because doing so ends up tying individuals to practices that might be oppressive to some members.

In both cases, the objection of essentialism is tied to the idea that communities change. Even if the communities, traditions, practices, and values that inform identity are important to human well-being, they may still be unsuited to legal or political protection because identity is reformulated through every human interaction and on the basis of changing historical circumstances. Cultural identity is negotiated in the context of power relations, and therefore it is putatively not the sort of thing that ought to be subject to adjudication and to the reification that occurs in the context of the law. According to some critics, we should pay more attention to the historical processes and political agendas by which traditions arise rather than protecting a given tradition just because it is centrally important at a particular time (Narayan 1997).

Together, these two types of essentialism constitute the most frequently cited criticism of identity protection and assessment. No group wants its traditions frozen in time or shaped by historical anthropologies that view the group through the majority's eyes. Nor should those working to change their community's sexist traditions or its hostility to dissenters have to contend with decisions made by outsider institutions that reaffirm the legitimacy of the conservative traditions they are working to change.

Any method of assessing identity claims has to consider essentialism in one way or another. Such a method would take into account questions about the historical origins of a practice, how the practice functions to sustain a culture's identity, what sort of capacities it gives to members, and which members it benefits. These questions are more likely to be precluded by approaches that ignore identity and, instead, for example, merely try to determine whether a law restricting a particular practice was passed in a procedurally correct manner or whether it contradicts other legally recognized rights.

The best method would entail carefully considering the type of essentialism that might result from alternatives to protecting a group's identity. The problem of historical essentialism, at least as the critics raise it, is not simply that the wrong practices will be protected because of the biased nature of the majority or of institutions such as courts,[9] but that *any* practice that is protected is eventually the wrong practice because of the dynamic nature of identity. Yet it is difficult to understand how to avoid this sort of essentialism in a practical context whether identity claims are accommodated or not. In the cases that actually arise in which a minority claims protection for a practice because it is central to its identity, the alternative to protecting the group's claim is often to reify the identity and values of the majority that dominates the state in which the group is a minority. In other words, the accommodation of minorities sometimes exists in a zero-sum relation to powerful ideologies about the importance of national unity and homogeneous national identity, particularly in cases that involve national minorities and indigenous peoples. For instance, what is sometimes presented in Canada as the alternative to carving out room for Aboriginal practices in Canadian law are approaches in which no group is granted such exemptions and in which Aboriginal peoples are encouraged to assimilate into mainstream Canadian society (see, for example, Flanagan 2000).

Even when the intention is not to impose a substantively thick set of national values on minorities, often solutions that embrace market mechanisms accomplish similar aims. For instance, one alternative to recognizing reindeer husbandry as central to Sami culture in Finland is to allow regional development schemes that treat all group interests as appropriately vetted through competitive market forces and thus dependent on the sovereign values of the market. In general, the alternative to protecting minority practices is to opt for an essentialized notion of the state as homogeneous in character, with laws and values that apply to every citizen in the same way and that protect a similar basket of opportunities for everyone (see Kymlicka 2005, 22n29).

Although minorities should not have to embrace static self-understandings in order to fend off coercive assimilation, it seems undeniable that defending identity-based arguments is sometimes the best means available to combat assimilation. Groups seek legal recognition for their distinctive practices because denying legal recognition, for whatever reasons, often shapes cultural practices and influences their importance in a minority community in ways that many within the community think is undesirable. As many critics point out, culture is largely relational and not a "natural or essential" sort of thing. But this observation does not help at all in resolving the problems of essentialism. Rather, it raises the questions of whether relations ought to be ones of restriction or accommodation and how we ought to decide. Whether they are restricted or accommodated, the practices of one community will be influenced and shaped by its relation to other communities. So the question of whether one community ought to accommodate the practices of another community through its laws and public policies must be decided on a basis other than the fact that accommodation constitutes a form of cultural interference or that it essentializes minority practices because, in many cases, the alternatives also entail interference and sometimes a more hostile form of essentialism.

The risk of internal oppression, that protecting group practices could end up tying individuals to practices they find oppressive, raises the question of whether the alternative to protecting group practices is also oppressive. In some cases, the alternative to tying individuals to their own cultural practices is to tie them to the practices and standards of another group, such as the cultural majority. In cases where a form of essentialism is a problem either way, the best solution appears to be to develop means that detect oppression and protect individuals from it, no matter what its source.

Consider, in this regard, cases in which, on one hand, individuals claim that their community's practices oppress them and, on the other hand, the community represents these practices as central to its identity. Cases of this sort often reveal that considerations based on identity can clarify rather than further confound the issues at stake. For instance, in *Sandra Lovelace v. Canada*, the United Nations Human Rights Committee examined the effects of a law that revoked the Aboriginal status and benefits of women who marry outside their communities on the cultural identity of Aboriginal women to whom this law applied. The Canadian government defended the law on identity grounds by arguing that it helped protect communities from being dominated by non-Aboriginal men. The UN committee approached the problem by balancing the effects of the law on Aboriginal women with its purported effects on Aboriginal communities more generally. It found that the effects of the law on women were devastating,[10] while the role of the law in sustaining Aboriginal identity was minor. Therefore, using criteria related to identity, the committee decided against Canada. In contrast, in *Kitok v. Sweden,* the committee upheld a law that denied a Sami man the right to partake in reindeer husbandry because he was not a Sami village member. Again, criteria related to identity were invoked. The committee recognized "reindeer husbandry to be so closely connected to the Sami culture that it must be considered part of the Sami culture itself" (para. 9.7). But the rule passed by the Swedish government, purportedly to protect the welfare of the Sami people, restricted the right to reindeer herding to village members and not to all individuals who are Sami. The committee urged Sweden to find "objective ethnic criteria in determining membership in a minority" (ibid.), yet it nonetheless recognized that the objective of a rule favouring village membership was valid, and on this basis the law should stand.

These cases illustrate that sometimes it is impossible to protect group practices in a manner that avoids imposing practices on individuals. However, where this is impossible, the extent to which a law jeopardizes group identity can be compared to its effects on individuals. In some cases, such as *Lovelace,* it seems clear which side, on balance, has a stronger claim on the basis of whose identity is more jeopardized by the regulation. Not all cases are likely to be so clear. But as with other challenges that public institutions confront, this challenge can be met only by developing transparent and fair criteria to assess and compare the identity claims of groups and their members and not by abandoning the assessment of such claims altogether.

Are Identity Claims Unconstrainable and Thereby Anti-Democratic?

A third general objection is that the public assessment and potential rejection of identity claims will lead to or heighten social conflict. This is partly because an approach that frames conflicts in terms of identity claims engages values that are at the same time integral to a person's sense of self and not widely understood. This combination of characteristics has the effect of creating some incentives for people to engage in strategic reason-giving of a sort that raises the stakes in democratic discourse so that compromise becomes impossible.[11] The worry is that people use identity to make their interests appear special and more worthy of resources than other interests.

This third objection has two sides. One side is the suspicion that groups make lavish claims. For example, in the case of Van der Peet, this concern would be that Van der Peet sold salmon not because she thinks selling salmon is important to her "identity" but because she can claim that it is important to her identity and because selling salmon is lucrative. The concern is that an identity-based framework invites Van der Peet to employ her identity strategically and that, more generally, this framework promotes an identity-driven discourse of lavish claims. The second side is the worry that too much is at stake when people are required to justify their actions using identity-based criteria. The risk of social conflict follows when courts or legislatures deny claims that others view as closely related to their entire sense of self.

Although the first concern, about lavish claims, is worth bearing in mind, it is not without some ironic features. In political practice, the opportunities to frame claims in terms of identity are on the rise but, ironically, some scholars suspect that this is because framing conflicts in terms of protecting identity narrowly restricts the sorts of claims that groups can make and often fails to capture the interests most relevant to some cases, especially those involving national minorities and indigenous peoples. For example, some Aboriginal people are concerned that opportunities to argue for the protection of discrete identity-related practices are replacing venues to argue for broader claims to self-determination and self-government (see Borrows 1997-98, 47-48). Whereas the critics worry that identity claims will open the floodgates for all sorts of group-based interests, whether they are about identity or not, the concern expressed by Aboriginal peoples, who are often in the position of making such claims, is that identity arguments unfairly restrict and narrow the sorts of claims that they can make because forums to argue effectively for self-determination are unavailable. This problem has increased the pressure on international institutions to develop parallel institutional processes for the recognition of self-determination and the negotiation of self-government agreements.[12]

The second concern, about the sensitive nature of identity claims, is, again, worth bearing in mind, but is also easily exaggerated and often mitigated by the real possibility of compromise in most cases that involve cultural traditions or religious practices. Courts often hear evidence about different ways in which practices can be followed and how they can be altered without jeopardizing whole traditions. In the case of religious minorities, the laws are full of such examples. For example, the issue of whether Sikh boys can wear kirpans to school led to policy compromises in British Columbia and Ontario that restrict the size of the dagger and specify how it should be strapped to the child's body so that it is difficult to remove. Controversies about circumcision, minority education, and religious animal slaughter are also examples in which accommodation has involved compromising the precise way in which groups practise their traditions without restricting the tradition entirely. While not all the outcomes in these disputes are satisfactory, they each nonetheless show that most claims are amenable to some compromises regarding how they are carried out and by whom. Moreover, often these compromises are reached in the context or aftermath of legal and political decisions that establish the need to protect practices in the first place because of their importance to the group's identity.

In sum, the three general objections examined here raise concerns worth bearing in mind. But none provides good reasons to avoid the public assessment of identity in all cases, and some of the problems raised by the objections, such as essentialism, are problems minorities may confront regardless of whether or not they seek protection for their identity claims. The problem of inscrutability raises a normative objection to assessing identity only because it mischaracterizes the aim of publicly assessing identity claims. It then relies on a mistaken understanding of the extent to which identity claims are empirically mysterious. The problem of historical essentialism usually fails to account for the realistic alternatives to protecting the practices of minority groups, which in many cases entail more threatening forms of essentialism that end up tying groups to the nationalist values of the majority or to values generated by the market. With respect to the problem of internal oppression, although protecting groups sometimes ties individuals to oppressive group practices, rather than constituting a reason not to protect groups at all, this problem suggests that individual and group claims sometimes have to be balanced with each other. Identity can sometimes provide a helpful framework for such comparisons and a means to balance claims. Finally, with respect to the problem of social conflict, this objection underestimates the extent to which identity claims are amenable to compromise. The objection is also out of touch with what is often a more serious problem, which is that identity narrows the terms upon which some groups, especially national minorities and Aboriginal groups, can advance their claims for self-determination.

Are There Benefits to Assessing Identity Claims?

Perhaps because the problems surrounding identity politics have been exaggerated, there exists in political theory a general reluctance to consider the benefits of framing conflicts in terms of identity and designing criteria to guide the public assessment of identity claims. One of the most obvious benefits (though perhaps less a reason than an acknowledgment of reality) is that developing fair criteria will help ensure that identity claims are assessed in a more fair and systematic manner. This is a significant benefit partly because public institutions are confronted with identity claims all the time. Minority groups often frame their claims against the state in terms of how their way of life is adversely affected by policies that the majority has passed, but which fail to take account of the minority's distinctive interests. Minority claims are often framed in these terms because individuals and groups view the harm that is done to them by state regulations or mainstream practices as a harm done to their way of life or their understanding of how they should conduct their life. One benefit of developing fair criteria of assessment is that doing so offers institutions an expanded conceptual vocabulary to employ in cases that involve identity claims.

A second benefit is that expanding the conceptual vocabulary of public institutions in this way appeals to the moral intuition of equal respect, which holds that people ought to be recognized on their own terms. These terms will often require a deeper public understanding of identity-related considerations and how these relate to social institutions and public regulations. While nothing guarantees that all individuals and groups can lead their lives precisely as they want to lead them, equal respect ensures that the restriction of some ways of life can only be decided after a full and demonstrated understanding of what is at stake for the group or individual being restricted. This kind of understanding requires the fair assessment of considerations of identity.

A third benefit is that a public and transparent set of criteria for assessing identity claims is a means to confront the mainstream biases that currently inform many institutional practices and methods used to assess the claims of minorities. To understand, even imperfectly, the commitments that other people claim are important to them is a means to better understand how mainstream institutions and practices are often not neutral, but rather create advantages for some and disadvantages for others. It may be impossible for public institutions to rid themselves of all cultural, religious, or other identity-related biases. Nonetheless, the project of pinpointing where these biases lie, whether they are opportunistic, and whether they can or ought to be eliminated is still worthwhile. Perhaps the law that restricts a particular practice is crucial to averting harm or protecting the vulnerable. Or perhaps it is mostly convenient for the majority or is a means to control and manage groups in objectionable ways.[13] One concern that could be raised about the pervasive insistence among political theorists and practitioners that identity claims not be entertained within public institutions is that this insistence, and the putative neutral principles of proceduralism or liberalism that are usually used instead of identity-related criteria, can be used strategically against minorities and as a proxy in a power struggle among majorities and minorities. To take identity claims seriously is one way of ensuring that the "liberal inclination" *not* to engage in a fair politics of identity cannot be used as a means of clinging to the myth that liberal institutions and practices are neutral when they are not. Therefore, the development of criteria to be used in the public assessment of identity claims has the potential to strengthen and clarify standards of public reasons that are more comprehensive and inclusive.

Is the Canadian Test a Success?

In light of these potential benefits, is the Canadian experiment with devising a distinctive culture test a step forwards in devising fair criteria for the assessment of identity or in positioning the Canadian majority and Aboriginal peoples in a more equitable relation to each other? Has the distinctive culture test successfully expanded the conceptual vocabulary available to public institutions in their fair dealings with Aboriginal peoples? In general, the consensus, from which my assessment does not depart, is that the test is seriously flawed along several dimensions, some of which have been mentioned already. But it also contains some positive dimensions that have received (perhaps unsurprisingly) less attention.

One positive dimension is that the test recognizes that claims of identity are not empirically mysterious and need not be accepted at face value. The promise of this test is that conflicts will be resolved in light of arguments that seek to determine whether, for instance, the Sto:lo claim that trade in salmon is central to Sto:lo identity is stronger than the claim of other communities or other considerations. In the context of assessing this case in terms of identity, the Sto:lo can argue that their claim to trade in salmon is different in character from the claims of other peoples and that it is more important than other considerations because, for instance, their way of life is jeopardized without being able to trade in salmon, because historical records show that they have resisted giving up that way of life, and because evidence suggests that their way of life is unsustainable if trade in salmon is widely shared with non-Aboriginal fishers in British Columbia. In contexts where cultural and identity claims are disallowed, these arguments are irrelevant.

A second positive dimension is that the court recognizes the necessity of developing transparent criteria to respond to the claims as they are presented to the court in terms of identity. The *Van der Peet* decision reflects a recognition not only that the interests at stake are potentially important to the identity of the Sto:lo, but also that the evidentiary standards used to establish these claims can properly depart from the standards used in private litigation and "should not undervalue" the kinds of evidence presented by Aboriginal claimants (para. 68, *per* Lamer J.), including the use of oral history. These are hopeful signs insofar as they indicate that the project of developing a test to assess the identity claims of Aboriginal people has implicated the court in the broader project of considering what sorts of institutional reforms will ensure that the context for considering identity claims is inclusive and fair to the perspectives and experiences of Aboriginal people.

Critics may argue that, in light of the "precontact requirement" – i.e., that only Aboriginal practices predating European contact count as ones eligible for protection – what *Van der Peet* and the distinctive culture test actually show is the unwillingness of the court to develop transparent criteria directed at assessing identity claims. They may plausibly argue that if the court were serious about assessing identity, it would have to be willing to consider whether, in some cases, the only or best way to protect a community's identity is through territorial autonomy or self-determination.[14] Rather than taking identity seriously, the provisions, both domestically and internationally, for considering identity claims explicitly prohibit groups from arguing for the connection between identity protection and group self-determination. For instance, a general comment on Article 27 by the United Nations Human Rights Committee specifies that nothing in Article 27 may be interpreted so as to confer on a minority the right to self-determination (UN Human Rights Committee 1994, paras. 2 and 3.1). A similar provision is built into Canada's distinctive culture test through the precontact requirement. Clearly this requirement has little to do with a credible interpretation of Aboriginal identity.[15] It is included in the test because, in the absence of this requirement, the assessment and protection of Aboriginal identity using a distinctive culture test would have a far-reaching and possibly dramatic impact on Canadian law.

This observation leads to the immediate problem raised by the critics of *Van der Peet*, which is that an approach that focuses on identity is unjust because it serves as a convenient way for the courts to avoid the larger issue of self-determination. The Canadian court was able to take a case that involved the questionable sovereignty of the Canadian state over Aboriginal people and turn it into a case about whether trading salmon is integral to Sto:lo cultural identity and whether or how it can accommodated within existing Canadian law.[16] To frame conflicts in terms of identity seems to obscure what often motivates conflicts that involve national minorities and indigenous peoples. Often these conflicts turn on the denial of self-determination, regardless of whether or not cultural differences exist between groups. Therefore, approaches that focus on accommodating identity-related differences may be just another way of seeking to legitimize colonial rule (see Green 2000).

This final problem captures one of the key challenges of most identity politics. When institutions and especially courts focus on sorting out identity claims, they tend to interpret cases narrowly and in ways that are limited to assessing whether a particular practice or tradition can be accommodated within an unchanged legal order.[17] These decisions are unlikely to challenge in any fundamental way state sovereignty or the overall legitimacy of the legal or political order of the mainstream society. Yet they may motivate changes that have the potential to be fundamental in other ways. In Canada, for instance, judicial decisions, which have stopped well short of overturning Canadian sovereignty, have nonetheless provided much-needed motivation for governments to settle land claims, sort out resource sharing, participate in treaty negotiations, and even establish negotiation processes that have led to successfully negotiated self-government agreements.

It is important to recognize the limited role played by legal tests and institutions, such as courts, that apply these tests. But even within these limits, the development of fair criteria by which the identity claims of minorities, including Aboriginal peoples, can be fairly assessed has important benefits. These criteria demystify claims and thus deepen public understanding of the good reasons that exist to recognize different ways of life. They may provide motivation for institutional reform and, on some occasions, even expose the limited capacity of institutions to respond to identity claims fairly. When some critics suggest that Western institutions provide an inadequate context to discuss the identity claims of Aboriginal peoples, what they mean is not that cultural understanding and accommodation is impossible per se, but rather that institutions through which such discussions take place, such as the Canadian courts or legislatures, do not provide a fair context in which the requirements of Aboriginal identity can be discussed in an equitable manner. In this sense, the process of thinking about how to deliberate fairly about the identity of a particular group can drive the need to consider different sorts of institutional responses and preconditions to the fair consideration of cultural conflicts and resolutions to them.

Acknowledgments

I want to thank Michael Asch, Colin Macleod, and James Tully for helpful comments on a previous draft.

Notes

1 Section 35 of the *Constitution Act, 1982* reads: "(1) The existing aboriginal and treaty rights of the aboriginal peoples of Canada are hereby recognized and affirmed; (2) In this Act, 'aboriginal peoples of Canada' includes the Indian, Inuit and Métis peoples of Canada; (3) For greater certainty, in subsection (1) 'treaty rights' includes rights that now exist by way of land claims agreements or may be so acquired; (4) Notwithstanding any other provision of this Act, the aboriginal and treaty rights referred to in subsection (1) are guaranteed equally to male and female persons."

2 See *R. v. Powley* and *Mitchell v. M.N.R.* Only in *Powley* was the Aboriginal claimant successful.

3 Article 27 reads: "In those States in which ethnic, religious or linguistic minorities exist, persons belonging to such minorities shall not be denied the right, in community with the other members of their group, to enjoy their own culture, to profess and practise their own religion, or to use their own language" (UN Human Rights Committee 1994, para. 1).

4 *Hopu* was not decided on the basis of Article 27 because France has made a reservation to Article 27. Instead, the committee relied on articles that recognize the rights to family such as 17(1) and 23(1). For commentaries on these cases see Macklem (2004) and Scheinin (2000).

5 See Deckha, this volume. Two other excellent discussions of the use of identity in power struggles are Deveaux (2005) and Phillips (2005).

6 James Tully's notion of mutual recognition requires that people understand each other (including the reasons for each other's practices, traditions, and beliefs) in full and deep ways. I agree with Tully that just and stable relations among people can be enhanced by mutual understanding, and this includes understanding why different practices are important to people. I also agree with Tully that our political institutions should be designed to facilitate this kind of mutual understanding. However, this aim, as Tully acknowledges, is highly ambitious and difficult to attain. An approach that focuses on identity claims is, I hope, one that has the aim of mutual understanding, but could nonetheless be successful even where mutual understanding is imperfect, as it inevitably will be (see Tully 1995).

7 In this way, the approach is distinct from approaches that require merely that individuals and groups live together under conditions of stability. Chandran Kukathas (1998), for instance, argues that liberal institutions have no business debating identity or culture, and that liberalism is about leaving people to form the associations and communities they choose and enabling them to do so and coexist peacefully. But if by "peacefully" we mean that we should live not simply under conditions of stability but also under conditions that are just, then some deliberation about the traditions and practices that different communities adhere to is important to ensure that each is treated in a fair manner.

8 On this problem in anthropology see Asch (1992). In relation to historical evidence see Fortune (1993). On controversies about archival evidence see McRanor (1997). And finally, on the use of oral histories as authentic evidence see *Delgamuukw v. British Columbia*. Also see Borrows (2001).

9 There is no doubt that, in assessing identity, the wrong practices may gain protection. The controversy over *Van der Peet* provides a good illustration of how this happens. The distinctive culture test ties eligible rights-bearing practices to precontact times and, in this sense, "freezes rights" to practices that, while of ancient origin, may be only incidental to how contemporary Aboriginal peoples survive as distinctive communities.

10 In particular, the committee accepted Lovelace's claim that "the major loss to a person ceasing to be an Indian is the loss of the cultural benefits of living in an Indian community, the emotional ties to home, family, friends, and neighbours, and the loss of identity" (Canada 1981, 9.9(1)). In contrast, the rule was in place because "in farming societies of the nineteenth century, reserve land was felt to be more threatened by non-Indian men than by non-Indian women" (*Lovelace*, para. 5).

11 For a critical assessment of the strategic use of cultural identity claims see Johnson (2000) and Weinstock (2001).

12 International institutions have gone to substantial lengths to recognize this problem and address it, in part by insisting on a strict divide between instruments used to establish cultural rights and those used to establish the right to self-determination. See UN Human Rights Committee (1994).

13 For a development of this argument in relation to multiculturalism see Day (2000), especially Chapter 8.

14 As Kymlicka argues, this sort of implication is precisely what various "liberal nationalist" political theorists have argued. Both Yael Tamir and Joseph Raz have used the right to culture as the basis to defend a right to national self-determination (see Kymlicka 2005, 8n9). Similarly, Benedict Kingsbury has argued that Article 27 may be violated where individuals "are not allocated the land and control of resource development necessary to pursue economic activities of central importance to their culture" (1992, 482).

15 Moreover, it deviates from the criteria applied internationally to similar cases through Article 27. The UN Human Rights Committee has applied a broad set of criteria that includes, for instance, the need to ensure "the survival and continued development of the cultural, religious and social identity of the minorities concerned" (1994, para. 9).

16 Thanks to Hamar Foster for pointing this out.

17 This criticism is discussed in relation to *Van der Peet* by Borrows (1997-98, 46-47).

References

Books, Articles, and Public Documents

Asch, Michael. 1992. Errors in *Delgamuukw:* An Anthropological Perspective. In *Aboriginal Title in British Columbia: Delgamuukw v. The Queen,* ed. Frank Cassidy, 221-43. Lantzville, BC: Oolichan.

Barsh, Russell, and James Youngblood Henderson. 1996-97. The Supreme Court's *Van der Peet* Trilogy: Naïve Imperialism and Ropes of Sand. *McGill Law Review* 42(4):993-1009.

Benhabib, Seyla. 2002. *Claims of Culture: Equality and Diversity in the Global Era.* Princeton, NJ: Princeton University Press.

Borrows, John. 1997-98. Frozen Rights in Canada: Constitutional Interpretation and the Trickster. *American Indian Law Review* 22:37-64.

–. 2001. Listening for a Change: The Courts and Oral Tradition. *Osgoode Hall Law Journal* 39(1):1-38.

Brom, Frans W.A. 2004. WTO, Public Reason and Food: Public Reasoning in the "Trade Conflict" on GM-Food. *Ethical Theory and Moral Practice* 7:417-31.

Canada. 1981. Communication No. (CCPR/C/13/D/24/1977) [1981] UN HRC 13 (30 July).

Constitution Act, 1982, being Schedule B to the *Canada Act 1982* (U.K.), 1982, c. 11.

Day, Richard. 2000. *Multiculturalism and the History of Canadian Diversity.* Toronto: University of Toronto Press.

Deveaux, Monique. 2005. A Deliberative Approach to Conflicts of Culture. In *Minorities within Minorities: Diversity, Rights and Equality,* ed. Avigail Eisenberg and Jeff Spinner-Halev, 340-62. Cambridge: Cambridge University Press.

Dryzek, John S. 2005. Deliberative Democracy in Divided Societies. *Political Theory* 33(2):218-42.

Flanagan, Thomas. 2000. *First Nations? Second Thoughts.* Montreal and Kingston: McGill-Queen's University Press.

Fortune, Joel L. 1993. Construing *Delgamuukw:* Legal Arguments, Historical Argumentation, and the Philosophy of History. *University of Toronto Faculty of Law Review* 51(1):80-101.

Green, Joyce. 2000. The Difference Debate: Reducing Rights to Cultural Flavours. *Canadian Journal of Political Science* 33(1):133-44.

Johnson, James. 2000. Why Respect Culture? *American Journal of Political Science* 44(3):405-18.

Kingsbury, Benedict. 1992. Claims by Non-State Groups in International Law. *Cornell International Law Journal* 25(3):481-514.

Kitok v. Sweden. 1987/88. Communication 197/1985, *Official Records of the Human Rights Committee,* vol. II.

Kukathas, Chandran. 1998. Liberalism and Multiculturalism: The Politics of Indifference. *Political Theory* 26(5):686-99.

Kymlicka, Will. 2005. The Moral Foundations and Geopolitical Functions of International Norms of Minority Rights: A European Case Study. Paper presented at the IVR World Congress, Granada, Spain.

Macklem, Patrick. 2004. Indigenous Peoples and Human Rights: International Developments, Domestic Consequences. Unpublished manuscript.

McRanor, Shauna. 1997. Maintaining the Reliability of Aboriginal Oral Records and their Material Manifestations: Implications for Archival Practice. *Archivaria* 43:64-88.

Narayan, Uma. 1997. "Westernization," Respect for Cultures, and Third-World Feminists. In *Dislocating Cultures: Identities, Traditions, and Third-World Feminism,* ed. Uma Narayan, 3-39. London: Routledge.

Phillips, Anne. 2005. Gender versus Culture: Not Always a Deep Disagreement. In *Minorities within Minorities: Diversity, Rights and Equality,* ed. Avigail Eisenberg and Jeff Spinner-Halev, 113-34. Cambridge: Cambridge University Press.

Quong, Jonathan. 2002. Are Identity Claims Bad for Deliberative Democracy? *Contemporary Political Theory* 1(3):307-28.

Sandra Lovelace v. Canada. 1984. Communication No. 24/1977, U.N. Doc. CCPR/C/OP/1 at 83.

Scheinin, Martin. 2000. The Right to Enjoy a Distinct Culture: Indigenous and Competing Uses of Land. In *The Jurisprudence of Human Rights Law: A Comparative Interpretive Approach*, ed. Theodore S. Orlin, Allan Rosas, and Martin Scheinin, 159-222. Turke, Finland: Institute for Human Rights, Abo Akademi University.

Scott, David. 2003. Culture in Political Theory. *Political Theory* 31(1):92-115.

Tully, James. 1995. *Strange Multiplicity: Constitutionalism in an Age of Diversity*. Cambridge: Cambridge University Press.

United Nations. General Assembly. 1966. *International Covenant on Civil and Political Rights*. G.A. res. 2200A (XXI), 21 UN GAOR Supp. (No. 16) at 52, UN Doc. A/6316 (1966), 999 UNTS 171.

United Nations. Human Rights Committee. 1994. *General Comment 23: The Rights of Minorities (Art. 27)*, CCPR/C/21/Rev.1/Add.5, General Comment No. 23. (General Comments).

Waldron, Jeremy. 2000. Cultural Identity and Civic Responsibility. In *Citizenship in Diverse Societies*, ed. Will Kymlicka and Wayne Norman, 155-76. Oxford: Oxford University Press.

Weinstock, Daniel. 2001. Les "identités" sont-elles dangereuses pour la démocratie? In *Repères en mutation: Identité et citoyenneté dans le Québec contemporain*, ed. Jocelyn Maclure and Alain-G. Gagnon, 227-50. Montréal: Éditions Québec-Amérique.

Cases

Delgamuukw v. British Columbia, [1997] 3 S.C.R. 1010.

Mitchell v. M.N.R., [2001] 1 S.C.R. 911.

R. v. Powley, [2003] 2 S.C.R. 207.

R. v. Van der Peet, [1996] 2 S.C.R. 507 [*Van der Peet*].

3
The Imperative of "Culture" in a Colonial and *de facto* Polity
Shauna McRanor

The dominant understanding of indigenous struggles for freedom, an understanding that inhabits, among other things, liberal political theory and state practice, tends to rest on two separate but related assumptions. It tends to assume, first, that the liberal social order, one exemplified by the settler state, its sovereignty, and its constitutional regime of rights, is an unproblematic or legitimate limit to these struggles.[1] It also tends to assume that, given this putatively legitimate limit, the only reasonable way to address the problem that indigenous peoples are struggling against – namely, the problem of being governed in a way that severely disables their capacity to pursue life together with others as they see fit – is to interpret the limit represented by the liberal social order in a way that seemingly allows for the accommodation of the indigenous peoples' political goal. In other words, the dominant understanding of the problem assumes that it can be overcome not by resisting the modern liberal-democratic state but, instead, by enlisting it and its system of law to secure certain rights, most often so-called minority or cultural rights. For brevity's sake, this dominant understanding of indigenous struggles for freedom is referred to in this chapter as the "dominant paradigm."[2]

Within the realm of political theory, one particular approach that I consider to fall within this dominant paradigm has become, according to Will Kymlicka, so prevalent that debates surrounding diversity and equality, debates that include how indigenous freedom might be achieved, now largely address the question of "how to develop and refine" that approach, rather than the question of "whether to accept it in the first place" (2001, 42).[3] The approach referred to, which takes up the imperatives of both liberal nationalism and liberal multiculturalism, is known as liberal culturalism (39, 41).[4] Kymlicka, one of its best-known proponents, can see "no clear alternative" to it, a conclusion that leads him to declare liberal culturalism the winning approach "by default" (43).

This apparent triumph of liberal culturalism is, in my estimation, tightly linked to the first assumption of the dominant paradigm, noted above. That assumption – that the settler state's rights regime is an unproblematic or legitimate limit to indigenous freedom – gives liberal culturalists the grounds to understand indigenous peoples surrounded by the borders of those states as "minorities" relative to the rest of the population; relative, that is, to a settler majority, and hence vulnerable to mistreatment by that majority. As a result, liberal culturalists argue (but not in a single, undifferentiated voice) that group-specific or "cultural" rights ought to accrue to indigenous peoples to protect or promote their difference and their capacity to live their lives accordingly. There is, however, an important caveat to this argument. As Kymlicka, for one, says, these cultural rights ought to be recognized only if they and the "familiar set of common civil and political rights of [liberal state] citizenship" remain compatible with each other (2001, 42); that is, as long as the special rights held by indigenous groups do not clash with the fundamental or universal freedoms of individual group members, who are always considered by liberals to be, at some level, citizens of the liberal state.[5]

But these clashes do indeed arise, and when they do, the courts of the state are often enlisted to levy judgments (the enlisters frequently include indigenous individuals and groups). Taken at face value, most of these judgments seem to consider indigenous rights seriously. Indeed, the jurisprudence in settler states like Canada indicates that, despite their collective nature, minority or group-specific interests do not always lose out in contests that appear to pit them against the fundamental or universal freedoms of individuals. Via her "difference" approach to rights-based conflicts, Avigail Eisenberg has attempted to explain why this is the case. In her view, the courts decide which kind of right, a group or individual one, is more worthy of protection or promotion by first translating the rights in question "into the identity-related differences that some rights are meant to protect" (2001, 165), and then comparing, on the basis of the adduced evidence, the importance of those differences to the lives of the parties to the conflict. This, Eisenberg says, is the principled method that the courts use – perhaps never or not always perfectly – to arrive at decisions that might otherwise be viewed as arbitrary ones between equally valued rights (see also Eisenberg 1994).

That said, in the realm of indigenous-settler politics there is a deeper issue, one that involves much more than the principled method by which settler-state institutions can act nonarbitrarily while adjudicating conflicts between so-called special and universal rights.[6] In the realm of indigenous-settler politics there is also the issue of legitimacy – specifically, the legitimacy of the state's institutions in adjudicating these conflicts, the legitimacy of the state's constitutional regime of rights, the legitimacy of the state's ultimate sovereignty, and, indeed, the legitimacy of the liberal state itself (see, for example, Alfred 1999, 2002; Green 2000; Tully 2000). In this chapter, I foreground this issue of legitimacy and assert that, in its present political configuration, the settler state called Canada cannot be justified; that the relations of power between indigenous peoples and Canadian settlers are fundamentally colonial; and that, insofar as this *de facto* (as opposed to *de jure*) polity acts to frustrate indigenous peoples' aspirations to determine for themselves how they shall be governed (i.e., their aspirations for freedom), it demands to be called into question.

Given that the dominant paradigm tends to take the legitimacy of the liberal order characterizing the Canadian state for granted, I argue that it works against the very freedom that it claims to support. One of the main tasks of this chapter is to disclose this hidden cruelty of the dominant paradigm (following Brown 2002a, 421), this unintentional complicity in the colonizing impulses of the state.[7] This disclosure proceeds with a rather Foucaultian attitude. As he once wrote, "Those who resist or rebel against a form of power cannot merely be content to denounce violence or criticize an institution. Nor is it enough to cast blame on reason in general. What has to be questioned is the form of rationality at stake ... Liberation can only come from attacking ... political rationality's very roots" (1988, 71).

According to Wendy Brown (2001, 114-15), what Foucault calls political rationality (or "governmentality") can be thought of in many ways, such as the legitimating structure of any government, a mode of governance or modality of power, an order of practice or of discourse, or, for that matter, any technique that releases governments from the need to use physical violence.[8] To attack a particular political rationality (e.g., a colonial rationality) at its very roots, as Foucault directs, is to interrogate and unmask the sorts of things just listed, to remove their temporally transcendent cast and reveal them as, in fact, particular in time, as the conditions in which we happen to live in the present, as "historical, contingent, partial, and thus malleable, such that 'that-which-is' can be thought of as 'that-which-might-not-be'" (112, 116). To launch this sort of attack, therefore, is essentially to undertake a genealogy, "to call into question the most heavily naturalized features and encrusted relations of the present" and hence "expose as a consequence of power what is ordinarily conceived as divinely, teleologically, or naturally ordained" (118). In short, it is to detach "the power of truth from the forms of hegemony ... within which it operates at the present time" (Foucault 2000a, 133), "unfix the terms of the contemporary political situation" (Brown 2001, 120), and thereby open up the possibility for alternative futures.

To that end, I inquire into the political rationality of the dominant paradigm and, specifically, into how the concept of culture is used in discourses that understand indigenous freedom as that which is attainable within the liberal state. Serving as the focal point for this inquiry is the way culture operates in liberal political theory and the practice of liberal states, as exemplified by the liberal culturalism of Kymlicka and selected Canadian case law on Aboriginal rights. I propose that, in these contexts, the concept of culture does more to frustrate than facilitate indigenous freedom. That is to say, in the context of Canadian state practice and Kymlicka's political theory, the concept helps to exercise a certain colonial imperative, one that seeks to govern indigenous peoples as marked minorities, as those who are normatively different from (i.e., *politically* inferior to) the majority making up the settler state, and hence "naturally" or inevitably subject to that state's authority. Culture operates this way in these liberal accounts because the concept is strongly articulated with a rationality that works to domesticate or neutralize the political dimensions of indigenous difference, a difference that would otherwise represent a formidable challenge to the liberal social order and all that it entails. In other words, in these accounts the concept functions to sabotage the social capacity, or what I call the authentic freedom, of indigenous peoples "to participate in shaping the conditions of their collective existence" (Hayward 2000, 39), to help determine how and with whom they will lead their lives, and to "have a say and a hand over" (Tully 2002, 552) the ways in which they will govern their interactions among themselves and with others.[9] As a result, the use of the concept of culture in the liberal treatments of Kymlicka and Canadian state practice does not – in fact, *cannot* – work in the service of indigenous peoples, as claimed. Instead, it works in the service of a colonial polity called Canada, which will continue to exist in a *de facto* and illegitimate condition until it comes to terms with its colonialism and with the defective relations of power that have never ceased to animate indigenous-settler politics in this part of the world, as well as in others.

Having said all that, I do not mean to suggest that Kymlicka's brand of liberalism is the same as the liberalism of Canadian state practice in all respects, nor that liberalism is applied across all or even a few state institutions in the exact same way. Still, key aspects of Kymlicka's theoretical framework reinforce the way in which the Canadian state has treated indigenous individuals and groups at common law, and these aspects are particularly visible when a certain understanding of culture is invoked.

This chapter shows that these aspects undercut the emancipatory goals of Kymlicka's approach and the approaches developed by Canadian courts. I begin the argument by turning to the concept of culture at issue. Next, I explain how the concept of culture used in Kymlicka's work and Canadian case law on Aboriginal rights effectively marks indigenous peoples as normatively different (politically inferior) and thereby inevitably subject to state authority. I argue that, insofar as liberal political theory and Canadian state practice leave unexamined both the understanding of culture used and the standpoint of the liberal social order from which the concept is mobilized, they reinscribe rather than redefine the relations of power that currently exist. To put it another way, they declare colonialism dead at the precise moment they provide it with the means to live. I therefore advocate that the assumption that the liberal social order constitutes a legitimate limit to the exercise of indigenous freedom ought to be abandoned, as should the related assumption that this limit ought to be interpreted in terms of cultural rights.

Culture

Figuring centrally in liberal culturalism and its treatments of indigenous minorities is the so-called fact of difference, the consideration of which, for liberals at least, is a relatively new and perhaps surprising venture into the realm of equality. Indeed, it was once believed that the *only* way to pursue the liberal goal – namely, that we should all be treated equally by the state – was to denude us, the citizens, of our differentiating characteristics; to think of us all, abstractly, as essentially the same. In this account, what grounds our basic rights or fundamental freedoms as citizens is our common humanity, our universal inclusion in the category of "Man" or "Everyman." But what if treating people as though they were all the same does not effect equal treatment but, instead, unequal treatment and the promotion of injustice? What if the category "Everyman" is biased towards the interests of a white, heterosexual, male elite; towards, that is, this elite's (unspoken) difference, its (tacit) identity-based commitments? Perhaps it is, after all, as Clifford Geertz writes, that "to be human *here* is ... not to be Everyman," but "a particular kind of man, and of course men differ" (1973, 53). As such, should the "here" in Geertz's passage – the social and historical context – be morally relevant to equality? Should difference matter?

As we know, for many liberals difference has indeed come to matter. In their view, the liberal culturalist view, difference no longer opposes the political, a position that other liberals would find hard to entertain. Clearly, then, whether difference ought to matter, and, if so, how it should be treated, are hardly settled points within the liberal school of thought or across political theory more generally. Moreover, some political theorists, many of whom cannot be called straightforwardly or in any way "liberal," have suggested that difference is not only relevant to the political; it is also an "irreducible and constitutive aspect" of it (Tully 1995, 5). Whatever their theoretical stripe, however, the difference that has invaded the discipline of politics is almost always understood by commentators as cultural, irrespective of the difference concerned, whether it is of, say, indigenous peoples, immigrants, women, gays, lesbians, or the disabled.[10] As David Scott explains it, "the being of culture, the otherness of the Other as culture, is taken for granted. We now, literally, *experience* difference *as* culture" (2003, 103; emphasis in original). The latter consumes the former, and this would appear to hold true in disciplines other than politics, if not in other areas of life.

Culture is therefore the difference that, according to liberal culturalists, ought to be protected and promoted by cultural rights. But as Kymlicka has observed, the practice of liberal democracies in relation to culture – the "is" of the situation – has for a long period of time gone without an "ought." His culturalist project therefore aims to close this gap between reality and ideal, to explain and justify the way various classes of minorities should be identified and treated by liberal states (2001, 51-52). What has emerged out of Kymlicka's work, then, is a cultural rights taxonomy that provides a standard against which state practice with respect to minorities can be measured. Broadly speaking, these minorities are categorized within Kymlicka's taxonomy as either "national" or "non-national," with cultural rights accruing to both groups.[11] Everyone, in Kymlicka's estimation, is entitled to a culture, inasmuch as it is thought to provide the liberal subject with a meaningful context of choice, one instrumentally valuable to a good life. This assertion – that all are entitled to a culture – is premised, in part, on the belief that the Self is autonomous and separable from any given culture or context of choice, from that which might make the Self distinctive in a particular way (the Self is prior to its ends) (Kymlicka 1995, 75). For communitarians like Charles Taylor, whom Kymlicka includes in the liberal culturalist camp, this sort of qualification cannot be made, for the Self, in Taylor's mind, is always situated, always already a product of cultural difference – a difference that cannot be suspended, discarded, or made in any way morally irrelevant (the Self is constituted by its ends) (Taylor 1991, 37).[12]

Interestingly, however, Kymlicka must make what essentially amounts to a communitarian argument for those who fall into his national group, such as indigenous peoples and Quebecers. This is because, in his account, individuals belonging to national minorities are entitled to more than just *a* culture; they are entitled to *their own* culture, an entitlement that does not extend to those belonging to minorities designated non-national, such as immigrants and refugees. For these latter groups, access to a culture simply means differentiated access to the culture of the dominant settler group. The reason for the distinction between the national and non-national categories appears to relate to what Kymlicka perceives as a greater degree of significance to membership in the "historical communities" that make up the national type. In these cases, as he writes, "people *are* bound, in an important way, to their *own* cultural community. We can't just transplant people from one culture to another ... Someone's upbringing isn't something that can just be erased; it is, and will remain, a *constitutive* [emphasis added] part of who that person is. Cultural membership affects our very sense of personal identity and capacity" (1989, 175).[13] In this account, the Self seems to be constituted by, rather than prior to, its ends, just as a communitarian would argue.

Kymlicka has been determined to maintain that the Self is autonomous, however. For example, in responding to Rainer Forst, who asserts that Kymlicka presents culture as important not for its function as a context of choice (i.e., the conditions for autonomy) but instead for its function as a context of identity (i.e., situatedness), Kymlicka suggests that autonomy and identity are interdependent: "Considerations of identity provide a way of concretizing our autonomy-based interest in culture. In principle, either the minority's own culture or the dominant culture could satisfy people's autonomy-interest in culture, but considerations of identity provide powerful reasons for tying people's autonomy-interest to their own culture. Identity does not displace autonomy as a defence of cultural rights, but rather provides a basis for specifying which culture will provide the context for autonomy" (2001, 55n7).

But while identity might specify which culture will (or ought to) provide the context of choice needed for autonomy, it would appear, to Kymlicka at least, that not all cultures within a liberal state *can* provide such a context. Indeed, for him, the only ones so equipped are those that constitute a "societal culture" – a culture that is both "territorially concentrated" and "centred on a shared language," a "language that is used in a wide range of societal institutions, including schools, media, law, the economy, and government" (1998, 27). While the cultures of non-national minorities are presumably perceived to lack these elements, the cultures of national minorities are seen to have them. As such, Kymlicka says that "the aim of a liberal theory of minority rights is to define fair terms" for the integration of non-national groups into the majority societal culture "and to enable national minorities to maintain themselves in distinct societies [i.e., distinct societal cultures]" (2001, 55n7), albeit within the confines of the state and in virtue of state-mediated rights and delegated state authority.

There is no question in my mind that Kymlicka understands the concept of culture in a highly reified, depoliticized, and uneven way, as something that to some extent stands outside its social field of creation and re-creation, outside of human agency and intention, as though it were always already extant somewhere, functioning as a pre-existing tool box. It is an understanding that has left him open to criticism, of which he is very much aware. Among the critical comments, he notes (2001, 45), is the view that his idea of culture overestimates the role of shared norms or beliefs in generating group cohesion (culture as integrative) and thus underestimates group dissension and conflict (culture as contested). While Kymlicka acknowledges that this sort of criticism is valid, he is nonetheless unsure of what its implications might be for liberal culturalism in particular. After all, he says, the problem of culture is an issue that, like others, permeates political theory, thus making it a professional hazard, one that cannot be reduced to any theory or position. He does not believe, therefore, that the problem of culture is any worse in liberal culturalism than in other approaches, nor that the problem is fatal to it (46).

Kymlicka may be right that the problem of culture permeates all of political theory. Indeed, Scott has recently pointed out that the idea of culture itself has been rarely theorized or historicized in this context and therefore operates as a rather unexamined convention in the field. Culture appears as "merely and fundamentally *there,* like a nonideological background, or a natural horizon" (2003, 111; emphasis in original). But I wonder whether this lack of reflexivity about culture is not more significant in the case of liberal culturalism; whether, that is, Kymlicka is right to claim that the problem of culture in this liberal approach is no worse than in other strains of political thinking. I am skeptical of that claim, especially since Kymlicka's entire project seeks to provide the grounds for how liberal states ought to treat cultural diversity in practice. In other words, the liberal order of those polities – and, more specifically, their unity and stability *as* states – operates as a point of departure rather than a target of critique in his approach. This obvious investment in already-constituted political arrangements has led Sujit Choudhry to point to that investment as precisely the reason Kymlicka conceives culture using the specific criteria he does – namely, to limit the range of groups that can claim self-government rights or a degree of autonomy from the state (2002, 71-72).

I want to probe things a little further, however. I want to know why Kymlicka thinks that indigenous peoples, as groups that he believes are entitled to these rights of self-government, should still be *ultimately* subject not to their own authority (i.e., free) but to Canadian parliamentary authority (i.e., to self-government *within* the liberal order).[14] I want to examine the assumptions that inform these theoretical prescriptions and to discuss, in terms of its implications for indigenous freedom, the nature of Kymlicka's givens, the situatedness of his pursuit, and the effects of power that work on and through his liberal approach. In short, I want to ask why the state and the concept of culture are themselves unenculturated in his account; why difference, in what I perceive to be its entirety, is left unaddressed.

By "difference in its entirety" I mean true, relational, political difference or, to put it another way, the "authentic" difference that ebbs and flows in the negotiation of power. This difference – what we call "culture" or "identity" – is formed *in* society. It cannot be separated from the social sphere; it cannot be abstracted from human relationships, the processes of socialization, the contestation of power; it cannot be reified and given a laundry list of traits (as Kymlicka does with his criteria). This is because society and

culture are mutually constitutive, and difference is produced and reproduced, made and unmade, at this site of reciprocity via human interaction
and intention (Ortner 2001, 674-75). As a result, society and culture do not
exist before this human element; they cannot step outside of it and transcend the context that defines and redefines their particularity. This lack of
transcendence also applies, of course, to any specific conceptualization of
culture, including the one I have just presented here, which is, to put it
simply, that the idea of culture is itself *of* culture. And to the extent that it is
of culture, it is also an irreducible aspect of social life, that is to say, of
politics or relations of power (Nash 2001, 77).[15]

It is important to connect the idea of culture to the realm of the political
and to relations of power, and to maintain that connection in theoretical and
methodological discussions of diversity and equality. This prescription stands
whether the concept of culture is given an essentialist or anti-essentialist
cast; whether it is seen as fixed, bounded, and internally uniform or as
shifting, unbounded, and infinitely differentiated. Indeed, it is not enough
to assume that essentialism is fundamentally about domination and thus
always wrong, or that anti-essentialism is fundamentally about liberation
and thus always right. It is not enough, in other words, to assume that once
we understand what culture truly is – for example, anti-essential – all will be
fine. How we use the concept is perhaps a more important question, and it
is in the asking and answering of that question that we can establish whether,
in some specific case, an essentialist view of culture is indeed being used as
a tool of oppression, or whether an anti-essentialist take on the concept, if
dead to the issue of power, is undermining the point of its own critique
(Johnson 2000, 22; also see Dirlik 1996). Consequently, it is prudent to keep
in mind that insofar as the idea of culture is articulated and employed within
relations of power, it is an effect of that power. It is not disinterested or
detached.

All of this is to say that if culture is constitutive of our human condition,
then a culturally neutral state, one that can recognize and accommodate
difference without at the same time reifying and depoliticizing that difference, is an impossibility. To insist otherwise, to insist that the state is impartial with respect to culture, is to deny the fact it is also *of* culture and to
deny that it, too, is born of and sustained by the negotiation of power. For
what is the state if not a particular way of ordering social life and human
interaction and intention? What, indeed, are institutions if not the regu-
larization of particular human interactions and the power dynamics that invariably animate those relations?[16] In my estimation, the Canadian state and
its institutions are no exception to the rule: they do not exist in the absence
of human agency; they are neither self-generating nor self-regulating. Canada
and its current institutional arrangements for recognizing and accommodating difference – for example, its rights regime – do not represent some

impartial framework; rather, they are themselves produced and managed by difference, by relations of power and their effects. For that reason, it is not enough for the Canadian state and its institutions to recognize and accommodate the indigenous difference at issue; they themselves – that is, the state and its institutions – must be subject to radical change if indigenous peoples are truly to have a say in determining the ways in which they will govern their interactions among themselves and with others.

Those who subscribe to the dominant paradigm, however, seem to suffer from a certain blindness to the particularity of these institutions and the state form of social organization of which they are a part. Although liberal democracies are no less cultural than the diverse forms of life they include, it would seem that Kymlicka's approach to indigenous rights resists fully acknowledging this point. For instance, in a discussion about nationalism, he appears to suggest that, whereas the form of culture of liberal nations is "thin," the form of culture of illiberal nations is "thick" (2001, 40n2). This distinction is similar to one that, according to Wendy Brown, gets drawn in liberal political theory more generally, where, as she says, culture is largely "treated as a kind of primal, transhistorical, and subrational good," as something that is "especially cherished and valued by oppressed minorities" and is "counterposed to liberalism," which is "presumed to be relatively cultureless" (2002b, 576n8). As the next section shows, this treatment of culture is also the norm in Canadian state practice.

Normative Difference

If culture is treated as something *in* which minorities are immersed, on the one hand, and *from* which liberal democracies are abstracted, on the other, then it would seem to me that the concept works in liberal theory and practice to mark those who differ from the liberal standard.[17] When it comes to indigenous peoples, this marking proceeds in a very specific way. To be more precise, it does not simply denote their descriptive or *mere* difference; rather, it signals their normative difference, a difference that is worse than or inferior to the undisclosed difference – the apparent lack of culture – of the liberal settler state.

A certain irony attends this development, for the location of the presence of culture and the location of its absence have been seemingly reversed. Evidence for this reversal is captured in the word "culture" itself. In what are known as Standard Average European languages, Richard Waswo instructs, the "cult/cultivate/culture" triad derives from the Latin *colo* (or *cultum* in its past participle form) and refers to many things, including taming and nurturing vegetation and animals, tilling the soil, instituting law to govern settled farming folk, refining human tastes, and developing the human intellect (1997, 6).[18] Therefore, it refers fundamentally to the domestication of food and, following from that, the domestication of humans themselves.

Indeed, since the ability to make your own food removes the necessity to forage for it and move about the land, "culture" is what develops in the fixed location of the city, the *civitas,* the locus of civilization (4). The exportable units of civilization are "colonies" (6), the satellites of empire that introduce that culture and all that it entails (i.e., social order) to new places (34-35). But if this is what culture is, then the condition that exists elsewhere and prior to the arrival of that wholesale domestication must be thought of as something else. This condition is savagery, "and what is savage – *silvestris, silva* – is literally 'of the woods'" and thus of nature (6).[19] It is wild, unsettled, and entirely without rule or rulers. It is, in a word, cultureless.

This linguistic heritage tells us that when the colonizers arrive at their new destination, the indigenous peoples they find there will be without society or social order – without, for instance, law or government.[20] The "culture-bringers," the settlers, give them what they lack and, in so doing, assimilate indigenous peoples to (domesticate them under) this "better" or "more advanced" European condition, always legitimately, always with good reason, or so the story goes (see Waswo 1996). This view – that Europe had culture while indigenous peoples did not – fell out of favour in the twentieth century, when, with the addition of an "s," "culture" was transformed into "cultures" (Stocking 1982, 203),[21] pluralized to account for the varied ways in which humans live their ineluctably social lives. But could the granting of culture to indigenous peoples (i.e., seeing them as bearers of culture) be operating in the same way that the withholding of culture from them once did (i.e., seeing them as cultureless)? Could the understanding of culture noted above be marking indigenous difference as something that, in its failure to be and measure up to the liberal settler state, is *still* justifiably dominated by it (i.e., by societies once thought to be the only bearers of culture, but which are now commonly perceived as cultureless)? I think that this is indeed what this understanding of culture might be doing, and I will explain why by returning to Kymlicka's minority rights taxonomy and by briefly reviewing some selected jurisprudence in the area of Canadian Aboriginal law. I address these two items in turn.

As already noted above, Kymlicka draws a broad distinction between national and non-national minorities. But he has also brought attention, in some of his work, to a more detailed and, for my purposes here, more salient distinction drawn in international regulatory instruments within the national category, and specifically the distinction made between indigenous nations and non-indigenous or "stateless" nations, such as Quebecers. According to Kymlicka's analysis of international state-centred practice, the division of these groups into separate classes may find its source in Article 1 of the *United Nations Charter,* "which says that all 'peoples' have the right to 'self-determination,'" and in Article 27 of the *International Covenant on Civil and Political Rights,* "which says that 'members of minorities' have the right to 'enjoy their own culture ... in community with other members of their group" (Kymlicka 2001, 123). But, Kymlicka continues, because Article 1 is considered too strong and Article 27 too weak to apply to national minorities, a number of other international instruments have attempted to accord these minorities "substantive rights of autonomy and self-determination (unlike article 27) ... within the framework of larger states (unlike article 1)" (124). It would seem, then, that although these instruments appear to emphasize, for stateless nations, only a reinforced version of Article 27 – that is, an expanded right to culture – the emphasis for indigenous peoples appears to be "an expanded but more modest version" of Article 1 – that is, an extension of "self-determination to include indigenous peoples," but in a way that "provides a more limited account of what self-determination means, focussing on internal autonomy rather than independent statehood" (125). Hence, the right to self-determination that indigenous peoples ostensibly ought to enjoy is still *not quite the same as* the one enjoyed by states (i.e., enjoyed by the people comprising the majority in each state). Rather, in the indigenous case it is an internal rather than external right to self-determination, which is not, I would emphasize, a right to self-determinat at all (as in Article 1), but a right to self-government, an entitlement to delegated state authority.

Given that this appears to be the practice in the wider liberal order – the "is" of the international situation – Kymlicka provides an explanation as to why groups that fall within the national category have been treated differentially in this context:

A desire to remedy past wrongs is surely part of the explanation, but I suspect another, more important, reason is the belief that the cultural differences between majorities and indigenous peoples are much greater than with stateless nations. Indigenous peoples do not just constitute distinct cultures[;] they form entirely distinct forms of culture, distinct "civilizations," rooted in a premodern way of life that needs protecting from the forces of modernization, secularization, urbanization, "Westernization," etc.

In other words, the basis for international protection of indigenous peoples is not so much the scale of mistreatment in the past, but rather the scale of cultural difference. It is important to realize that these are, in principle, quite different grounds for rights. (128-29)[22]

Indeed, they are. And in the case of indigenous peoples, the grounds for rights are diverted from those that would address relations of power – specifically, colonialism or the scale of mistreatment – to those that concern the degree of dissimilarity, the order of magnitude, separating premodern and modern "civilizational" forms, or separating "distinct" indigenous cultural difference from settler existence. Moreover, in making this separation there is an implicit suggestion that the way of life of the settler is "better" than indigenous varieties of the same, for to describe indigenous peoples as "premodern" is to signal a belief in a progressive cast to the human condition, one that envelops all peoples into a single universal history and unceasing march of "progress." In this account, to be "modern" is to be liberal and therefore farther along this directional path towards some putative apex of human achievement. In addition, when the "more advanced" civilization, the settler one, comes into contact with "less advanced" indigenous ones, the modern liberal state must benevolently intervene to stop what certain evolutionary strains of anthropology would call acculturation – an otherwise "natural" or "inevitable" assimilation to the "higher" form.[23] After all, a premodern way of life, where in this account indigenous difference apparently resides, is simply too vulnerable, too weak, to be left to its own devices. Thus, it ought to be protected and promoted, via rights, to counteract the unrelenting assimilative forces of "progressive" settler society.

Kymlicka presents this grounding of indigenous rights as a widely unspoken norm of practice, as the basis for recognizing and accommodating indigenous peoples through these sorts of entitlements. He claims, however, not to agree with that grounding. Indeed, for Kymlicka, the reason that indigenous peoples ought to be recognized and accommodated is not because of their status as distinct premodern cultures, but rather because of their status as distinct societal cultures, specifically ones that were "involuntarily incorporated into the state" (2001, 40-41).

Still, even though Kymlicka claims not to agree with the argument that the rights of indigenous peoples are grounded in their normative difference, the colonial reasoning that informs that justification is nonetheless evident in his own approach. Recall, for instance, his comment that the form of culture of the liberal nation is "thin" relative to that of illiberal nations, which is "thick." This framing makes it appear as though the liberal form of culture – that is, the difference of the liberal state – is barely discernible, as if its difference is neutral or inconsequential to the recognition and accommodation of minority difference, and as though it were simply operating as a generic social organizing device with no interests of its own. It does, however, have these interests, not least among them the reinforcement of its unity and stability. This, then – the sound integrity of the state – is the assumed legitimate limit of liberal (and sometimes even nonliberal) accounts of freedom. While these accounts may present different ways of interpreting this limit (as, for example, cultural rights), the limit itself is never transcended; the legitimacy of the liberal social order, the state, remains unproblematized.

If, however, incorporation into the state was never agreed to by indigenous peoples in the first place (i.e., if it was involuntary), then ought not the legitimacy of this limit – the legitimacy of the state itself – be precisely the issue? And if, as in Kymlicka's approach, it is not, then what are the grounds for differentiating between, on the one hand, self-determining settler states and, on the other, merely self-governing indigenous peoples? In other words, why should the latter always be ultimately subject to the former? It may well involve a notion of normative difference, a notion that sees indigenous peoples as politically inferior. If this were not the case, the recognition that these peoples were incorporated into the state without consent should, if anything, undermine the idea that the freedom they ought to enjoy is *not quite the same as* the freedom enjoyed by the settler majority. Kymlicka maintains the distinction between groups with entitlements to self-determination (settler majorities) and groups with entitlements to self-government (indigenous peoples). His approach thereby supports, rather than undermines, the "not quite the same as" idea. So although, in his account, he recognizes indigenous peoples as different and hence entitled to cultural rights to protect that difference, he depicts their difference as normative, not just descriptive (see, for example, 2001, 39-48 and 120-32).

Normative difference, then, tends to ground indigenous freedom in the liberal theory and international practice detailed above. This grounding is also evident in the practice of individual settler states. In Canada, for instance, the notion of a marked divide between the liberal and indigenous condition is alive and well and has been invoked frequently in the jurisprudence developed under section 35 of the *Constitution Act, 1982,* the provision under which Aboriginal and treaty rights are recognized and affirmed, and specifically so within and by the Canadian state.

In 1996 the section 35 provision was given substance by the Supreme Court of Canada in its landmark *R. v. Van der Peet* decision. Then and there, the court laid out the factors that judges were henceforth to consider when evaluating section 35 claims. Among these factors, collectively known as the "integral to a distinctive culture" test (see paras. 55-67), two are of particular importance. First, to qualify as an Aboriginal right, the practice, custom, or tradition that constitutes the substance of the claim must be of central significance to the group in question. To be centrally significant, the court notes that a practice, custom, or tradition must amount to "one of the things that truly made the society what it *was*" (para. 55; emphasis in original). It must be distinctive of, but not necessarily unique to, a given group; it must, in short, be a defining feature of the indigenous community at issue.[24] Second, the practice, custom, or tradition at issue must also display continuity with those that existed among that same group prior to contact. Although this continuity between precontact (or "premodern") and current forms need not remain unbroken, there must be a clear indication that what the group does today is clearly rooted in what the group's ancestors did in the past, before European arrival; before, that is, "modern" and "naturally" assimilative settler difference appeared on the scene.

This "distinctive culture" approach developed in *Van der Peet* also plays an essential role in the Aboriginal title test devised by the Supreme Court in *Delgamuukw*, a decision it released a year later, in 1997. In this judgment, Aboriginal title was deemed to be a "species" of Aboriginal right, specifically a right to land (see *Delgamuukw v. British Columbia*, paras. 2 and 127). As a result, if a group were able to demonstrate, to the satisfaction of the court, that it occupied and used a territory to the exclusion of other indigenous groups prior to the assertion of European sovereignty, and that it had done so continuously since, then that exclusivity of occupation and use would indicate that the territory in question is integral to the distinctive culture of that particular group (para. 142). In other words, the reference point for the proof of Aboriginal title in particular is the same as the reference point for the proof of Aboriginal rights in general, namely, so-called modern Europe – when it arrived (in the case of rights), when it asserted its sovereignty (in the case of title), when, in short, its assimilative tendencies were unleashed on "premodern" indigenous life.

Any number of legal cases could be adduced to support this argument – that is, to demonstrate that indigenous difference is always adjudicated with reference to a European standard and how, "at the pleasure of the Crown," what is "properly" indigenous is invariably conceived as falling a bit short of that standard, as normatively different to Europe. It will suffice to discuss two more cases. In the *Baker Lake* decision of 1979, a decision upon which both *Van der Peet* and *Delgamuukw* draw (Asch 2000a, 120-23, 126), the Federal Court of Canada suggested that, among other things, indigenous peoples could actually lack, in fundamental contradistinction to modern European peoples, any form of society worthy of the name.[25] What facilitated this suggestion was the reliance of the *Baker Lake* court upon *Re Southern Rhodesia* (Asch 2000a, 121 and citations therein), a decades-old British Privy Court ruling that placed indigenous and European peoples at polar ends of a primitive-civilized scale, as revealed most explicitly in the following extract from the judgment: "Some tribes [indigenous peoples] are so low in the scale of social organization that their usages and conceptions of rights and duties are not to be reconciled with the institutions or legal ideas of civilized [European] society. Such a gulf cannot be bridged" (233).

The decisions in *Baker Lake, Van der Peet,* and *Delgamuukw* exhibit the same colonial rationality from which this sort of comment issued. This is not to say, however, that the decisions of the Canadian courts were in error simply because they relied directly or indirectly on an irredeemably bad prior judgment, that of *Re Southern Rhodesia*. On the contrary, the point to be made here is that, given the colonial imperative working on and in these Canadian institutions, no other decisions could have been rendered. To put it plainly, the reasoning of *Re Southern Rhodesia* "works" in this liberal context, a context informed by a colonial rationality, one that governs the way indigenous difference and freedom can even be imagined (i.e., as legitimately limited by "superior" settler difference or by the liberal social order).

Power

I therefore suggest that this is the colonial rationality at play in both the case law on Aboriginal rights just reviewed and Kymlicka's liberal culturalism, outlined earlier. It is a rationality wedded, I believe, to the idea that indigenous peoples are normatively different, and, insofar as it informs how state practice and Kymlicka's theory treat those peoples, it is difficult to see how either practice or theory could advance the realization of indigenous freedom. Indeed, I would argue that this way of thinking operates instead as a "discourse of conquest" (Williams 1990, 8),[26] and precisely one that assists the state in shielding a specific set of European (and even more specifically British) institutions – and the encrusted relations of power that they hold in place – from the realm of deliberation and thus from the realm of the political (Day 2000, 225). As Richard Day has said before, although these institutions are more strongly articulated with a European-mediated difference than with any other, an articulation enforced and reinforced by asymmetrical relations of power, they are nonetheless promoted as belonging to no group in particular, as cultureless and universal, as accepting of all difference (223). The situatedness of state institutions, not to mention of the state form itself, is therefore disavowed precisely at the moment that the situatedness of indigenous peoples (among others) is purportedly recognized by the state's institutions and accommodated within their "multicultural" expanse.

This expanse, however, is a façade behind which these institutions work, in effect, to exclude and obliterate a difference that is true, relational, and political – in short, authentic – as previously defined above. The Canadian state, as the beneficiary of asymmetrical relations of power, says that this should be so; it says that what is integral to a distinctive indigenous culture can only exist up to, but not at, the point of contradiction with the state. This point was recently driven home in 2001, when the Supreme Court issued its decision in *Mitchell v. M.N.R.* There, the court declared that the British common-law doctrine of sovereign incompatibility still applies, and therefore made it clear that when the territorial integrity or political unity of the state is threatened by an indigenous difference asserting something akin to a political personality, it will refuse to recognize that difference and "mark" it into juridical irrelevancy. As the court wrote in its summary to the judgment:

> British colonial law presumed that the Crown intended to respect aboriginal rights that were neither *unconscionable* nor *incompatible* with the Crown's sovereignty. Courts have extended this recognition to practices, customs or

traditions integral to the aboriginal community's distinctive culture. While care must be taken not to carry forward doctrines of British colonial law into interpretations of s. 35(1) without careful reflection, s. 35(1) was not a wholesale repudiation of the common law. The notion of incompatibility with Crown sovereignty was a defining characteristic of sovereign succession and therefore a *limitation* on the scope of aboriginal rights. (*per* Major and Binnie JJ.; emphasis added)

Simply put, Canada's source of sovereignty can, according to colonial law, decide the scope of indigenous difference. It should come as no surprise, then, that indigenous difference is invariably interpreted, in this context, as being *merely* cultural rather than political. After all, since what is "Aboriginal" must be reconciled with and hence domesticated by the "fact" of ultimate state sovereignty, it cannot compete with the thing with which it is to be reconciled (Asch 2000a, 134); it cannot compete with a settler majority that is, magically, always already *more* self-determining than indigenous peoples. Thus, whatever the state deems to constitute the meaning of "Aboriginal," that meaning cannot be politicized, in the sense that it cannot challenge the state's fundamental authority over indigenous peoples, and therefore cannot capture what is meant by authentic indigenous freedom.

But how did the state come to attain this authority, this insurmountable limit? How has it been able to evacuate indigenous difference of all its political force, or at least apparently so? Some commentators have fingered the retrospectively imposed fiction of *terra nullius* as the culprit (see, for example, Asch 2000a, 2000b). This fiction, from the vantage point of the present, imagines Canada at the time of colonization as a land without people, or at least without people socially organized enough to warrant political recognition.[27] Though the operation of this fiction is never officially admitted, it is the crucial component of the *ex post facto* justification for the present concentrated power of the Canadian state. In other words, according to state-centric thinking, which is heavily invested in a concept of sovereignty that promotes the enforcement of state borders and the ideal of noninterference (Patton 1996, 165; Young 2000), this power gives the Canadian polity the authority to pre-empt – through simple adjustments – any move that might threaten its politically undifferentiated unity (its *de facto* condition) or that might transform the colonial relationship into one of politically differentiated equals and allow Canada to rightfully come into being.

These simple adjustments include, as I have already shown above, placing an emphasis on culture and, in particular, the cultureness of indigenous peoples. In virtue of this cultural emphasis, the liberal state, that "cultureless" order, avoids addressing the supposedly *terra nullius*-derived relations of power that cause and perpetuate indigenous unfreedom, and that therefore continue to inform the colonial dynamic between the settler state and the indigenous peoples living within its borders. Consequently, in the practice of liberal recognition, which often occurs in Canada via section 35 adjudication, those state-privileging relations of power are reinscribed, thereby domesticating the indigenous culture-bearer "*back into* the community of abstract [state] citizenship" (Povinelli 2002, 185; emphasis in original); that is, back into the community of the politically unified and non-culture-bearing liberal condition. With the colonial fiction of *terra nullius* in active (but unacknowledged) circulation, and with the preeminent sovereignty of the Crown considered an unassailable fact, the way to best manage the interests people, as individuals, have in their respective cultures – as Kymlicka, for instance, would put it – comes to be understood as a common way to interpret the limit within which the problem of indigenous unfreedom can be resolved. To believe this, however, is to believe that indigenous freedom *is* possible within the confines of the settler state. It is to believe that justice will indeed be served if the difference that is crucial to the autonomy of the indigenous individual, to his or her flourishing as a state citizen, is judged worthy of recognition by the institutions of that liberal order and deemed to be, via state courts, a group right – that is, one vested in the distinctive indigenous culture to which the indigenous individual may lay claim.

Reified or depoliticized difference is thereby recognized at the exact same time that authentic (interactional or political) difference is thwarted, and the net result is called cultural accommodation. For the liberal subject, it has to be this way, for he or she must be delivered into a world made safe for difference (Scott 2003, 97 and citations therein),[28] into a world in which difference in the form of disagreement and conflict is neutralized and governed by a host of cultural rights, of normalized identities and encrusted social relations, of oppression and domination. And in this world, in the "fantasy space" where indigenous difference, on the one hand, and liberal theory and practice, on the other, "coexist without conceptual violence or producing social antagonism" (Povinelli 1999, 21), true, relational, political (i.e., authentic) freedom, as James Tully (1999) tells us, is not possible. Simply put, a world made safe for difference is one that has been emptied of politics, emptied of the sites of interaction that are not only acted on by difference, but that also issue and reissue difference.

Conclusion

Richard Day and Tonio Sadik have summarized at least part of the problem at the heart of this chapter in the following way: "Preserving a [reified and depoliticized] culture within a multinational federation is one thing; offering up *competing* models for the articulation of peoples with polities and economies is quite another" (2002, 29; emphasis added). Indeed, it is the difference between unfreedom and freedom. I have argued that Kymlicka's liberal culturalism (as an instance of liberal political theory) and Canadian case law on Aboriginal rights (as an instance of state practice) operate to effect the former; they work to eradicate those competing models by disabling their political dimensions (i.e., depoliticizing them) through an emphasis on a certain understanding of the term "culture," and by domesticating indigenous peoples into the settler state and homogenizing them "into a 'native slot' on the ethnic landscape" (Day and Sadik 2002, 25 and citations therein). In so doing, these liberal approaches refuse to acknowledge indigenous peoples' specificity, which is precisely their social capacity, their freedom, "to express that specificity on [their] own terms" (ibid.). They instead transform indigenous subjects into liberal subjects and into citizens of the state.

This is the predicament that a colonial and *de facto* polity creates, a state in which the apparent liberal commitment to indigenous difference, to "the interests in culture," turns out to be a commitment to recognizing and accommodating – in short, governing – reified or depoliticized indigenous minorities (based, that is, on a reified and depoliticized sense of culture), and thus really to fostering political sameness (the unity and stability of the state). In other words, as strange as it may sound, when indigenous struggles for freedom and for the radical reconfiguration of an existing order of social life (e.g., the "legitimate" limit of the state) are reduced to liberal calls for the recognition of difference (e.g., through the interpretation of that limit as cultural rights), such a reduction could very well work towards the assimilation of indigenous difference and to misrecognizing what difference might really mean to those desiring emancipation. Thus, the assumption of the legitimate limit of the state and the interpretation of that limit as cultural rights ought to be abandoned, for in the moment of reduction to this form of liberal recognition, the liberal comes to be revealed as implicated in the structures of oppression and in the perpetuation of indigenous unfreedom, and as working in the same colonial rationality as the one the liberal purports to criticize (see Brown 2001, 210).

I do not see how liberal thinking can escape that rationality if it insists on the viability of the state in its current organization; if it insists, that is, on this one particular arrangement of human relationships as a legitimate limit on all others. As Kate Nash reminds us, "'the state' is always an unstable and temporary outcome – however long a particular formation may last – of ongoing ... politics" (2001, 88), of ongoing social life, of ongoing effects of power. The state, at any given time and place, cannot escape itself. And so while there is no doubt that we will disagree over how to best interact with one another, how to best relate to and order our polities (and economies, for that matter), the contingency of those interactions and orderings – that is, the contingency of our societies and the diffuse power that animates them – means that we are not endlessly condemned to an ineluctable fate.

We must resist the thinking that would have us believe that. It is, after all, in that resistance, in the throes of struggle, in the dust of conflict, that we find the space for social possibility, the room for alternative futures.

Acknowledgments
I wish to thank Avigail Eisenberg for the engaging conversations that led to this essay; Jim Tully, Taiaiake Alfred, and Michael Asch for their inspiration and helpful comments on earlier drafts; and Jocelyn Maclure for his thoughtful reading of the manuscript.

Notes

1 For the purposes of this chapter, I use "state" to mean, following Trouillot, "the apparatus of national governments" (2001, 131). That said, I realize, again following Trouillot, that "in the age of globalization, state practices, functions, and effects increasingly obtain in sites other than ... the national order" (ibid.), and while they perhaps never entirely bypass that order, they certainly broaden the notion of what the word "state" might signify.

2 For a highly useful historical review of this paradigm and others for understanding and addressing these sorts of struggles see Tully (Chapter 1, this volume).

3 Kymlicka has expressed this view elsewhere: "I think we can see an emerging consensus, or at least a dominant paradigm," for which one of the central claims is "that some or other form of multiculturalism is now unavoidable – 'we are all multiculturalists now,' as Nathan Glazer puts it ... – and that the interesting debate is not whether to adopt multiculturalism, but rather what kind of multiculturalism to adopt" (2000, 217).

4 Whereas liberal nationalism holds that "it is a legitimate function of *the state* to protect and promote the national cultures and languages of the nations within its borders," liberal multiculturalism posits that "non-national cultural groups ... such as immigrant and refugee groups, religious minorities, or even non-ethnic cultural groups like gays or the disabled ... have a valid claim, not only to tolerance and nondiscrimination, but also to explicit accommodation, recognition, and representation within the institutions of *the larger society*" (Kymlicka 2001, 39, 41; emphasis added). In short, liberal nationalism pertains to national minorities, while liberal multiculturalism attends to non-national minorities. Kymlicka's grounds for this distinction are later explained briefly in the present chapter.

5 On this account, if indigenous groups wish to secure external freedom (or rather group-based rights), they cannot restrict the internal freedom (or rather the individual rights) of their members. They cannot, in short, be illiberal.

6 In elucidating this "principled method," I believe Eisenberg is committed to explaining how the law of liberal states deals and ought to deal with difference when those states and their rights regimes are taken as the limits to the debate: "Because the most attractive feature of rights is the political and legal power they promise, *by framing our fundamental values in terms of rights* we implicate ourselves in the project of determining how to resolve conflicts between these fundamental claims in a non-arbitrary manner. The difference perspective is part of that project" (2001, 168; emphasis added).

7 While I acknowledge a distinction is possible between those who might actively support colonialism as a "good thing," on the one hand, and, on the other, those (perhaps like liberal culturalists) who fail to sufficiently recognize colonial relations of power that they would, if they were aware of them, likely disavow – a difference rightly pointed out to me by Colin Macleod – I would nevertheless maintain that, since colonialism is reinscribed in either case, the distinction is easily (and conceivably even ought to be) elided.

8 Scott is instructive on the analysis of political rationality in the context of the present chapter and writes that "in order to understand the project of colonial power at any given historical moment one has to understand the character of the political rationality that constituted it" (1995, 204).

9 For Hayward, this "social capacity to help shape the terms of one's life with others" is the essence of political freedom (2000, 10) and is what I mean by "authentic" (or, alternatively, "true, relational, political") freedom. For more on the idea of freedom expressed here see Tully (2002, especially 551-52).

10   In terms of state policy, the application of the term "culture" to religious and nonethnic difference occurs with more frequency in the United States than in Canada or Australia. In the two latter cases, the idea of culture is largely reserved for racial or ethnic difference. (See Day 2001, 174-75.)

11   See note 4, above, for Kymlicka's general distinction between "national" and "nonnational" minorities.

12   As Taylor writes, "it follows that one of the things we can't do, if we are to define ourselves significantly, is suppress or deny the horizons against which things take on significance for us" (1991, 37).

13   Kymlicka offers this comment in the context of a discussion about "history-based groupist" claims, ones that appeal to "the importance of membership in historical communities," such as those of national minorities (1989, 175). For more on Kymlicka's communitarian cast see Lenihan (1991, 417).

14   "In Native politics," according to Alfred, "there are two approaches to the future: one that seeks to resurrect a form of indigenous nationhood (a traditional objective), and another that attempts to achieve partial recognition of a right of self-government within the legal and structural confines of the state (an assimilative goal). It is this divergence in the political positions of various indigenous organizations that allows the state to manipulate the so-called decolonization process towards its own objectives" (1999, 99).

15   The intersectional formulation of culture, society, politics, and power that I outline here fits well with some of the thinking presented by Hardt and Negri: "The political is understood here as the foundation of every social relationship and the originary evaluation or 'decision' that constructs the sphere of power and thus guarantees the space of life" (2000, 463n6). It also fits well with Foucaultian offerings, for example: "One sees why the analysis of power relations within a society cannot be reduced to the study of a series of institutions or even to the study of all those institutions that would merit the name 'political.' Power relations are rooted in the whole network of the social" (2000b, 345).

16   Of course I do not mean to suggest that all human interactions and relations of power are institutionalized, for this is evidently not the case.

17   I find it interesting that the treatment of liberalism as cultureless appears to mirror the way liberalism once invariably treated the idea of the citizen, that is, as something that must be denuded of its differentiating characteristics.

18   For example, the triad appears in French as *culte/cultiver/culture,* in Italian as *culto/colitvare/ coltura,* and in German as *Kult/kultivieren/Kultur* (Waswo 1997, 6).

19   The word "autochthonous," which is applied to indigenous peoples, literally means "sprung from the land itself" (Waswo 1997, 35).

20   That is to say, indigenous peoples will be found without society or social order because they will be in a state of nature, in a condition of natural equality. Here, in this condition, every person is an island, left to fend for himself or herself. In this situation, the basis for "society" is wanting: there are no hierarchies of power to organize; no politics; no social relations requiring regulation through law.

21   As Stocking reports, "In extended researches into American social science between 1890 and 1905, I found no instances of the plural form in writers other than [Franz] Boas prior to 1895. Men referred to 'cultural stages' or 'forms of culture,' as indeed [E.B.] Tylor had before, but they did not speak of 'cultures.' The plural appears with regularity only in the first generation of Boas' students around 1910" (1982, 203).

22   With reference to Kymlicka's use of the phrase "forms of culture" see Stocking's comment at note 21, above.

23   For an example of the "acculturation" thesis in the anthropological literature see Murphy and Steward (1956).

24   I would note here that there is no consistency as to how, exactly, the "community" is construed in any given case – whether by band, tribal council, language, or otherwise – simply because the community of "relevance" emerges out of the deliberations of the court, based on the evidence provided.

25   I refer here to the first criterion of the four-point test that came out of the *Baker Lake* proceedings, namely, that to secure legal recognition of Aboriginal title, a group had to

establish that "they and their ancestors were members of an organized society" (*Hamlet of Baker Lake v. Minister of Indian Affairs and Northern Development et al.*, 557-58). As Bell and Asch have pointed out, this statement, which is part of what they call the "legal theory of culture" (1997, 64), allows for the possibility that people can live together in groups yet entirely lack, or have very little, social organization.

26 A "discourse of conquest" is a technique (in the Foucaultian sense) whereby "demands for further ... examinations of the colonizing enterprise" are dismissed or deflated (Williams 1990, 8).

27 I use "retrospectively" here because, as some scholars have noted, in virtue of entering into treaty relationships with indigenous peoples at, after, and well beyond contact, European colonizers clearly acknowledged the political personalities of the former (see, for instance, Schulte-Tenckhoff 1998, 239-89). I would also add that the *terra nullius* hypothesis has been explicitly repudiated as justification for the dispossession of indigenous peoples by, for example, the International Court of Justice in *Western Sahara* and the High Court of Australia in its decision in *Mabo v. Queensland*. For more on this point see, for example, Asch (2000a, 134, 2000b, 152) and Patton (1996, 165).

28 On the same "made safe for difference" theme see Michaels (2000), who distinguishes between "difference *without* disagreement" and "difference *as* disagreement."

References

Books, Articles, and Public Documents

Alfred, Taiaiake. 1999. *Peace, Power, Righteousness: An Indigenous Manifesto*. Don Mills, ON: Oxford University Press.

–. 2002. Sovereignty. In *A Companion to American Indian History*, ed. P.J. Deloria and N. Salisbury, 460-74. Malden, MA: Blackwell.

Asch, Michael. 2000a. The Judicial Conceptualization of Culture after *Delgamuukw* and *Van der Peet*. *Review of Constitutional Studies* 5(2):119-37.

–. 2000b. First Nations and the Derivation of Canada's Underlying Title: Comparing Perspectives on Legal Ideology. In *Aboriginal Rights and Self-Government: The Canadian and Mexican Experience in North American Perspective*, ed. C. Cook and J.D. Lindau, 148-67. Montreal and Kingston: McGill-Queen's University Press.

Bell, Catherine, and Michael Asch. 1997. Challenging Assumptions: The Impact of Precedent in Aboriginal Rights Litigation. In *Aboriginal and Treaty Rights in Canada: Essays on Law, Equality, and Respect for Difference*, ed. Michael Asch, 38-74. Vancouver: UBC Press.

Brown, Wendy. 2001. *Politics out of History*. Princeton, NJ: Princeton University Press.

–. 2002a. Suffering the Paradoxes of Rights. In *Left Legalism / Left Critique*, ed. W. Brown and J. Halley, 420-34. Durham: Duke University Press.

–. 2002b. At the Edge. *Political Theory* 30 (August):556-76.

Choudhry, Sujit. 2002. National Minorities and Ethnic Immigrants: Liberalism's Political Sociology. *Journal of Political Philosophy* 10(1):54-78.

Constitution Act, 1982, being Schedule B to the *Canada Act 1982* (U.K.), 1982, c. 11.

Day, Richard J.F. 2000. *Multiculturalism and the History of Canadian Diversity*. Toronto: University of Toronto Press.

–. 2001. Who Is This "We" That Gives the Gift? Native American Political Theory and "The Western Tradition." *Critical Horizons* 2(2):173-200.

Day, Richard J.F., and Tonio Sadik. 2002. The BC Land Question, Liberal Multiculturalism, and the Spectre of Aboriginal Nationhood. *BC Studies* 134 (Summer):5-34.

Dirlik, Arif. 1996. The Past as Legacy and Project: Postcolonial Criticism in the Perspective of Indigenous Historicism. *American Indian Culture and Research Journal* 20(2):1-31.

Eisenberg, Avigail. 1994. The Politics of Individual and Group Difference in Canadian Jurisprudence. *Canadian Journal of Political Science* 27(1):1-21.

–. 2001. Using Difference to Resolve Rights-Based Conflicts: A Reply to Joyce Green. *Canadian Journal of Political Science* 34(1):163-68.

Foucault, Michel. 1988. Politics and Reason. In *Politics, Philosophy, and Culture: Interviews and other Writings, 1977-1984*, ed. Lawrence D. Kritzman, 57-85. New York: Routledge. Cited in Brown 2001, 115.

–. 2000a. Truth and Power. In *Power: Essential Works of Foucault 1954-1984,* Vol. 3, ed. J.D. Faubion. Trans. R. Hurley et al., 111-33. New York: The New Press.
–. 2000b. The Subject and Power. In *Power: Essential Works of Foucault 1954-1984,* Vol. 3, ed. J.D. Faubion. Trans. R. Hurley et al., 326-48. New York: The New Press.
Geertz, Clifford. 1973. *The Interpretation of Cultures.* New York: Basic Books.
Green, Joyce A. 2000. The Difference Debate: Reducing Rights to Cultural Flavours. *Canadian Journal of Political Science* 33(1):133-44.
Hardt, Michael, and Antonio Negri. 2000. *Empire.* Cambridge, MA: Harvard University Press.
Hayward, Clarissa Rile. 2000. *De-Facing Power.* Cambridge: Cambridge University Press.
Johnson, Rebecca. 2000. Power and Wound: A Study of the Intersection of Privilege and Disadvantage in *Symes v. Canada.* SJD dissertation, University of Michigan. Later published as *Taxing Choices: The Intersection of Class, Gender, Parenthood, and the Law* (Vancouver: UBC Press, 2002).
Kymlicka, Will. 1989. *Liberalism, Community, and Culture.* Oxford: Clarendon Press.
–. 1995. *Multicultural Citizenship.* Oxford: Oxford University Press.
–. 1998. *Finding Our Way: Rethinking Ethnocultural Relations in Canada.* Don Mills: Oxford University Press.
–. 2000. American Multiculturalism and the "Nations Within." In *Political Theory and the Rights of Indigenous Peoples,* ed. D. Ivison, P. Patton, and W. Sanders, 216-36. Cambridge: Cambridge University Press.
–. 2001. *Politics in the Vernacular: Nationalism, Multiculturalism, and Citizenship.* Oxford: Oxford University Press.
Lenihan, Don. 1991. Liberalism and the Problem of Cultural Membership: A Critical Study of Kymlicka. *Canadian Journal of Law and Jurisprudence* 4 (July):401-19.
Michaels, Walter Benn. 2000. Political Science Fictions. *New Literary History* 31:649-64.
Murphy, Robert F., and Julian H. Steward. 1956. Tappers and Trappers: Parallel Processes in Acculturation. *Economic Development and Cultural Change* 4:335-53.
Nash, Kate. 2001. The "Cultural Turn" in Social Theory: Towards a Theory of Cultural Politics. *Sociology* 35(1):77-92.
Ortner, Sherry B. 2001. Theory in Anthropology since the Sixties. In *Readings for a History of Anthropological Theory,* ed. P.A. Erickson and L.D. Murphy, 642-87. Peterborough, ON: Broadview Press. Originally published in *Comparative Studies in Society and History* 26(1984):126-66.
Patton, Paul. 1996. Sovereignty, Law, and Difference in Australia: After the *Mabo* Case. *Alternatives* 21:149-70.
Povinelli, Elizabeth A. 1999. Settler Modernity and the Quest for an Indigenous Tradition. *Public Culture* 11(1):21-48.
–. 2002. *The Cunning of Recognition: Indigenous Alterities and the Making of Australian Multiculturalism.* Durham: Duke University Press.
Schulte-Tenckhoff, Isabelle. 1998. Reassessing the Paradigm of Domestication: The Problematic of Indigenous Treaties. *Review of Constitutional Studies* 4(2):239-89.
Scott, David. 1995. Colonial Governmentality. *Social Text* 13(43):191-220.
–. 2003. Culture in Political Theory. *Political Theory* 31 (February):92-115.
Stocking, George W. Jr. 1982. *Race, Culture, and Evolution: Essays in the History of Anthropology.* Chicago: University of Chicago Press.
Taylor, Charles. 1991. *The Ethics of Authenticity.* Cambridge, MA: Harvard University Press.
Trouillot, Michel-Rolph. 2001. The Anthropology of the State in the Age of Globalization: Close Encounters of the Deceptive Kind. *Current Anthropology* 42(1):125-38.
Tully, James. 1995. *Strange Multiplicity: Constitutionalism in an Age of Diversity.* Cambridge: Cambridge University Press.
–. 1999. The Agonic Freedom of Citizens. *Economy and Society* 28(May):161-82.
–. 2000. The Struggles of Indigenous Peoples for and of Freedom. In *Political Theory and the Rights of Indigenous Peoples,* ed. D. Ivison, P. Patton, and W. Sanders, 36-59. Cambridge: Cambridge University Press.
–. 2002. Political Philosophy as a Practical Activity. *Political Theory* 30 (August):533-55.

Waswo, Richard. 1996. The Formation of Natural Law to Justify Colonialism, 1539-1689. *New Literary History* 27:743-59.

–. 1997. *The Founding Legend of Western Civilization: From Virgil to Vietnam.* Hanover, NH: Wesleyan University Press.

Williams, Robert A. Jr. 1990. *The American Indian in Western Legal Thought: The Discourses of Conquest.* Oxford: Oxford University Press.

Young, Iris Marion. 2000. Self-Determination and Global Democracy. In *Inclusion and Democracy,* 236-75. Oxford: Oxford University Press.

Cases

Delgamuukw v. British Columbia, [1997] 3 S.C.R. 1010 [*Delgamuukw*].

Hamlet of Baker Lake v. Minister of Indian Affairs and Northern Development (1980), 1 F.C. 518 (T.D.) [*Baker Lake*].

Mabo v. Queensland, [No. 2] (1992), 175 C.L.R. 1 (High Court of Australia).

Mitchell v. M.N.R., [2001] 1 S.C.R. 911.

R. v. Van der Peet, [1996] 2 S.C.R. 507 [*Van der Peet*].

Re Southern Rhodesia (1919), A.C. 210 (P.C.).

Western Sahara (1975), I.C.J. 12.

4
Culture as a Basic Human Right
Cindy Holder

Most political theorists and philosophers now accept that there are cultural rights of some sort. But what kind of rights are they? For example, can interests in culture generate entitlements and duties on their own? Or do they do so only derivatively, in virtue of their contribution to interests that are more important?

International human rights norms treat the interest individuals have in culture as of basic importance, or capable of generating entitlements and duties on its own merits. Canadian cases have played a prominent role in this, especially in the articulation of the right to culture set out in Article 27 of the *International Covenant on Civil and Political Rights (ICCPR)* (UN General Assembly 1966). Key cases include *Ominayak v. Canada* (UN Human Rights Committee 1990), in which Canada was found to have violated the complainants' cultural rights when it permitted a provincial government to expropriate ancestral lands, *Lovelace v. Canada* (UN Human Rights Committee 1988a), in which the complainant's cultural rights were found to be violated by the *Indian Act*'s denial of status and benefits to women who married non-Indians, and *Ballantyne/Davidson/MacIntyre v. Canada* (UN Human Rights Committee 1993), in which the Article 27 rights of Canada's francophone minority were found to be insufficiently threatened by the use of English in commercial settings to justify restrictions on freedom of expression.

Most political philosophers are reluctant to treat cultural rights as basic. Instead, the predominant view is that cultural interests are only important derivatively, in virtue of their contribution to some other interest. In this chapter I argue that we ought to follow international human rights norms regarding the importance of culture. Not only do international human rights courts and committees come to the right conclusion about the significance of culture, but, as importantly, they come to this conclusion because they think about what cultural rights protect in the right way. Contemporary political philosophers prefer to treat cultural rights as derivative in part because they tend to treat culture as a "resource" or a "good," but this is a mistake.

Cultural rights are better understood as protecting and promoting an activity. Respecting and promoting cultural participation is a constitutive element of showing respect for human dignity because, like free expression, political participation, and freedom of conscience, cultural participation is something persons do as part of making a life for themselves.

International Human Rights Norms as a Model for Theory

One may ask: "Why think that normative theory has anything to learn from a branch of international law?" The relationship between theory and law is usually thought to be the other way around. In this regard, international law seems a particularly unlikely resource from which to draw normative principles. International legal norms are in large part the product of power politics, and they are negotiated against the background of a global system that is manifestly unjust and in which the primary actors, and so the primary influences, are representatives of states.

Nonetheless, there are (at least) two reasons for thinking that international human rights law has something to offer normative theories of cultural rights. First, international human rights norms offer a model for movement between normative principles and laws or policy decisions that theorists of cultural rights would do well to emulate. Second, international human rights norms explicitly confront the question of jurisdiction and, in particular, the question of who gets to make the call when authorities disagree. I will discuss these reasons in turn.

Moving between Principles and Policy

Although most theorists in the literature on cultural rights are careful to distinguish between the *principles* that ought to direct public policy regarding cultural rights and the *policies* that such principles imply, the use of real-world examples of criminal cases, institutional demands, and constitutional interpretations in debates tends to blur this distinction. There is a tendency to treat criminal cases and demands for institutional accommodation as "problems" that cultural rights pose or resolve. For example, Susan Okin (1999) frames cultural rights as posing a problem for feminism. Jacob Levy (2000), in contrast, frames cultural rights as a solution to a problem liberalism faces. This makes sense if rights are understood as legal entitlements to performances, goods, privileges, or immunities. Rights understood in this way are implied by principles, but they are not synonymous with them.

However, many theorists present these real-world cases not as examples pointing to rights that are implied by certain principles, but as counter-examples: as outcomes that are implied by the principles that justify cultural rights even though they should be rejected, or that are not implied by the principles even though they should be (Okin 1998; Barry 2001). The problem is that using a real-world case in this way requires an argument to the effect that the example is necessarily implied (or necessarily fails to be implied) by the principles in question. When such an argument is lacking, the use of these examples can conflate arguments about whether a normative principle ought to underwrite political decision making with arguments about what a normative principle implies in particular contexts.

In contrast, international human rights norms maintain sharp distinctions between arguments against the propriety of recognizing the existence of a legal entitlement in a particular case, arguments regarding the proper interpretation of the content of various principles, and arguments against the propriety of applying certain principles in the first place. International human rights treaties, declarations, treaty-monitoring bodies, and tribunals have been developed for the express purpose of helping states determine whether and in what respects their institutions are compatible with a set of normative principles (i.e., the basic elements of human dignity as articulated in the international bill of rights). They are intended to apply across a variety of institutional and cultural contexts, and so they are specifically designed to separate arguments about the principles that political decisions and institutions must respect from arguments about what respect for those principles looks like in a particular context.

International human rights norms accomplish this distinction in part by using rights to refer to a set of interests that must be accorded a special status in political reasoning such that they may not be traded off in certain ways. Particular legal entitlements may be owed to persons and groups as a matter of (human) right; however, questions of whether interests ought to be accorded a special status, and what this special status implies for particular cases, are treated separately. This separation is an important conceptual tool as it forces interlocutors to spell out the relationships they see among interests, between interests and institutional arrangements, and between interests and goods.

Confronting the Problem of Jurisdiction

A second useful feature of international human rights norms is their explicit attention to questions of jurisdiction. International treaty-monitoring bodies and tribunals are specifically designed to distinguish questions about what international norms require (i.e., questions about the right way to interpret various rights' content) from questions about whether and in what way it is appropriate to enforce a tribunal's judgment on what the norms require when this diverges from the opinion of a state. This distinction may be a by-product of the statist character of the system within which such mechanisms have developed. Even so, it has had the valuable effect of developing norms in which questions about the proper interpretation of principles are separated from questions about jurisdiction and political legitimacy (i.e., questions about the authority to compel compliance).

This feature is useful for discussions about cultural rights because of the way it frames disagreements between governing authorities over whether and how normative principles ought to apply. International human rights norms frame the proper handling of such disagreements as a question not of tolerance but of authority, of legitimately acquired power and proper jurisdiction. In doing so, they distinguish questions about the rightness of one's judgment from questions about the grounds on which one may insist that one's own judgment be the one to prevail in cases of interpretive disagreement. In the case of cultural rights, this means that questions about what makes one policy regime better than another for a group of people are distinguished from questions about what makes one level of political authority a more appropriate (or inappropriate) location for decisions. This allows one to separate pragmatic reasons (such as "Local decision makers will do a better job") from principled reasons (such as "This decision is outside the scope of that level of government's authority").

This distinction (between what makes decisions better and what makes them legitimate) is important for theories of cultural rights. Most theoretical discussions of cultural rights focus on issues that arise in the municipal or national contexts of liberal states, almost all of which have a history of racism, internal colonialism, state-sponsored violence, and economic discrimination in the public policy that has been pursued within their borders (as well as outside them). Because of this fact one cannot assume that liberal states may properly insist that their judgments about the compatibility of certain cultural practices with human dignity should prevail. International human rights norms put issues of jurisdiction and legitimacy at the forefront when liberal states claim for themselves the authority to legislate in areas such as culture.

Two Views of Cultural Rights

Cultural Rights as Basic

International human rights norms treat cultural rights as basic: as constitutive elements of the minimal standard for respecting human dignity. Retaining and participating in one's own culture is one of a core set of rights that appears as a matter of course in human rights declarations, treaties, and interpretive documents.[1] For example, in Article 5 of the *Declaration on the Human Rights of Individuals Who Are Not Nationals of the Country in Which They Live*, the right of aliens to retain their own language, culture, and tradition is included with the rights to life, to protection against arbitrary interference with privacy, to equality before the law, to freedom of conscience, and to marry and found a family (UN General Assembly 1985, Article 5). And in a 1996 supplementary report to the UN Commission on Human Rights, the Special Rapporteur described the purpose of her study into the protection of the cultural heritage of indigenous peoples as advising "how these universally recognized principles of human rights should best be interpreted and applied in particular contexts, such as the context of indigenous peoples" (16).

The Human Rights Committee (HRC, the treaty-monitoring body for the *ICCPR*) notes in General Comment 23 that Article 27 (the article naming cultural rights) establishes a right "distinct from, and additional to, all the other rights which, as individuals in common with everyone else, they [the members of a minority] are already entitled to enjoy under the Covenant"; that "the protection of these rights is directed towards ensuring the survival and continued development of the cultural, religious and social identity of the minorities concerned"; and that, accordingly, "these rights must be protected as such and should not be confused with other personal rights"(1994a, 1, 9). This view has been clearly reflected in the committee's treatment of complaints. For example, in *Ominayak v. Canada* (UN HRC 1990), the committee found that the Canadian government had violated the complainants' cultural rights by allowing the provincial government to grant leases for oil and gas exploration within their territory. And in *Länsman v. Finland* (UN HRC 1994b, 1995), the HRC explicitly rejected the state's argument that the right to culture could not serve to ground claims to noncultural goods (such as the resources to practise one's culture and to make it one's primary source of livelihood), stating that Article 27 protects the capacity of indigenous groups to practise their traditional way of life as a livelihood and that in so doing it protects their access to the resources that are essential to this.

In this view of cultural rights, depriving individuals of their culture is treated as wronging them directly, over and above any wrong done to them by undermining other aspects of their dignity. Cultural participation is treated as a constitutive element of the minimum standard of human dignity in its own right and not – or not only – in virtue of its contribution to some more important interest. Respect for cultural integrity is taken to be of sufficient importance to ground other entitlements, such as claims to resources or land. This is illustrated not only in the United Nations system but also in the Organization of American States (OAS) system. For example, the *Additional Protocol to the American Convention on Human Rights in the Area of Economic, Social and Cultural Rights* [*Protocol of San Salvador*] commits the states who are party to it to recognizing the right of everyone "to take part in the cultural and artistic life of the community" (OAS 1988, Article 14.1(a)). This last has been interpreted by the Inter-American Commission on Human Rights as a right of persons to participate in the culture of their minority communities as well as that of the majority. In its 1999 *Report on the Situation of Human Rights in Colombia,* the commission included "creating opportunities needed for attaining respect for their social and cultural particularities as well as for their unique organizational forms" as an advance in the recognition and development of indigenous peoples' human rights

(OAS 1999, X.7). And its 1997 *Report on the Situation of Human Rights in Brazil* named "the introduction of infrastructure (roads, dams, etc.) that destroys and threatens the physical and cultural integrity of the indigenous areas" as a rights-violating situation that must be addressed (OAS 1996, VI.41).

One worry about this treatment of cultural rights is that it is too open-ended and that statements to the effect that persons must be able to "enjoy" or "practise" their culture are too vague and must be more explicitly and specifically defined to properly serve as a basis for adjudication or policy. However, various international treaty-monitoring bodies and human rights courts have not found it difficult in practice to circumscribe what counts as an infringement of culture and to differentiate between justifications based in cultural integrity and justifications based in other human rights. For example, in a case in Colombia where members of an indigenous community argued that authorities had violated the group's rights under Article 27 in addition to violating individuals' rights under other articles when the group's leaders were murdered, the tribunal rejected the Article 27 claim (UN HRC 1997a). The HRC has also distinguished between cultural rights per se and the implications of cultural plurality in its interpretation of other *ICCPR* rights. In *Hopu v. France,* the committee rejected the state's argument that the complainants could only claim a violation of their right to family in a case of a development planned for an indigenous community's burial grounds if they could demonstrate clear and recent blood ties to the persons buried there. The tribunal pointed out that the state's argument rested on a culturally specific understanding of who counts as a family member, which members of the complainants' community did not share, and that, based on the conception of family that the complainants' community accepted, the complaint had merit (UN HRC 1997b, 10.3).

Cultural Rights as Derivative
Most political philosophers and political theorists have been reluctant to accord the fundamental normative significance to culture that one sees in international human rights law. For example, Will Kymlicka (1995) argues that the integrity of one's culture is important because it is a precondition to personal autonomy and so to rights of personal self-determination, and that it must give way in cases where it puts such rights at risk. Jacob Levy (2000) argues that respect for culture ought to be grounded in a healthy fear of the consequences of a state that does not show such respect. Jeremy Waldron (1992) argues that culture is simply not important enough by itself to ground the kind of constraint that rights imply, an argument that has been deployed against ascriptive obligations more generally by John Simmons (1996). Susan Okin (1999) and Marilyn Friedman (2001) have argued that, at the very least, the interests at stake in cultural rights must be subservient to the value of autonomy.

This reluctance reflects skepticism about the propriety of comparing the significance of participating in a culture with the significance of physical integrity or of equality before the law. And such skepticism is not surprising given the way individuals' interests in culture have been represented. In much of the existing literature, culture is presented as important because of its role in the "inner lives" of individuals: as a source of beliefs, interpersonal skills, or informational capacities that the individual can deploy in the pursuit of well-being or moral agency. Culture is treated as a kind of mental or psychological operating system, on the basis of which individuals gain the ability to appreciate, define, and pursue their human needs.

Such a conception of cultural rights sets them up to fare poorly in comparison to other claims. Insofar as a person is functioning as an agent or self-definer at all, it looks as though his or her minimal cultural needs are being met. But when a person fails to function as an agent, it is difficult to demonstrate that the inability to access his or her culture is the particular factor to blame, rather than other features of the environment. When held up against tangible and specific harms such as loss of income or inability to voice one's view, the harms experienced as a result of loss of culture look vague and difficult to measure. The effects seem liable to a wide degree of interpersonal variation; the actual impact seems difficult to verify.

Moreover, cultures and cultural practices are in part external to the individuals who participate in them, but only in part; a significant chunk of what constitutes a culture seems to be its embodiment in and effects on its members' statements and lives. This raises a particularly worrisome problem: one important component of the cultural resources external to an individual is the set of past, present, and future co-participants. Thinking of the right to culture as a right to access a good or to achieve a state seems to imply that one should think of the other persons with whom an individual participates in the culture as either vehicles for the delivery of some resource – the culture – or as themselves resources to which their co-participant ought to be secured access or use. This possibility becomes even more worrisome if one takes seriously the possibility that some of the resources that culture provides are "beliefs" or "ways of thinking." Beliefs and ways of thinking involve mental states, and these are ultimately lodged within a person. It is little wonder then that talking of the continuation of a culture as of sufficient normative weight in and of itself to establish the constraints on others that rights imply has made most normative theorists uneasy.

Diverging Treatments

The worries that keep most theorists from treating culture as of fundamental importance in its own right are genuine and pressing. So why don't these worries keep international human rights norms from treating cultural rights as basic? International human rights norms are committed to ethical individualism and to developing and maintaining internal coherence in their norms. How are these features to be reconciled with their treatment of cultural rights?

A preliminary (but mistaken) explanation might be that international human rights norms and the philosophical literature on cultural rights are talking about two different things. International human rights norms set limitations on the actions that states may take with respect to minority groups, so they are concerned with *external protections* (i.e., with rights of a minority not to be undermined by outsiders). Philosophical discussions of cultural rights, on the other hand, are primarily concerned with what states ought to allow individuals to do to and with one another, and so they are concerned with *internal restrictions* (i.e., with rights of a minority to restrict the liberties of its own membership) (Kymlicka 1995, 150-52). In this explanation, international human rights norms do not offer a competing view of groups; they offer a complementary one.

This attempt to explain away the divergence does not quite work. International human rights norms establish restrictions on the actions that states can take with respect to minorities *as groups.* This includes restrictions on what they can require of these groups. In *Lovelace v. Canada,* for example, the HRC found in favour of the complainant (a woman who had been excluded from membership after marrying a non-band member) not because the membership rule violated her human rights, but because Canada had violated her right *in concert with other band members* to determine for themselves the conditions of membership (UN HRC 1988a; Anaya 1996, 98-104). The membership rule violated the complainant's rights because it had been imposed upon her by Canada for its own purposes, not the purposes of the group. In contrast, in *Kitok v. Sweden,* the HRC ruled that membership restrictions did not violate the complainant's right to culture by excluding him, because such restrictions could be justified as a measure to protect the Sami as a whole (1988b). In both these cases, protecting the group from the state that hosted it was taken to imply that the state must not interfere with certain kinds of internal decision making (such as decisions about who counts as a member). This is a general feature of international norms in this area: the human right to cultural integrity imposes limits on the range of actions that states may take with respect to minorities and their ways of life, and this includes limits on the extent to which states may interfere with a group's internal restrictions (Lerner 2003, 1-24).

A more promising explanation is a difference in the two approaches' willingness to recognize fundamental rights for groups as such. Philosophers and political theorists have been very reluctant to accept groups as such as rights-bearers on a par with individuals, but the practice and comments of international human rights treaty-monitoring bodies and courts have long treated groups as bearing human rights in their own right. Nonetheless, this explanation is incomplete. For example, one of the reasons that international norms are much more likely to treat at least some group rights as on a normative par with individualistic ones is that the international bill of rights has come to be interpreted holistically, as a unified statement of the minimum conditions of respect for human dignity. In particular, the inclusion of groups as such as potential rights-bearers has been a direct consequence of perceived limitations in the ability of individualistic approaches to protect groups and individuals from assaults on their cultural, linguistic, and religious distinctiveness. This suggests that the group-friendliness of international human rights norms is a consequence of the view of culture as much as an explanation of it. In fact, Natan Lerner and others have argued that the shift in recent years to a more group-friendly model reflects inadequacies in a more individualistic framework's capacity to protect cultural and self-determination interests (Lerner 2003, 16-19; Franck 1999, 213, 216).

The difference in attitude towards cultural rights in large part reflects a difference in the ways philosophical approaches and international human rights norms conceive persons' interest in culture. Philosophical approaches tend to conceive the interest in culture as an interest in accessing or securing a resource (analogous to food in the right to adequate nutrition) or as an interest in preserving a certain feature of oneself (analogous to physical integrity in the right to health). In contrast, international human rights norms tend to conceive the interest in cultural integrity as an interest in doing something, in performing or developing an activity. What cultural rights are about is very different in these two approaches, and this explains their different attitudes towards the normative status of the constraints and entitlements that such rights generate.

Cultural Integrity and the Interest in Culture

Interests in Culture as Interests in Goods

In most philosophical accounts, cultural rights are first and foremost about maintaining or preserving access to a resource or good, namely, "culture." This may require governments to ensure that the resource is not depleted below a level necessary for those who depend on its consumption to maintain it, or it may require governments to ensure that arbitrary or unjustified impediments to individuals' access are removed or prevented from developing. Under either interpretation, the interests that individuals have at stake in a cultural rights claim will be served by reliable access to, consumption of, or use of "culture," a resource. Motivating and defending (or undermining and criticizing) the idea that individuals' cultural interests are sufficiently important to ground rights and duties focuses on articulating what it is about this resource or good – culture – that makes it so important that individuals are able to access, consume, or use it. The most popular arguments appeal to the importance of having or accessing a culture (in particular, the culture that is one's own) for one to be able to do or have the capacity to acquire other important things (Kymlicka 1989; Miller 1995; Tamir 1993). Other arguments focus on the inherent value of cultural goods; on the inherent disvalue of being denied cultural goods; and on the unequal treatment inherent when a government refuses to provide a good for some that it does provide for others (Svennson 1979; Kymlicka 1989, 185-200; Margalit and Raz 1990).

These arguments treat cultural rights as rights to a sort of primary good: as primarily about securing or maintaining some *thing* or set of things, namely, "culture." The most striking example of this is Will Kymlicka's influential definition of a societal culture as a territorially based set of institutions (1995, 75-80). It is also apparent in the tendency of some writers to use the word "culture" as a synonym for "group" (Kernohan 1998; Kymlicka and Almagor 2000, 237; Ripstein 1997), in Jeremy Waldron's description of culture as a set of norms (2000, 234), and in Susan Okin's description of cultures as patriarchal when they have specific effects on women (1999, 16).

Such interpretations of cultural rights require a clear definition of what it is for something to be a culture, or at the very least an explicit set of circumstances in the world to which one can point and say definitively, "Yes, the government provided (or no, the government failed to provide) culture for you because *x, y,* and *z* were (or were not) present." Analogous rights would be the right to personal property, the right to adequate nutrition, and the right to due process. The relationship between cultural rights' groupness and the nature of the interests at stake look contingent and instrumental: cultural rights imply group rights because groups are best placed to secure the cultures that individuals need.

One obvious problem with this approach is that cultures are not plausibly thought of as resources or goods. They don't seem to have the kind of stability, persistence of identity across time, or distinctness from other social factors that one needs to establish the requisite empirical link between a culture's persistence and individual members' consumption of the good, capacity, or internal state that is supposed to be at stake (Holder 2002; Narayan 1998). This in part explains the popularity of Kymlicka's societal culture definition. Institutions and territory have the kind of stability and perdurance that a goods-based conception of cultural interests needs. Even better, institutions and territory allow one to continue to talk about the benefits that cultures confer in psychological terms without raising the unsettling possibility that one of the interests at stake in a cultural right is other people developing a belief or exhibiting a character trait or other personal quality.

However, institutional definitions have their own drawbacks. For example, there does not seem to be anything particularly cultural about cultural rights understood in this way. Instead, cultural rights look to be synonymous with some sort of political right: either the right to some particular legal regime or the right to an independent governing system. This is not the same as arguing that cultural rights may *ground* political rights under particular circumstances; in the institutional definition, cultural rights just are rights to a particular political regime.

For example, in Will Kymlicka's view, polyethnic groups don't have cultural rights per se; they have rights not to be excluded from citizenship or subject to impediments to participation in virtue of the ways in which they differ from the rest of the citizenry (i.e., rights of equal participation and of nondiscrimination). This is because, unlike societal cultures, *polyethnic groups do not have interests in a distinct political regime.* Cultural interests and political interests are reduced to one another, so that the extent to which members of a group are recognized as having genuinely cultural interests at all is determined by looking at the extent to which they have interests in political autonomy.

Moreover, these political rights are not rights that allow a group's members to freely determine how they will live. Rather, they are rights to live together authentically: to live together as the group they constitute. Such rights are not rights *to do* and *to decide;* they are rights *to be* and *to have.* In particular, they are rights to exhibit certain properties and to have certain institutions. The institutional definition of culture justifies cultural rights by appealing to the need for "suitable" political institutions, for a proper fit between a group's (objectively identifiable) characteristics and its form of governance. In so doing, it establishes a plausible object for groups' rights claims at the price of emphasizing congruence with a group's true properties as the hallmark of legitimacy.

This means that the institutions that groups may claim as a matter of cultural right are not justified in terms of their giving voice to the aspirations of a group of persons, or even by their having been affirmed by those persons. Rather, they are justified in terms of their being either especially suited for a population or authentic reflections of the people that a population constitutes. In this view, cultural rights direct a government to show respect for a population's choices as a people for instrumental reasons: as a reliable mechanism for ensuring that groups get the institutions they are entitled to. The point of cultural rights is not to secure respect for persons' communal decisions, but to secure respect for the characteristics that distinguish them as members of this or that group.

This view does not require that one be essentialist about cultures, but it does require that one talk about cultures as if they had essences. For example, the entitlements that a group's cultural rights establish will depend on one's description of what characterizes that particular group: what distinguishes it *as a culture* such that dominant institutions are not appropriate. Getting accurate descriptions or definitions of the cultures that characterize peoples becomes very important; it becomes something that theorists must do before they can figure out whether a group has cultural rights at all.

Interests in Culture as Interests in an Activity

In contrast, international human rights norms do not treat cultural rights as in themselves rights to particular institutions. Rather, cultural rights are rights to produce, develop, and participate in institutions that express, embody, and reflect the culture of one's people. In the context of a particular people, this will often carry the implication that a specific institution must be respected or promoted as a matter of right. But claims to specific institutions are derivative of the basic right, which protects the activity of producing, maintaining, changing, and participating in such institutions.

In this view, what is at stake for individuals in cultural rights is the capacity to pursue, develop, or engage in an activity. It is an interest in being able to do something. This view is most striking in Article 27 of the *ICCPR*, where the right to cultural integrity has been interpreted to imply rights of self-determination, which is understood as a right to freely determine the terms on which a group lives together and in relation to other groups within the state (UN HRC 1988a, 1994a, 6.2.) It is also apparent in discussions of indigenous peoples' human rights, where culture has been interpreted as closely linked to rights of self-government and to land use, and it is a general theme in international documents and decisions treating culture (UN Commission on Human Rights 1995).

For example, Article 14 of the *Protocol of San Salvador,* which treats "Rights to Benefits of Culture," recognizes "the right of everyone: a. To *take part* in the cultural and artistic life of the community; b. To enjoy the benefits of scientific and technological progress; c. To benefit from the protection of moral and material interests deriving from any scientific, literary or artistic production of which he is the author" (OAS 1988; emphasis added). Here, culture benefits people by enabling them *to engage in cultural life,* in addition to benefiting them instrumentally by providing scientific and technological advance and personal and material rewards.

This is also illustrated in the UNESCO *Declaration of the Principles Governing International Cultural Cooperation,* which states that "1. Each culture has a dignity and value which must be respected and preserved. 2. Every people has *the right and the duty to develop its culture.* 3. ... all cultures form part of the common heritage belonging to all mankind" (1966, Article 1; emphasis added). In this case the document uses culture as a noun when indicating attitudes that ought to be adopted towards cultural differences, but describes the right that peoples have regarding their cultures as the right to *do* something: to *develop* its culture.

The UN *Declaration on the Rights of Persons Belonging to National or Ethnic, Religious or Linguistic Minorities* directs states "to protect the existence" of minority identity and encourage the conditions of its promotion in Article 1. But when it goes on to articulate the rights of minorities in Article 2, it names actions and activities: "the right to *enjoy* their own culture," "the right to *participate effectively* in cultural, religious and social life," "the right to *establish and maintain* their own associations" and free and peaceful contacts with other members of their group (UN General Assembly 1992; emphasis added).

This way of thinking about what persons have at stake in cultural rights is reminiscent of Dan Sperber's description of culture as participation in a shared process or activity (1996). Cultural rights are essential to human dignity not because they secure individuals in their ability to get or achieve something, but because cultural participation is one of the things people do when they are living their lives. The appropriate analogies for cultural rights in this understanding are the right to express oneself freely, to get married if one so desires, to move about the country as one wishes, or to participate in political institutions. These rights to engage in a certain kind of activity are all acknowledged to have a certain instrumental value in contributing to the security of individuals' physical well-being and access to goods. Yet individuals are also thought to have a fundamental interest in being able to engage in them apart from any contribution such activities make to securing important goods.

So being able to lay claim to specific institutions or accommodations as a matter of right may be implied by the right to culture in a specific set of circumstances, but this does not require that a claim to institutions or accommodations of that type be built into the concept of culture. For example, specific features of an indigenous people may mean that respecting that people's cultural integrity requires the state to accept constraints on its decision making with respect to land that the people lives on or uses, but it does not require the state to accept such constraints with respect to land that another, non-indigenous people within its borders lives on or uses. Such a difference would not imply that indigenous peoples' rights to culture are different in kind from the rights of other peoples. Rather, it would imply that for that particular indigenous people, but not for all peoples, the human right to culture establishes claims regarding the state's decision making about land. Differences in what the human right to culture establishes a claim to as a matter of right reflect differences in circumstances (Anaya 1996, 75-128).

In other words, what grounds the right to culture is individuals' interests (both personally and as members of a group) in being able to access, express, and develop a language, world view, history, and identity that respond to and reflect aspects of life that they share with specific others. As a description of the interests that ground the right, this is fairly narrow and does not require one to think about cultures themselves as static, all-consuming, or centred on any particular set of institutions or goods. Of course, what a group may claim as a *matter* of right on the basis of this interest may be quite extensive and (depending on the circumstances and the group) may well involve very specific objects, institutional arrangements, or tracts of land. But that one cannot respect a particular group's right to culture without allowing them to use land in a certain way does not imply that the interest in culture in itself includes an interest in land. Analogously, to say that one can respect a person's interest in marrying freely even when she's marrying someone of whom the family disapproves does not imply that the right to marry freely in itself includes an interest in marrying someone of whom one's family disapproves.

Activity: The More Promising View

Understanding what it means to describe cultural participation as an interest in question of persons *in groups* and not just persons in separation becomes easier when activities such as getting married or freely expressing oneself are taken as its models. Cultural rights of groups are to the speech rights of individuals as self-determination rights of peoples are to individual rights of political participation. Cultural rights are in part the rights of groups of persons to express themselves *as a collective,* just as self-determination rights are the rights of groups to collectively determine the political institutions under which they live (Holder 2005).

   This comparison explains why normative theorists' worries about treating culture as of more than derivative importance seem to ring true but are ultimately misplaced. In the international human rights view, objects, beliefs, and institutions that cultural activity produces (things that commonly come to mind when "culture" is used as a noun) gain their significance derivatively, as a necessary means to, or an indicator of the presence of, something else. That "something else" is not noncultural; it is participating in a group of persons negotiating, articulating, changing, and expressing who and what they are, collectively and in relation to one another. An assault on a group's capacity to use, access, produce, or maintain the materials of that participation is an assault on their capacity to pursue the activity at all, and as such it is an assault on each of them as a human being.

   When one adds to this description of culture the observation that many cultural activities involve efforts, as a group and as individuals, to shape the physical and social world in which persons live and relate to one another, it is difficult to see how individuals' interests in preserving, developing, or controlling the cultures in which they participate can be anything other than of fundamental importance. In the same way that the ability to determine whether, with whom, and on what terms I will build a family is of key importance to my dignity as a person, so being able to determine whether, with whom, and on what terms I develop and interpret my social and economic history or conditions will be of fundamental importance to that dignity.

Once these features of cultural participation are recognized, it becomes implausible to claim that culture's importance is primarily psychological or related to the development and maintenance of belief systems or other internal states. If the above analysis is right, then culture is an important venue for and factor in determining the field within which a person *acts*, not simply determining the *beliefs* that he or she has. Culture matters not just because it "gives" us beliefs, nor even because it reflects the beliefs we want to have. Culture matters because it is one of the vehicles through which we act with others. Participating in culture is one of the ways we influence the beliefs of others, one of the ways we determine how their activities and ours will be patterned, and one of the ways we establish what we and others are doing when we undertake certain behaviours. Groups are sites of action and not just sites of affection or meaning. They are collections of people who act together, and this common action is as much an explanation as it is an effect of their affective ties and shared meanings. This makes culture important in the same way that politics is important: in part as a vehicle of expression, in part as a medium of action, and in part as a medium through which others express themselves and act. The importance of cultural activity not just to oneself but also to others, and the ways in which our own interests are entangled with those of others within cultural activity are such that the power to define our relationship to our co-participants in culture can only justly be exercised in concert with them. Making choices as part of one's group is part of making choices as an individual, *and this is true for every member.* This is why having a say in the symbols and social structures of one's group is an important part of what it is to have a say in the running of one's own life.

This implies two things about internal restrictions. First, it implies that there may be circumstances in which individuals may claim freedom from state interference with an internal restriction as a matter of human right. In such circumstances, the freedom from state interference will not be justified by a people's right to persist nor by a right of the individuals within the group to live in accordance with the properties that distinguish their group as the group it is. Rather, it will be justified by the right of the persons of whom that people is comprised to decide for themselves what their common life means and how it will proceed. This does not mean that peoples may be exempted from the duty to themselves to respect the right to culture of each of their members. In the same way that states must allow each person within to participate in the development of the national culture, peoples must allow the participation of each member.

This points to a second implication regarding internal restrictions. It is conceivable that in some circumstances respect for the human right to culture may not only be compatible with a people developing and maintaining certain internal restrictions, but may also require a people to develop and maintain certain internal restrictions. This is because peoples must not only allow the participation of each member, but they must also ensure that each member's participation leaves room for and does not discourage the participation of everyone else. Recognizing that peoples have this duty does not imply that peoples may impose just any restriction in the name of protecting participation. But neither does it imply that peoples must defer to the judgment of the states that host them regarding what is required for them to live up to the duty to protect participation. Whether peoples must allow all members to participate, and whether states may legitimately judge whether or not those duties have been fulfilled and compel compliance with those judgments are separate questions.

In this, it is instructive to look at the way the HRC (1993, 1994c) has handled complaints about legislation restricting the use of English in commercial settings in the province of Quebec, especially *Ballantyne/Davidson/MacIntyre v. Canada*. In these cases, unlike in *Lovelace*, the restriction was developed and imposed by a (linguistic) minority, so that the question before the committee was whether the state violated its treaty obligations in tolerating the restriction. The legislation did not exclude individuals from membership, but it did attempt to protect and develop certain properties of the population over which it enjoyed jurisdiction, and this makes it instructive.

In *Ballantyne*, the HRC (1993, 11.4) took the merits of the complaints to turn on the plausibility of the minority's claim that the restrictions it had imposed were necessary to secure its membership in their rights under Article 27 (their rights to language and culture). Because Article 27 was described as protecting francophones (as a linguistic minority) in their ability to use their language, the committee took the persuasiveness of the state's defence (that the legislation is necessary to preserve certain characteristics in the population, namely, using French in commercial transactions) to depend on whether those characteristics are in fact required for the minority to be secure in its ability to speak French. If preserving the use of French in commercial transactions could be shown to be necessary for the francophone minority as a whole to continue to use French, then the legislation would be an acceptable limit on the complainants' freedom of speech. But the majority of the HRC concluded that the legislation was not an acceptable limit. They rejected the state's claim that the characteristic in question was necessary for the minority as a whole to use French.

Conclusion

Thinking of cultural rights as primarily about protecting a kind of activity allows one to describe the wrongs of assaults on a people's or an individual's cultural identity in terms that are true to the experience of those on whom these wrongs are visited: as an assault on their dignity independent and apart from the consequences such assaults have for other aspects of their lives. Assaults on one's culture are wrong because they represent attempts to deny one the ability to exist in and move around the world as do others, including the assaulter. Conceiving culture as a good or resource encourages one to treat the interests at stake in assaults on culture in a way that misses this aspect of the wrongness.

In contrast, thinking of culture as an activity clarifies the interests at stake and makes it easier to recognize the ways in which assaults on culture are assaults on human dignity itself. It does this in part by making it easier to separate the symbolic or otherwise intangible aspects of culture itself from an appreciation of the effects, role, or function that participation in a culture usually plays in individuals' lives.

Thinking about cultural rights as protecting an activity also defuses at least some of the worries about the extent to which cultural rights involve claims over other people. Cultural rights have implications regarding other people because human lives are social; they are lived in concert with others. The group dimension of cultural rights is a reflection of that fact. Puzzles about how a person could have an interest in the product of cultural activity even if she personally rejects aspects of that product are analogous to puzzles about democratic legitimacy. The latter is a puzzle about when and to what extent connections between persons may legitimate constraining them to defer to group decision making in some aspect of their lives.

Cultural rights also have implications regarding access to and control over objects, institutions, and resources, because human lives are materially based and physical. These implications play themselves out in requirements and constraints regarding the way governments treat family structures, land tenure systems, medical practices, or other institutions and patterns of relationship. Because of this, cultural rights regularly raise issues about legislative authority and political jurisdiction. International human rights norms don't settle these issues, and they do not in any way make them go away. But I have suggested here that such norms may provide a more useful framework for thinking about the relevant questions than does the framework theorists currently use.

Note

1 For example, see UN General Assembly (1948, Article 27); United Nations (1969, Article 15); UNESCO (1978, s. 2); United Nations (1989, Article 30); UN General Assembly (1992, Article 2); UN World Conference on Human Rights (1993, 19).

References

International Documents

Organization of American States. 1988. *Additional Protocol to the American Convention on Human Rights in the Area of Economic, Social and Cultural Rights* [*Protocol of San Salvador*]. OAS Treaty Series 69. San Salvador: OAS.

–. 1997. Inter-American Commission on Human Rights. *Report on the Situation of Human Rights in Brazil*. OAS Doc. OEA/Ser.L/V/II.97 (29 September).

–. 1999. Inter-American Commission on Human Rights. *Report on the Situation of Human Rights in Colombia*. OAS Doc. OEA/Ser.L/V/II.102 (26 February).

UNESCO. 1966. *Declaration of the Principles Governing International Cultural Cooperation*. General Conference of the United Nations Educational, Scientific and Cultural Organization, 4 November 1966 (14th Session).

–. 1978. *Declaration of Bogota*. Intergovernmental Conference on Cultural Policies in Latin America and the Caribbean.

United Nations. 1969. *International Convention on the Elimination of All Forms of Racial Discrimination*. 660 UNTS 195.

–. 1989. *Convention on the Rights of the Child*. GA res. 44/25, annex, 44 UN GAOR Supp. (No. 49) at 167, UN Doc. A/44/49.

United Nations. Commission on Human Rights. 1995. Subcommission on the Prevention of Discrimination and Protection of Minorities. *Protection of the Heritage of Indigenous People: Final Report of Special Rapporteur, Mrs. Erica-Irene Daes*. UN Doc. E/CN.4/Sub.2/1995/26.

–. 1996. *Supplementary Report of the Special Rapporteur, Mrs Erica-Irene Daes, Submitted Pursuant to Sub-Commission Resolution 1995/40 and Commission on Human Rights Resolution 1996/63*. UN Doc. E/CN.4/Sub.2/1996/22.

United Nations. General Assembly. 1948. *Universal Declaration of Human Rights*. GA res. 217 A(III), UN Doc. A/810 at 71.

–. 1966. *International Covenant on Civil and Political Rights*. GA res. 2200A (XXI), 21 UN GAOR Supp. (No. 16) at 52, UN Doc. A/6316 (1966), 999 UNTS 171.

–. 1985. *Declaration on the Human Rights of Individuals Who Are Not Nationals of the Country in Which They Live*. GA res. 40/144 UN GAOR Supp. (No. 53) at 252, UN Doc. A/40/53 (1985), Article 5.

–. 1992. *Declaration on the Rights of Persons Belonging to National or Ethnic, Religious or Linguistic Minorities*. GA res. 47/135, 18 December 1992.

United Nations. Human Rights Committee. 1988a. *Lovelace v. Canada*. Communication No. R/24, UN GAOR, 43rd Sess. Supp. (No. 40) at 166, UN Doc. A/43/40, Annex 7(G).

–. 1988b. *Kitok v. Sweden*. Communication No. 197/1985, UN GAOR, 43rd Sess. Supp. (No. 40) at 207, UN Doc. A/43/40, Annex 7(G).

–. 1990. *B. Ominayak, Chief of the Lubicon Lake Band v. Canada*. Communication No. 167/1984, UN GAOR, 45th Sess. Supp. (No. 40, vol. 2) at 1, UN Doc. A/45/40, Annex 9(a).

–. 1993. *Ballantyne/Davidson/MacIntyre v. Canada*. Communication No. 359/1989:Canada, UN Doc. CCPR/C/47/D/359/1989.

–. 1994a. *General Comment 23: The Rights of Minorities (Art. 27)*. UN Doc. CCPR/C/21/Rev.1/Add.5, General Comment No. 23. (General Comments).

–. 1994b. *Länsman v. Finland*. Communication No. 511/1992:Finland, UN Doc. CCPR/C/52/D/511/1992.

–. 1994c. *Singer v. Canada*. Communication No. 455/199:Canada, UN Doc. CCPR/C/51/D/455/1991.

–. 1995. *Jouni Länsman et al. v. Finland*. Communication No. 671/1995, UN Doc. CCPR/C/58/D/671/1995.

–. 1997a. *Chapparo et al. v. Colombia*. Communication No. 612/1995 (19/08/97), UN Doc. CCPR/C/60/D/612/1995.

–. 1997b. *Hopu v. France*. Communication No. 549/1993:France, 29/12/97, UN Doc. CCPR/C/60/D/549/1993/Rev.1.

United Nations. World Conference on Human Rights. 1993. *Vienna Declaration and Programme of Action*. 25 June 1993, Vienna, UN Doc. A/CONF.157/24 (Part I) at 20.

Books and Articles

Anaya, S. James. 1996. *Indigenous Peoples in International Law.* Oxford: Oxford University Press.

Barry, Brian. 2001. *Culture and Equality.* Cambridge, MA: Harvard University Press.

Franck, Thomas. 1999. *The Empowered Self.* Oxford: Oxford University Press.

Friedman, Marilyn. 2001. Human Rights, Cultural Minorities and Women. Paper presented at the ninth annual McDowell Conference on Philosophy and Human Rights, American University, Washington, DC, 6 November.

Holder, Cindy. 2002. Are Patriarchal Cultures Really a Problem? Rethinking Objections from Cultural Viciousness. *Journal of Contemporary Legal Issues* 12:727-57.

–. 2005. Self-Determination as a Basic Human Right: The Draft U.N. Declaration on the Rights of Indigenous Peoples. In *Minorities within Minorities: Diversity, Rights and Equality,* ed. Avigail Eisenberg and Jeff Spinner-Halev, 294-316. Cambridge: Cambridge University Press.

Kernohan, Andrew. 1998. *Liberalism, Equality and Cultural Oppression.* Cambridge: Cambridge University Press.

Kymlicka, Will. 1989. *Liberalism, Community and Culture.* Oxford: Clarendon Press.

–. 1995. *Multicultural Citizenship.* Oxford: Oxford University Press.

Kymlicka, Will, and Raphael Cohen Almagor. 2000. Ethnocultural Minorities in Liberal Democracies. In *Pluralism: The Philosophy and Politics of Diversity,* ed. M. Baghramiau, 228-50. New York: Routledge.

Lerner, Natan. 2003. *Group Rights and Discrimination in International Law.* 2nd ed. Leiden, NL: Brill Academic Publishers.

Levy, Jacob. 2000. *The Multiculturalism of Fear.* New York: Oxford University Press.

Margalit, Avishai, and Joseph Raz. 1990. National Self-Determination. *Journal of Philosophy* 87:439-61.

Miller, David. 1995. *On Nationality.* Oxford: Oxford University Press.

Narayan, Uma. 1998. Essence of Culture and a Sense of History: A Feminist Critique of Cultural Essentialism. *Hypatia* 13:86-106.

Okin, Susan. 1998. Feminism and Multiculturalism: Some Tensions. *Ethics* 108(4):680-81.

–. 1999. *Is Multiculturalism Bad for Women?* Princeton, NJ: Princeton University Press.

Ripstein, Arthur. 1997. Context, Continuity and Fairness. In *The Morality of Nationalism,* ed. R. McKim and J. McMahan, 209-26. Oxford: Oxford University Press.

Simmons, A. John. 1996. Associative Political Obligations. *Ethics* 106:247-73.

Sperber, Dan. 1996. *Explaining Culture.* New York: Blackwell Publishers.

Svennson, Frances. 1979. Liberal Democracy and Group Rights: The Legacy of Individualism and Its Impact on American Indian Tribes. *Political Studies* 27:421-39.

Tamir, Yael. 1993. *Liberal Nationalism.* Princeton, NJ: Princeton University Press.

Waldron, Jeremy. 1992. Minority Cultures and the Cosmopolitan Alternative. *University of Michigan Journal of Law Reform* 3:195-230.

–. 2000. What Is Cosmopolitanism? *Journal of Political Philosophy* 8:227-43.

5
The Misuse of "Culture" by the Supreme Court of Canada
Neil Vallance

Jean-Claude Mahé, a francophone father of school-aged children, sued the province of Alberta on the grounds that its refusal to establish an independent francophone school board contravened section 23 of the *Charter of Rights and Freedoms*.[1] Dorothy Marie Van der Peet, a member of the Sto:lo First Nation, defended a charge of selling fish contrary to the *Fisheries Act* on the grounds that the act contravened section 35 of the *Constitution Act, 1982*.[2] What do these disputes have in common? They both ended up before the Supreme Court of Canada as, respectively, *Mahe v. Alberta* and *R. v. Van der Peet*. And both judgments made extensive use of the term "culture," though in very different ways.

The intent of this chapter is twofold. First, to demonstrate, by analysis of both cases, that the court's use of the term "culture" lacks critical awareness and consistency. Second, to demonstrate, by comparison of the cases, that the court uses the term in a manner that confers a benefit upon Canada's official language minorities and confers an unjust burden upon the First Nations of Canada.

The court's use of "culture" is assessed here against the standards established by anthropology in its long and arduous engagement with the concept. According to Michael Asch, "anthropology represents the primary approach developed in the western intellectual tradition to understand cultures other than one's own. It has developed its approach on the basis of over a century of purposive enquiry into the nature of culture" (1992, 505).

The Concept of Culture
In 1952 A.L. Kroeber and Clyde Kluckhohn produced a classic study, *Culture: A Critical Review of Concepts and Definitions* (1966), containing 164 definitions. Many more definitions have been produced (and then reproduced in introductory anthropology texts) over the last half century. Novel definitions continue to crop up (see Shweder 2001, 437), but no one definition has achieved uncontested acceptance.

The definitions of culture catalogued so relentlessly by Kroeber and Kluckhohn can be categorized in many ways. For example, there is the lengthy omnibus definition (inclusive of everything).[3] There are also short-hand definitions, such as "way of life" or "design for living."[4] A third category comprises definitions that emphasize the passing on and preservation of tradition.[5] Finally, there are definitions that stress the knowledge acquired by learning as opposed to instinct.[6]

Many of the definitions contain elements from more than one category. The number of possible permutations and combinations is astronomical. Therefore, any one definition is subject to criticism for being short and incomplete or long and unwieldy. As well, many of the definitions are contradictory, with the result that espousing one implies partial or total rejection of others.

In 1974, Roger Keesing provided a useful update on the ongoing debate. He opened with a complaint that "the holistic, humanistic view of culture synthesized by Kroeber and Kluckhohn includes too much and is too diffuse either to separate analytically the twisted threads of human experience or to interpret the designs into which they are woven" (73). Keesing proposed four "new" definitions. For example, he described "adaptive systems," better known today as "cultural ecology," as follows:

> Technology, subsistence economy, and elements of social organization directly tied to production are the most adaptively central realms of culture. It is in these realms that adaptive changes usually begin and from which they usually ramify. However, different conceptions of how this process operates separate the "cultural materialism" of Harris from ... the "cultural evolutionism" of Service and distinguish the cultural ecologists of the Steward tradition from human ecologists such as Rappaport and Vayda. However, all ... would view economies and their social correlates as in some sense primary, and ideational systems – religion, ritual, world view – as in some sense secondary, derived, or epiphenomenal. (76)

In the last two decades, commentators have directed most of their attention away from formulating new definitions and towards criticism of the concept of culture in general (Kuper 1999). The criticisms usually refer to one or more of four interrelated features: boundedness, homogeneity, absence of change, and lack of agency. These criticisms are essential to the assessment of the court's use of the concept of culture in the minority education and Aboriginal rights cases. There are two criticisms that are particularly effective. The first is by Eric Wolf: "Once we locate the reality of society in historically changing, imperfectly bounded, multiple and branching social alignments ... the concept of fixed, unitary, and bounded culture must give way to a sense of the fluidity and permeability of cultural sets. In the rough-and-tumble of social interaction, groups are known to exploit the ambiguities of inherited forms, to impart new evaluations or valences to them, to borrow forms more expressive of their interest, or to create wholly new forms to answer to changed circumstances" (1982, 387). The second is by George Marcus and Michael Fisher: "The [present] task ... is ... to revise ethnographic description away from [a] self-contained, homogeneous, and largely ahistorical framing of the cultural unit toward a view of cultural situations as always in flux, in a perpetual historically sensitive state of re-sistance and accommodation to broader processes of influence that are as much inside as outside the local context" (1986, 78). As well, some anthro-pologists argue that the concept of culture is too broad, fuzzy, and conten-tious to be of any value and should be dropped from academic discourse (Barth 2001; Kuper 1999; Rodseth 2001).

This brief history of the concept of culture within anthropology dem-onstrates the necessity for extreme care in its use in all but the most casual contexts. "Extreme care" means that before the term is used in research, the researcher must assign a specific content to it with an explicit working definition.

Anthropological experience is relevant to the court's use of the term "cul-ture" because while isolated, incidental use of the term in judgments is not problematic, that changes in cases where a judge makes repeated use of the term without providing a definition. Uncritical use of a term with such a long history of overlapping, contradictory, contested, and changeable mean-ings *is* problematic. The reader is left to guess which meaning (if any) the judge had in mind, and this lack of certainty provides an inadequate guide for those who must interpret and follow the court's judgments as binding precedents. In the absence of definition, the court, without realizing it, may also use the term differently from one case to the next. Again, this lack of consistency places an unfair burden on subsequent litigants and lower-court judges. It is even more problematic to use the term as the basis for a legal test without providing a clear definition for the guidance of those who must apply it. However, the court appears to have done just that with the "dis-tinctive culture test" developed in the pivotal Aboriginal rights case *R. v. Van der Peet*.

R. v. Van der Peet and Section 35 Aboriginal Rights
In *Van der Peet*, the word "culture" is used far more than in any other deci-sion of the court in any area of law.[7] To be specific, the term is used over two hundred times in the report of the case. However, even though the judg-ment in *Van der Peet* is peppered with references to culture, the term is never explicitly defined. A survey of twenty Aboriginal rights decisions rendered by the court since 1982 found 494 references to "culture." None of the judg-ments stated a need to define the term (Vallance 2003). This is particularly

surprising because the judgments in *Van der Peet* contain five definitions of other key words used in the course of the decision: Chief Justice Lamer resorted to *Le Petit Robert* for a definition of "ancestral" and to the *Concise Oxford Dictionary* for definitions of "tradition" (*Van der Peet,* para. 40), "distinct," and "distinctive" (para. 71); and Justice McLachlin had recourse to the *Shorter Oxford English Dictionary* for a definition of "integral" (para. 256). Lamer even came up with a working definition of "Aboriginal" as "prior to the arrival of Europeans in North America" (para. 62). However, counsel and lower courts are left with the problem of applying a test that depends on the term "culture" – an undefined term capable of almost infinite meanings.

The facts in the case are brief: when Dorothy Van der Peet was charged with selling ten salmon contrary to the *Fisheries Act,* she alleged in her defence that the restrictions imposed by the act infringed her Aboriginal right to sell fish and therefore violated her section 35 rights (para. 6). Section 35(1) of the *Constitution Act, 1982* states that "the existing aboriginal and treaty rights of the aboriginal peoples of Canada are hereby recognized and affirmed." Section 35 does not define Aboriginal rights. A series of conferences held pursuant to section 37(1) of the act were intended to "identify and define" Aboriginal rights. However, no agreement was reached (Asch and Macklem 1991, 504), and it was left to the court to interpret the meaning of the phrase. In *R. v. Sparrow,* Dickson and La Forest made a single reference to Musqueam salmon fishing as "an integral part of their distinctive culture" (1099). This phrase was transformed six years later into the distinctive culture test by Chief Justice Lamer in his reasons for judgment in *Van der Peet.*

Lamer promulgated the test as part of his interpretation of Aboriginal rights: "The following test should be used to identify whether an applicant has established an aboriginal right protected by s. 35(1): in order to be an aboriginal right an activity must be an element of a practice, custom or tradition integral to the distinctive culture of the aboriginal group claiming the right" (para. 46). He provided "further elaboration" intended to assist in the "practical" application of the test. First, the Aboriginal "perspective" must be taken into account, provided that it is "framed in terms cognizable to the Canadian legal and constitutional structure" (para. 49). Second, he directed future courts to identify integral practices, customs, and traditions in "the period prior to contact between aboriginal and European societies" (para. 60). Third, he defined "integral" as the opposite of "incidental," with the result that a court cannot look at practices, customs, or traditions that are "only incidental or occasional to that society" (para. 56).

Lamer decided that the exchange of fish was not central to Sto:lo culture and affirmed the conviction of Dorothy Van der Peet (para. 93). He justified this conclusion on the grounds that specialization, such as the trade of fish, occurs only at the tribal level, while the Sto:lo were at the band level, where "division of labour tends to occur only on the basis of gender or age" (para. 90).

The first criticisms of Lamer's test are to be found in the dissenting reasons for judgment of Justices L'Heureux-Dubé and McLachlin. For example, McLachlin came out strongly against the "indeterminacy" of the test on the grounds that "different people may entertain different ideas of what is distinctive, specific or central. To use such concepts as the markers of legal rights is to permit the determination of rights to be coloured by the subjective views of the decision-maker rather than objective norms, and to invite uncertainty and dispute as to whether a particular practice constitutes a legal right" (para. 257). L'Heureux-Dubé also took a different position from Lamer on the "integral versus incidental" distinction: "Simply put, the emphasis would be on the significance of these activities to natives rather than on the activities themselves" (para. 157).

This theme was taken up by Barsh and Henderson (1997), who objected to the court's quest for the "grail of 'centrality'": "The extent to which an idea, symbol or practice is central to the cultural identity of a particular society is inescapably subjective to that society – or, in the jargon of anthropologists, *emic* (a matter of subjective meaning)" (1000). They described Lamer's treatment of Aboriginal culture as objective, or *etic* ("a phenomenon which can be reliably and consistently measured by outsiders") (ibid.). They also observed that to make a distinction between "integral" and "incidental" implies that the component parts of a culture can exist independently of one another. "This presumption of independence is, in and of itself, utterly incompatible with Aboriginal philosophies, which tend to regard all human activity (and indeed all of existence) as inextricably inter-dependent" (ibid.).

Lamer's emphasis on "integral" versus "incidental" and on the difference between "band level" and "tribal level" subsistence economies is clearly an (implicit) application of the cultural ecology concept of culture as described by Keesing (1974) earlier in this chapter. It is also therefore subject to the criticism levelled by Wolf (1982) and Marcus and Fisher (1986) that this conception tends to view cultures as bounded, homogenous, static, and without agency.

Barsh and Henderson provide a fascinating explanation of Lamer's presumption in formulating the test:

Anthropologists long regarded "culture" as something that could be observed, counted, measured and then compared, and tribal societies were routinely characterized as simple, transparent and static. The aim of fieldwork for more than a century was to produce a comprehensive ethnography – a book that contained everything that was useful or interesting about a society. From this conceit – that a "simple" society could be described adequately in one book when European society has not even begun to exhaust its possibilities (and its ambiguities) in a hundred thousand books – arises the presumption that a Euro-Canadian jurist today can sit in judgment of what a Heiltsuk or Sheshaht once believed or valued most. (1997, 1002)

Their criticism is well-taken and is now acknowledged by anthropologists: "The popular conception that a group is defined by a distinctive culture and that cultures are discrete, clearly bounded and internally homogenous, with relatively fixed meanings and values ... echoes what was until recently a dominant if contested ... understanding of 'culture' within the discipline of anthropology" (Cowan et al. 2001, 3). While anthropology has moved on, the court has not. There is no indication in the Aboriginal rights (or non-Aboriginal rights) cases of any awareness of these cogent criticisms (Vallance 2003, 71-72).

As Barsh and Henderson point out, the requirement that the existence of Aboriginal rights be determined on a case-by-case basis has a startling consequence: Canada's courts face the prospect of reviewing evidence on various aspects of precontact culture from over six hundred First Nations (1997, 1005). Since Barsh and Henderson's analysis, the test continued to attract critical comment as well as suggestions for its amendment (Slattery 2000) and replacement (Macklem 2001).

The test was reconsidered in the case of *Mitchell v. M.N.R.* By this time McLachlin was chief justice. She delivered the majority decision of the court and made only one reference to criticism of the test: "Determining what practices existed, and distinguishing central, defining features of a culture from traits that are marginal or peripheral, is no easy task at a remove of 400 years. Cultural identity is a subjective matter and not easily discerned" (para. 32). This statement was followed by citation, without comment, of three commentaries on *Van der Peet*, including that of Barsh and Henderson (1997).[8] It also echoes one of the criticisms of the test contained in McLachlin's own dissent in *Van der Peet*, namely that the test is indeterminate, subjective, and invites "uncertainty and dispute" (*Van der Peet*, para. 257). However, rather than amending or replacing the test, she applied the test and concluded that the Aboriginal right claimed in the case was "not a practice integral to the distinctive culture of the Mohawk people" (*Mitchell*, para. 60). Therefore, the distinctive culture test remains the law of the land.

Mahe v. Alberta and Section 23 Minority Language Education Rights
In a 2002 judgment, Justice Le Bel remarked that "most constitutional litigation on cultural issues has arisen in the context of language and education rights" (*Kitkatla Band v. British Columbia*, para. 51). A survey of the

court's use of the term "culture" confirms that he was almost right. Aboriginal rights is the one area of constitutional litigation with greater reference to cultural issues (Vallance 2003, 123). The court's 1990 judgment in *Mahe*, delivered by Chief Justice Dickson, used the term "culture" a total of twenty-two times. This broke the previous record of fourteen references in the 1973 Aboriginal rights case *R. v. Calder*. *Mahe* held the record for most use of the term until 1996, when it yielded the title to *Van der Peet*.

The facts in *Mahe* are brief: Jean-Claude Mahé and two other parents of school-aged children claimed that the provision of French language education in Edmonton did not meet the requirements of section 23 of the Charter. Specifically, the relevant authorities had denied their request for a separate francophone school board. Section 23 holds that parents whose first language is French or English, and who live in a province where that language is in the minority, have the right to have their children receive publicly funded primary and secondary schooling in that language, and in "minority language educational facilities," wherever the number of qualified children "warrants."[9]

Dickson, in his analysis of the issues, declared that "the general purpose of s. 23 is clear: it is to preserve and promote the two official languages of Canada and their respective cultures." He went on to state: "My reference to cultures is significant: it is based on the fact that any broad guarantee of language rights, especially in the context of education, cannot be separated from a concern for the culture associated with the language" (*Mahe*, 362). Next he introduced a "sliding scale approach" to determine the extent of the obligation to provide minority language education. For example, in areas with a "small number" of minority language students, governments and school boards need do nothing, or at most they might provide some instruction in French. At the higher end of the scale, where there are many minority language students, governments and school boards must provide facilities for eligible students, ranging from a separate school to a separate school board. Dickson acknowledged that the test lacks precision, but he did not want to impose "specific modalities" requiring a specified number of students to trigger a particular level of instruction or facility. He justified the test as follows: "In some instances this approach may result in further litigation to determine whether the general requirements mandated by the court have been implemented. I see no way to avoid this result, as the alternative of a uniform detailed order runs the real risk of imposing impractical solutions. Section 23 is a new type of legal right in Canada and thus requires new responses from the courts" (376).

He then entered upon a consideration of the scope of the word "facilities" in section 23. He was able to infer that the obligation to provide facilities included providing the parents with some measure of "management and control" over those facilities. He reinforced his point by stating, "I think it incontrovertible that the health and survival of the minority language and culture can be affected in subtle but important ways by decisions relating to these issues." As examples he named decisions about curricula, hiring, and expenditures (371-72).

With respect to the situation in Edmonton, Dickson reviewed some statistics on present and potential enrolment and decided there were enough "section 23 students" to warrant the presence of "section 23 parents" on the existing school board, but not enough to mandate the establishment of an independent francophone school board (386-89).

Dickson's views on the use of culture were favourably reviewed and extensively quoted by his successor, Chief Justice Lamer, in *Reference re Public Schools Act (Man.)*. However, Lamer also emphasized that "the right should be construed remedially, in recognition of previous injustices that have gone unredressed and which have required the entrenchment of protection for minority language rights" (850). He reinforced this point in the following interpretation of a pre-*Mahe* decision: "In passing, one should note, as this Court held in *Ford v. Quebec (Attorney General)*, [1988] 2 S.C.R. 712, at pp. 777-78, that the focus on the historical context of language and culture indicates that different interpretative approaches may well have to be taken in different jurisdictions, sensitive to the unique blend of linguistic dynamics that have developed in each province" (851).

The court's most recent decision on minority language education rights is *Arsenault-Cameron v. Prince Edward Island*. The decision of the court was delivered by Justices Major and Bastarache. They devoted a section of the judgment to "The Remedial Purpose of Section 23," which stated that "the historical and contextual analysis is important for courts in determining whether a government has failed to meet its s. 23 obligations." However, the "analysis" of the trial judge was limited to "explaining the historical background of the official language minority in Prince Edward Island" (*Arsenault-Cameron v. Prince Edward Island*, para. 28). As well, my review of the decision of the trial judge in *Mahe* (Justice Purvis) indicated that the "historical and contextual analysis" in that case consisted only of a simple "Outline of French Language Instruction in Northwest Territories and the Province of Alberta Educational Systems" (*Mahe*, 34-38). While a brief review of the historical background is still a required introductory step in any section 23 applications, it has not matured into a significant threshold test for entitlement to section 23 rights. As in *Reference re Public Schools Act (Man.)*, the court in *Arsenault-Cameron* was careful to quote extensively and favourably from the references to language and culture in *Mahe*. Therefore, the stance on culture taken by Dickson in *Mahe* remains unchallenged.

To the best of my knowledge, there are no dissenting judgments in any of the major decisions of the court on minority language rights. The court's use of the terms "language and culture" in section 23 cases also remains largely unchallenged in the anthropological and legal literature (see L. Green 1987, 640; Paulston 1997). In a case comment, Maurice Green noted that "in reviewing the purpose [of section 23] the Court was definite in its opinion that language had to be linked to culture" (1990-91, 208). In fact, over the course of the judgment, Dickson used the phrase "language and culture" eleven times. However, the reasons for judgment at the trial and appeal levels did not cite "culture" as any part of the purpose of section 23. Why did Dickson make such a strong connection between these two terms?

One answer is provided by Maurice Green, who referred to a judgment of the Manitoba Court of Appeal, delivered just five weeks before *Mahe*. In the Manitoba case, one of the judges had rejected the notion that the purpose of section 23 was to give constitutional status to biculturalism: "The fundamental thesis of the Commission on Bilingualism and Biculturalism has been repudiated by the adoption of the principle of multiculturalism" (*Reference re s. 79(3), (4) and (7) of the Public Schools Act (Manitoba)*, 290, quoted in M. Green 1990-91, 207). That opinion was something the court "emphatically rejected" in *Mahe* (M. Green 1990-91, 207). Dickson specifically referred to the Royal Commission on Bilingualism and Biculturalism as "a major force in the eventual entrenchment of language rights in the Charter," and just to drive the point home he followed with a quote from the commission's report: "Language is also the key to cultural development. Language and culture are not synonymous but the vitality of the language is a necessary condition for the complete preservation of a culture" (Canada. Royal Commission on Bilingualism and Biculturalism 1968, 8, quoted in *Mahe*, 262).

A second explanation may be derived from an analysis of language rights conducted before the court heard the *Mahe* case. In "Are Language Rights Fundamental?" Leslie Green (1987) made reference to popular criticisms that had "cast doubt upon the fundamental importance of language rights." He discussed various arguments for the fundamental importance of language, including one that "[an ethnic group's] concern is not with the endangerment of a linguistic species, but with the continued flourishing of a group of speakers whose desire to transmit their culture to future generations is an aspect of their well-being" (656). He also referred to the desire that "one's language group should flourish" (658). Similar arguments are found in Dickson's judgment, which indicates the resonance between political and public debates at the time in terms that map Green's way of framing the problem.

A possible third answer lies in Dickson's decision to include "management and control" in his interpretation of "facilities." This constitutes a very expansive interpretation of "facilities." He needed to identify an important public purpose, beyond preservation of the language, that would be served by such a broad approach. He chose to invoke culture: "Such management and control is vital to ensure that their language and culture flourish," and he reinforced his stance by stating: "To give but one example, most decisions pertaining to curricula clearly have an influence on the language and culture of the minority students" (*Mahe*, 372). In other words, Dickson may have introduced culture and tied it to language to tip the scales in favour of the arguments for language preservation.

In *Mahe*, the court, of its own volition, introduced the concept of culture to flesh out its concept of language, without a parallel consideration of the nature of culture. Even though he used the term "culture" twenty-two times in the judgment, Dickson did not see fit to elaborate on what he meant by the term in general, nor did he inquire into the membership, extent, or content of French language culture in Edmonton. He merely assumed that there was such a culture and that it was worthy of preservation (in aspic) by the imposition of publicly funded minority language education.

Such goals as preserving the "health and survival" of a culture and ensuring that language and culture "flourish" seem to fit the mould of "preservation of tradition" definitions enumerated by Kroeber and Kluckhohn (1966). They are also reminiscent of the functionalist approach to culture, which holds that "the function of any element of culture, a rule of morality or etiquette, a legal obligation, a religious belief or ritual can only be discovered by considering what part it plays in the social integration of the people in whose culture it is found" (Radcliffe-Brown 1930, 3-4, quoted in Kroeber and Kluckhohn 1966, 160). None of these definitions deals with the aspects of culture raised by Wolf (1982) and Marcus and Fisher (1986), namely, boundedness, homogeneity, absence of change, and lack of agency.

These definitions are also examples of the reification of culture, which in turn leads to essentialism. In this case the essentialism takes the form of (erroneously) viewing language communities as homogenous and static (Keesing 1994, 303). The court has compounded the problem by overemphasizing the interdependence of language and culture, leaving the impression that they are conjoined twins unable to survive separation. While the extract from the *Report of the Commission on Bilingualism and Biculturalism* quoted by Dickson in *Mahe* (262) acknowledges that "language and culture are not synonymous" (Canada. Royal Commission on Bilingualism and Biculturalism 1968, 8), the judgment as a whole treats the concepts as interchangeable. In anthropology, language is a part of culture but never the whole of it: "As Harry Hoijer (1953) insisted, one should think of language *in* culture and not just of language *and* culture" (Duranti 1997, 336; emphasis in original). As in the case of culture, the anthropological approach reveals much about the complexity of language: "What is unique about linguistic anthropology lies ... in its interest in speakers as social actors, in language as both a resource for and product of social interaction, in speech communities as simultaneously real and imaginary entities whose boundaries are constantly being reshaped and negotiated through myriad acts of speaking" (6). And the problem with ignoring the mutability of culture is well summarized by Cowan et al.: "In the stark distinction between mass or majoritarian cultures, on the one hand, and disadvantaged minority cultures, on the other, internal homogeneity is too easily assumed and taken as natural. An endangered 'culture' is perceived as a pre-existing given which must be defended, rather than as something creatively reworked during struggles to actualize rights" (2001, 19).

Comparison of *Mahe* and *Van der Peet*

In 1990 the court handed down landmark decisions in both areas of law: minority language education rights and Aboriginal rights. *Mahe* was one, and the other was *R. v. Sparrow,* an Aboriginal rights case. Both cases contained optimistic statements as to how the court should interpret these rights. In *Mahe,* Chief Justice Dickson explained his approach to section 23 as follows: "Careful interpretation of such a section is wise; however, this does not mean that courts should not 'breathe life' into the expressed purpose of the section, or avoid implementing the possibly novel remedies needed to achieve that purpose" (365). Did the court make "novel" use of culture to "breathe life" into section 23 rights? I argue that it did.

Chief Justice Dickson and Justice La Forest, in *Sparrow,* made a forceful declaration with respect to section 35: "When the purposes of the affirmation of aboriginal rights are considered, it is clear that a generous, liberal interpretation of the words in the constitutional provision is demanded" (1106). However, *Sparrow* did not provide an interpretive framework for Aboriginal rights. Nor did it contain many explicit references to culture (only four) compared to *Mahe* (with twenty-two). The task of interpreting the scope and content of Aboriginal rights was postponed until 1996, the year of *Van der Peet,* with its two hundred references to culture. In that case, the majority judgment of Chief Justice Lamer quoted the above statement of Dickson and La Forest (para. 23). Did the court's use of the concept of culture contribute to a "generous, liberal interpretation" of section 35 rights? I argue that it did not.

There are some obvious similarities between the two sets of rights in addition to the optimistic statements contained in *Sparrow* and *Mahe.* Both minority language rights and Aboriginal rights were first granted constitutional status by the *Constitution Act, 1982.* While sections 23 and 35 of the act do not contain any reference to culture, the court used the term extensively in *Mahe* and *Van der Peet,* defining it in neither.

In both cases the court developed "novel" tests: a sliding scale test in *Mahe* and a distinctive culture test in *Van der Peet.* The court also acknowledged that the application of the tests to particular fact patterns might require further references to the court. However, there are over six hundred First Nations that can potentially offer different fact patterns relevant to the distinctive culture test, yet only ten provinces that might offer different patterns relevant to the guarantee of minority language education rights.[10] In this respect, the burden imposed on First Nations in Canada to show the court the different ways in which their rights should be guaranteed is much more onerous than the one placed on the (French and English) minority language communities.

There is another similarity between minority language education and Aboriginal rights cases: in both instances the concept of culture may have been introduced by the court to deal with political concerns. In its interpretation of section 35, the court used culture to keep the lid on the scope of Aboriginal rights because a truly "generous, liberal interpretation" could threaten the legality of Canada's assumption of sovereignty over First Nations (Asch 1999, 440). In its interpretation of section 23, the court was faced with the following narrow construction of language rights imposed by Justice Beetz in *Société des Acadiens du Nouveau-Brunswick Inc. v. Association of Parents for Fairness in Education:* "Unlike language rights which are based on political compromise, legal rights tend to be seminal in nature because they are rooted in principle ... Language rights ... although some of them have been enlarged and incorporated into the Charter, remain none-theless founded on political compromise ... The courts should pause before they decide to act as instruments of change with respect to language rights" (578, quoted in L. Green 1987, 645).

It was Justice Beetz's warning that "courts should be careful in interpreting language rights" which prompted Dickson to say that "this does not mean that courts should not 'breathe life' into the expressed purpose of the section, or avoid implementing the possibly novel remedies needed to achieve that purpose" (*Mahe,* 365). Dickson may have introduced the idea of culture in part as a justification for the implementation of "novel remedies," such as his liberal interpretation of "facilities."

Unlike most Charter rights, minority language rights are not universal. They are available only to Canadian citizens who meet the eligibility criteria set out in section 23. Aboriginal rights also are not universal. They are available only to "the Indian, Inuit and Metis peoples of Canada" (s. 35(2)). However, Lamer went on to further restrict the application of Aboriginal rights: "Aboriginal rights are not general and universal, their scope and content must be determined on a case-by-case basis. The fact that one group of aboriginal people has an aboriginal right to do a particular thing will not be without something more, sufficient to demonstrate that another aboriginal community has the same aboriginal right. The existence of the right will be specific to each aboriginal community" (*Van der Peet,* para. 69). The right only comes into existence once an Aboriginal community has satisfied the requirements of the distinctive culture test. But, as I have argued, it is diffi-cult to ascertain with any certainty the requirements of the test, let alone how to satisfy them.

On the other hand, all section 23 parents "have the right to have their children receive primary and secondary school instruction in that language in that province" (s. 23(1)). The application of the right does depend on "the number of children of citizens who have such a right" (s. 23(3)(a) and 23(3)(b)). However, culture is not used to restrict entitlement to the enjoy-ment of the rights. Instead, culture is linked to language in a way that bol-sters the importance of the rights and justifies an expansive interpretation of their scope and content. The applicant minority-language parents are assumed to belong to a culture. The culture is presumed to be worthy of preservation. No inquiry is made into the content of the culture.

So far, this comparison has identified significant differences in the treat-ment of culture in the two cases. Earlier sections of the chapter have also identified serious problems with the use of culture in both cases. What are the present consequences and future implications?

Conclusion

A survey of all the court's decisions disclosed the absence of any serious definition or discussion of culture in any area of law in Canada (Vallance 2003). It also found that no judicial test is remotely comparable to the dis-tinctive culture test in *Van der Peet*. It appears to be unique. My search of the court's reported decisions for any reference to culture as a "concept" turned up nothing as well.[11] In contrast, the court is on record as defining other ambiguous concepts. For example, in *R. v. Big M Drug Mart,* Dickson ac-knowledged that "freedom of religion" is a "concept" and proceeded to define it (336). This points to a key feature of the court's approach to culture: while the court treats freedom of religion as a concept, it treats Aboriginal culture as a fact. The corollary is that concepts need only be defined, whereas facts must be proven. The requirement that Aboriginal culture be proven rather than defined is consistent with Barsh and Henderson's interpretation of *Van der Peet*, namely that Lamer treated Ab-original culture as objective, "a phenomenon which can be reliably and consistently measured by outsiders" (1997, 1000).

In contrast, in *Mahe* the court did not treat culture as either a concept to be defined or a fact to be proven. At most, the court could be said to have taken "judicial notice" of culture: "Judicial notice may be taken only of 'facts' which are ... so notorious as not to be the subject of dispute among reasonable persons" (Hogg 1992, ch. 57, 10). It may be an example of what Cross calls "tacit applications" of judicial notice, where "a great deal is taken for granted" (1974, 143). It is difficult otherwise to explain the court's oblivi-ous attitude towards culture in this case.

I have argued that the pairing of "language and culture" in *Mahe* has paved the way for an expansion of minority language education rights, while the distinctive culture test has become a barrier to the achievement of Aboriginal rights. My survey found no cases, outside the area of Aboriginal rights, in which claimants were required to prove anything about their culture as a prerequisite for entitlement to rights (Vallance 2003, 82). In other words, claimants to Aboriginal rights are held to a higher standard than claimants to Charter or other rights. I believe that the creation of this double standard constitutes an injustice against the First Nations in Canada.

This chapter is also a cautionary tale about the uncritical use of the term "culture" by the court. Confusion and problems could be avoided if the court resists the temptation to introduce the concept into its future deliberations. The court's use of a complex and contested concept such as culture will always be prone to "the proclivity of legal systems to demand clearly defined, context-neutral categories (including categories of identity and membership) in order to be able to classify persons and deal with them on the basis of these categories – the *essentializing proclivities of law*, in other words – contributes to the strategic essentializing of culturally defined groups" (Cowan et al. 2001, 10-11; emphasis in original).

However, the court may have no choice if any of the current crop of residential school class actions come before it. The statement of claim in one, *Baxter et al. v. The Attorney General of Canada et al.*, claims damages on behalf of former Aboriginal residential school students ("Alumni") on many grounds, one notably being that "their culture and language was undermined and in some cases eradicated by the forced assimilation of the Alumni Class members into non-aboriginal culture through the Residential Schools" (26). If any trials proceed on this ground,[12] counsel and judges will undoubtedly look for guidance to section 23 and section 35 cases, such as *Mahe* and *Van der Peet*. Unfortunately, these cases have little to offer in the way of safe passage through the complexities of the concept of culture. As matters stand, I fear that a continuation of the court's simplistic and uncritical use of the term "culture" may well contribute to further injustices.

Notes

1 Section 23 of the *Canadian Charter of Rights and Freedoms* reads:
   (1) Citizens of Canada
   (a) whose first language learned and still understood is that of the English or French linguistic minority of the province in which they reside, or
   (b) who have received their primary school instruction in Canada in English or French and reside in a province where the language in which they received that instruction is the language of the English or French linguistic minority population of the province, have the right to have their children receive primary and secondary school instruction in that language in that province.

(2) Citizens of Canada of whom any child has received or is receiving primary or secondary school instruction in English or French in Canada, have the right to have all their children receive primary and secondary language instruction in the same language.

(3) The right of citizens of Canada under subsections (1) and (2) to have their children receive primary and secondary school instruction in the language of the English or French linguistic minority population of a province

(a) applies wherever in the province the number of children of citizens who have such a right is sufficient to warrant the provision to them out of public funds of minority language instruction; and

(b) includes, where the number of those children so warrants, the right to have them receive that instruction in minority language educational facilities provided out of public funds.

2 Section 35 of the *Constitution Act, 1982* reads:

(1) The existing aboriginal and treaty rights of the aboriginal peoples of Canada are hereby recognized and affirmed.

(2) In this Act, "aboriginal peoples of Canada" includes the Indian, Inuit, and Metis peoples of Canada.

(3) For greater certainty, in subsection (1) "treaty rights" includes rights that now exist by way of land claims agreements or may be so acquired.

(4) Notwithstanding any other provision of this Act, the aboriginal and treaty rights referred to in subsection (1) are guaranteed equally to male and female persons.

3 For example, "Culture, or civilization, ... is that complex whole which includes knowledge, belief, art, law, moral, custom, and any other capabilities and habits acquired by man as a member of society" (Tylor 1870, 1, quoted in Kroeber and Kluckhohn 1966, 81).

4 For example, "A culture refers to the distinctive way of life of a group of people, their complete 'design for living'" (Kluckhohn 1951, 86, quoted in Kroeber and Kluckhohn 1966, 98).

5 For example, "Culture means the whole complex of traditional behavior which has been developed by the human race and is successively learned by each generation" (Mead 1937, 17, quoted in Kroeber and Kluckhohn 1966, 90).

6 For example, "Culture is the sociological term for learned behavior, behavior which in man is not given at birth, which is not determined by his germ cells as is the behavior of wasps or the social ants" (Benedict 1947, 13, quoted in Kroeber and Kluckhohn 1966, 112).

7 This assertion and subsequent numerical references in the chapter are derived from a survey conducted by the author as part of a master's thesis on the use of the term in both Aboriginal rights and non-Aboriginal rights cases decided by the Supreme Court of Canada (Vallance 2003).

8 The other two are Borrows (1997) and Woodward (1989).

9 See note 1.

10 One could argue that there is the potential for hundreds of court applications from school boards across the country, but to date it has required applications by only one or two boards per province for the remaining ones to fall into line.

11 Data sheets for each of the 165 cases surveyed isolate any words, such as "concept," used in association with the term "culture" (or its adjectival form, "cultural").

12 According to counsel for several claimants, no trial as yet has proceeded with this head of damage because of a concern about limitation periods (Dumonceau 2003, pers. comm.).

References

Books, Articles, and Public Documents

Asch, Michael. 1992. Errors in *Delgamuukw*: An Anthropological Perspective. In *Aboriginal Title in British Columbia: Delgamuukw v. The Queen*, ed. Frank Cassidy, 221-43. Vancouver: Oolichan Books.

–. 1999. From *Calder* to *Van der Peet*: Aboriginal Rights and Canadian Law, 1973-96. In *Indigenous Peoples' Rights in Australia, Canada, and New Zealand*, ed. Paul Haverman, 428-46. Auckland: Oxford University Press.

Asch, Michael, and Patrick Macklem. 1991. Aboriginal Rights and Canadian Sovereignty: An Essay on *R. v. Sparrow. Alberta Law Review* 29(2):498-517.

Barsh, Russel Lawrence, and James Youngblood Henderson. 1997. The Supreme Court's *Van der Peet* Trilogy: Naïve Imperialism and Ropes of Sand. *McGill Law Journal* 42:993-1009.

Barth, Fredrik. 2001. Rethinking the Object of Anthropology. *American Anthropologist* 103(2):435-37.

Benedict, Ruth. 1947. *Race, Science and Politics.* Revised edition. New York: Viking.

Borrows, John. 1997. The Trickster: Integral to a Distinctive Culture. *Constitutional Forum* 8(2):27-32.

Canada. Royal Commission on Bilingualism and Biculturalism. 1968. *Report of the Commission on Bilingualism and Biculturalism.* Vol 2. Ottawa: Queen's Printer.

Canadian Charter of Rights and Freedoms, Part I of the *Constitution Act, 1982,* being Schedule B to the *Canada Act 1982* (U.K.), 1982, c. 11.

Constitution Act, 1982, being Schedule B to the *Canada Act 1982* (U.K.), 1982, c. 11.

Cowan, Jane K., Marie-Benedicte Dembour, and Richard A. Wilson. 2001. Introduction. In *Culture and Rights, Anthropological Perspectives,* ed. Jane K. Cowan, Marie-Benedicte Dembour, and Richard A Wilson, 1-23. Cambridge: Cambridge University Press.

Cross, Sir Rupert. 1974. *Evidence.* London: Butterworths.

Duranti, Alessandro. 1997. *Linguistic Anthropology.* Cambridge: Cambridge University Press.

Green, Leslie. 1987. Are Language Rights Fundamental? *Osgoode Hall Law Journal* 25(4):639-69.

Green, Maurice A. 1990-91. The Continuing Saga of Litigation: Minority Language Instruction. *Education and Law Journal* 3:204-15.

Hogg, Peter. 1992. *Constitutional Law of Canada.* Loose-leaf edition. Toronto: Carswell.

Keesing, Roger M. 1974. Theories of Culture. *Annual Review of Anthropology* 3:73-97.

–. 1994. Theories of Culture Revisited. In *Assessing Cultural Anthropology,* ed. Robert Borofsky, 301-10. New York: McGraw-Hill.

Kluckhohn, Clyde. 1951. The Concept of Culture. In *The Policy Sciences,* ed. D. Lerner and H.D. Lasswell, 86-101. Stanford, CA: Stanford University Press.

Kroeber, A.L., and Clyde Kluckhohn. 1966. *Culture: A Critical Review of Concepts and Definitions.* New York: Vintage Books. Originally published 1952, in Papers of the Peabody Museum, Harvard University, 47.

Kuper, Adam. 1999. *Culture: The Anthropologists' Account.* Cambridge, MA: Harvard University Press.

Macklem, Patrick. 2001. *Indigenous Difference and the Constitution of Canada.* Toronto: University of Toronto Press.

Marcus, George, and Michael M.J. Fisher. 1986. *Anthropology as Culture Critique.* Chicago: Chicago University Press.

Mead, Margaret. 1937. *Cooperation and Competition among Primitive Peoples.* New York: McGraw-Hill.

Paulston, Christina Bratt. 1997. Language Policies and Language Rights. *Annual Review of Anthropology* 26:73-85.

Radcliffe-Brown, A.R. 1930. Applied Anthropology. *Report of Australian and New Zealand Association for the Advancement of Science,* 1-14.

Rodseth, Lars. 2001. Another Passage to Pragmatism. *American Anthropologist* 103(2):440-42.

Shweder, Richard A. 2001. Rethinking the Object of Anthropology and Ending Up Where Kroeber and Kluckhohn Began. *American Anthropologist* 103(2):437-42.

Slattery, Brian. 2000. Making Sense of Aboriginal and Treaty Rights. *Canadian Bar Review* 79(2):196-224.

Tylor, E.B. 1870. *Researches into the Early History and Development of Mankind.* London: John Murray.

Vallance, Neil. 2003. The Use of the Term "Culture" by the Supreme Court of Canada: A Comparison of Aboriginal and Non-Aboriginal Cases since 1982. Master's thesis, University of Victoria.

Wolf, Eric. 1982. *Europe and the People without History.* Berkeley: University of California Press.

Woodward, Jack. 1989. *Native Law.* Loose-leaf update 2000, Release 2. Toronto: Carswell.

Cases

Arsenault-Cameron v. Prince Edward Island, [2000] 1 S.C.R. 3 [*Arsenault-Cameron*].

Charles Baxter et al. v. The Attorney General of Canada et al. Amended Statement of Claim. Ontario Superior Court of Justice, File No. 00-CV-192059CP, 25 October 2002. www.thomsonrogers.com/AmendedStatementofClaim.pdf.

Kitkatla Band v. British Columbia (Minister of Small Business, Tourism and Culture) (2002), SCC 31.

Mahe v. Alberta (1985), 22 D.L.R. (4th) 24 (Alberta Q.B.); (1987), 6 W.W.R. 331 (Alberta C.A.); [1990] 1 S.C.R. 342 (SCC) [*Mahe*].

Mitchell v. M.N.R., [2001] 1 S.C.R. 911 [*Mitchell*].

Reference re Public Schools Act (Man.), s. 79(3), (4) and (7), [1993] 1 S.C.R. 839.

Reference re s. 79(3), (4) and (7) of the Public Schools Act (Manitoba) (1990), 2 W.W.R. 289 (Man. C.A.).

R. v. Big M Drug Mart Ltd., [1985] 1 S.C.R. 295.

R. v. Calder, [1973] S.C.R. 313 [*Calder*].

R. v. Sparrow, [1990] 1 S.C.R. 1075 [*Sparrow*].

R. v. Van der Peet, [1996] 2 S.C.R. 507 [*Van der Peet*].

Société des Acadiens du Nouveau-Brunswick Inc. v. Association of Parents for Fairness in Education (1986), 27 D.L.R. (4th) 406.

6
Gender, Difference, and Anti-Essentialism: Towards a Feminist Response to Cultural Claims in Law
Maneesha Deckha

Feminist legal and political theory has recently grappled in divergent ways with the concept of culture and the desirability of inserting "culture talk" into legal discourse. Feminist consideration of just how receptive courts, legislators, and other legal actors should be to rights claims founded on cultural equality typically revolves around an assessment of the risk that multiculturalism or the legal recognition of individual and group cultural identities may pose to women's interests. The extent to which this risk is real, illusory, or misconceived is at the centre of ongoing feminist debate.[1]

We can group feminist scholarship in this area into three separate categories: universalist, postcolonial, and differentiated (Shachar 2001a, 2n3).[2] The common strand running through the literature is a general wariness of a discourse of culture, but the theoretical reasons for the wariness, and the practical conclusions reached, vary. Briefly stated, the universalist approach urges feminists to renounce the ideas of culture, multiculturalism, and cultural rights within legal discourse unless they are nearly certain that the circulation of cultural claims will not have adverse effects on gendered and other marginalized subgroups of the culture articulating the claims. It is highly critical of cultural relativism and is concerned that some of those advocating cultural equality are disingenuously using the cloak of postcolonial resistance to Western cultural hegemony as a moral shield to perpetuate or reinvent harmful gendered traditions that work to their benefit. The universalist position has little tolerance for multiculturalism or state recognition of cultural difference and is dramatically opposed to a cultural protectionist position that is less disturbed by the essentialisms that may flow from the recognition of cultural claims based on invented "traditions" (Deckha 2004, 20-24). The approach is exemplified in the writings of political theorist Susan Moller Okin, most forcefully in her lead essay "Is Multiculturalism Bad for Women?" in a collection of the same title (1999, 10).

Equally critical of the cultural protectionist position, but more sympathetic to the justice subordinated groups seek when they articulate such claims, are the postcolonial and differentiated approaches. Both of these approaches delve deeper into the instabilities of culture as a concept than the universalist approach, which affirms the fluidity of the concept but privileges a more stable formulation in its theorization. The postcolonial and differentiated approaches emphasize the hybridity, dynamism, and continuous invention of tradition within any given culture, as well as the individual and group identities associated with that culture. They seek to divorce culture from racially fraught modernist narratives implicated within colonialism and imperialism and to wed it to ideas of human agency in creating, subverting, and disrupting cultural meanings. They do not imagine culture as intact but as open to movement and play by actors from all social strata.

The difference between these two approaches lies in their attention to political strategy. To the extent that postcolonial accounts advocate a place for culture within legal discourse, they reserve their approval for those cultural claims that can generate new moments of cultural dissent. Postcolonialists will only tolerate cultural claims that do not essentialize, quell internal dissent, or otherwise silence internal cultural subalterns. The differentiated approach harnesses the postcolonial critique into pragmatic suggestions for promoting cultural equality and reducing cultural hegemony while adequately conceptualizing culture with respect to certain legal issues. Advocates of the differentiated approach would permit cultural claims to enter legal discourse as long as they did not violate the principle of anti-subordination. Thus, a cultural defence in a criminal case and other culturally oriented rights may be defensible given the appropriate circumstances (Deckha 2004, 24-29).

How do we reconcile these competing visions about what the "good" of pluralistic liberal societies requires in relation to cultural claims? More specifically, which formulation, if any, is to be preferred by feminists, especially feminists committed to intersectionality and the affirmation of differences among women? Which position should an intersectionalist feminist favour? From the brief review of the positions above, it is reasonable to conclude that all the theorists canvassed are aspiring to more or less the same end – an egalitarian social order free of oppression and exploitation based on (at least) sex or gender differences (Lacey 1998, 2n2).[3] Yet they advocate substantially different, and at times diametrically opposed, roles for cultural discourse. Some argue for its rejection, while others maintain that qualified cultural narratives should be respected in certain situations (Darwall 1977, 38).[4]

Trying to identify which theory is "right" suggests faith in the liberal legal project of creating universal rules to be applied in any given fact situation. This is a suggestion I do not wish to make. Rather, I wish to identify a standard we may use both to evaluate these positions (I suggest a framework of ethical feminism) and to develop a line of reasoning that probes the strengths and weaknesses of each position. I argue that though no standard is perfect, an intersectionalist approach should favour the differentiated approach and that, in the absence of a better noncultural discursive organizing principle for a particular cultural claim, a somewhat modified version of the differentiated approach as it is typically stated suggests a way forwards to respect the deconstructive critiques of cultural discourse as well as the assertion of certain cultural identities (Shachar 2001a and 2001b, 294-95).[5] It is the position most responsive to intersectionalist sensibilities. My plan is not to develop a systematic theory that will apply across all contexts to all cultural claims regardless of particularity, but to further refine existing proposals in feminist legal scholarship with the goal of moving "beyond a dilemma, paradox, or inconsistency" that the existing proposals contain (Young 1997, 5).

The preliminary task in this refinement project is to set out my idea of the "good" (Rawls 1971, 22-23).[6] My framework for evaluating the presence of cultural discourse within law is meant to bring about a state of justice or order in which all individuals are able to lead autonomous (but not isolated) lives, maximizing their potential for creative, intellectual, social, and sensory pursuits (Nedelsky 1989, 10-11).[7] This view of the "good" is one in which subordination, particularly in the form of violence, whether it occurs physically or epistemically, is absent. I find that this sense of the "good" is most aptly captured by a loose adoption of Drucilla Cornell's (1991) definition of "ethical feminism."[8] Cornell defines this term as the absence of doing violence to an Other, whether through literal or epistemic marginalization (1990, 688).

On the surface, this definition appears to resonate in part with a classic liberal formulation of liberty (Mill 1859; Berlin 1969).[9] Cornell is referring to something different though, namely, the differences in social identities that liberalism disavows. Her ethical starting point is to recognize social actors as embodied and connected agents. She affirms the interpretation of social reality that insists that hierarchies of difference such as sex, race, class, sexual orientation, ability, age, and so on, structure our experiences and affect our personhoods. Her term "ethical feminism" is meant to signal a commitment to a project of dismantling power hierarchies, rigid identities, and the affirmation of abject differences they sustain. Since liberalism does not take these embodied attachments into account in its formulation of liberty as a "right to live free as long as you do not violate someone else's rights," it is fundamentally different from Cornell's use of the term (1990, 645).

Cornell's definition of feminist ethics would attend to the hierarchies of differences that constitute our experiences of injustice as well as empowerment and would ask how these hierarchies can be flattened in any given sense so that physical differences are no longer ascribed negative social meanings. Cornell seeks an ethical position that can recognize the hierarchically ordered social meanings ascribed to "natural" or "physical" differences and undo the degrading effects of laws and policies that rely on these meanings, while at the same time affirming differentiated identities (Thurschwell 1994, 1643). One may discern within her concept of ethical feminism a vision of equality that unmasks the partiality of laws that privilege certain differences but masquerade as impartial (Cornell 1995, 214-16).[10] It is this multilayered, inherently intersectionalist, definition I adopt when I evaluate whether a particular theory about the use of culture is ethical under intersectionalist feminist standards. I ask the following question of each of the universalist, postcolonial, and differentiated positions: Does the use of culture in its position enact violence on Others (i.e., non-elite or marginalized members of society)? In what follows, I would like to assess what insights ethical feminism can bring to bear on whether culture should figure partially or even marginally within legal discourse.

What Is Wrong with the Universalist Approach?
Of the approaches sketched, it is easiest to dispense with the universalist one first. Okin's writings are paradigmatic in this regard and have been well canvassed by postcolonial feminists and others (Gilman 1999, 54; al-Hibri 1999, 46; Honig 1999, 35, 38; Post 1999, 67-68). I do not wish to linger on these concerns other than to note my general agreement with the critique of her universalist position (Volpp 2001). What is worth eliciting from this broad critique are the specific reasons why Okin's version violates the concept of ethical feminism as I have defined it above and thus cannot be favoured by intersectionalists seeking to affirm cultural differences without sanctioning subordination.

Okin wants members of Western liberal democracies to approach claims of culture with acute suspicion due to her belief that women belonging to marginalized cultures (read "Third World women") are more at risk of subordination from within their culture than from without. This perspective violates ethical feminism to the extent that it revives colonial dynamics of Othering. It does this in three steps. First, it relies on an Enlightenment theory of cultural ranking in which the West's purportedly superior state of gender relations marked it as a superior state of political being to which non-Western cultures should aspire (Volpp 2001). Consider Okin's logic in the following excerpt:

> While virtually all of the world's cultures have distinctively patriarchal pasts, some – mostly, though by no means exclusively, Western liberal cultures – have departed far further from them than others. Western cultures, of course, still practice many forms of sex discrimination ... But women in more

liberal cultures are, at the same time, legally guaranteed many of the same freedoms and opportunities as men. In addition, most families in such cultures, with the exception of some religious fundamentalists, do not communicate to their daughters that they are of less value than boys, that their lives are to be confined to domesticity and service to men and children, and that their sexuality is of value only in marriage, in the service of men, and for reproductive ends. This situation, as we have seen, is quite different from that of women in many of the world's cultures, including many of those from which immigrants to Europe and North America come. (1999, 16-17)

Implicit in Okin's thesis is the premise that the marginalized culture is usually more averse to gender equality than is the majority liberal culture of which it is a part. She asserts that such majority cultures are typically Western liberal democracies, while the gender-hostile marginalized cultures that are making the troubling cultural demands on them are Third World in origin. Okin's premise that non-Western cultures are more gender-hostile than Western ones (ibid.) is too reminiscent of the hierarchically ordered trajectory of social evolution on which non-Western cultures were forever lagging behind the West on all indicators of "progress," particularly gender relations.

Second, the universalist approach uncritically advances a trope of victimization for the women in these cultures, with a concomitant erasure of agency due to the disbelief that the "sexist practices" contested may also have positive meanings that culturally marginalized women may want to support. This resistance to alternative interpretations betrays Okin's construction of culture as relatively stable, with the meanings of any practice being the same despite the effects of migration, dislocation, and globalization, and despite the particular Western "home" to which these practices have been introduced (ibid.). Third, this investment in the colonial imaginary of gender provides the rationale for exposing non-Western cultures and peoples to the social engineering efforts of Western political norms and institutions, either through a partial enculturation of Western gender norms or, if necessary, by cultural extinction (22-23). This is the universalizing aspect of her approach to the interaction of gender and culture. Okin's solution is to enculturate culturally marginalized cultures into the Western liberal majority culture either by adjusting gender norms within the former so that they espouse gender equality or, alternatively, by integrating members of the former into the latter until the problematic culturally marginalized cultures become extinct (ibid.).

In short, the universalist approach as exemplified by Okin's work is too theoretically flawed if we choose to see culture as a continuous, scattered process of negotiating meanings and if we wish to write against a colonial script of how we think about controversies of culture. One has to undertake a meticulous reading of Okin in order to distinguish her arguments from those that lament the "special treatment" of minorities and the resulting denigration of and loss of pride in Western host cultures.

What Is Wrong with the Postcolonial Approach?

I agree with the deconstruction visited on the concept of culture in the postcolonial approach. My main reservation with the approach is its inattention to the political consequences of its cogent critique. Although, conceptually, postcolonialists portray culture in a less problematic way than do universalists, their close readings of its instabilities lead them too close to a path of nihilism; they would let culture into legal discourse only where it is strategically useful (i.e., where it enables cultural subalterns to speak), and even there they argue for its rejection. Postcolonialist proposals are too abrupt, shutting out invariably essentialist cultural claims made by cultural groups with whom they otherwise empathize.

But how helpful is support in theory or affect, but not in practice or law? Is it desirable for feminists and others who care about issues of social justice to work for the complete abolition of culture talk within political and legal discourse because of the inevitable essentialisms that will result when trying to describe a collective and compare and contrast it with other collectives? Might there be certain instances where we would wish to entertain claims about culture animated by our desire for a more egalitarian social order despite our postmodernist sensibilities against the concept? Postcolonial theorists concerned with issues of social justice have typically met such claims with the insistence that the concept of culture that cultural protectionists would like to preserve is a fiction, even a fantasy (Chanock 2000, 18). Their point is that we cannot make cultural claims because such claims rest on an inaccurate understanding of the term. They are a misrepresentation that the law should not support.

Is the misrepresentation issue, however, the right focus of concern? Perhaps we need to step back from asking what we should "do" about essentialism and instead ask why essentialism is so troubling when it comes to us in its cultural form. Certainly whether a claim is essentialist is one question, but it is not clear that it disposes of the issue of whether we should support, tolerate, or condemn culture talk in legal discourse. If the inaccurate claim results in a more socially just redistribution of goods, why does it matter that the right result (a more egalitarian social order) was achieved through the wrong means (a reliance on an essentialized concept of culture)? After all, utilitarianism has supported this instrumental political logic for centuries (Waldron 1987).[11] Of course, consequentialist theories have fallen sharply out of favour in the last century due to the harsh criticisms from rights theorists who insist that the means do matter, that there are certain things we must not do even if they would lead us to the laudable result we have set (Scheffler 1988). Thus, if torturing one person would prevent a bomb from going off and killing a hundred people, most theories of rights would proscribe the torturing despite everyone's desire for a terror-free society and a society where killing is kept at a minimum.

Yet relying on a false conceptualization of culture is not akin to a human rights violation. Certainly feminists and others have viewed some practices justified through cultural discourses, whether false or not, as human rights violations. Girls forced to wear head scarves because of cultural and religious interpretations, girls having their sexualized body parts painfully and permanently cut, and women pressured into marriages they do not want, or denied certain rights because of whom they marry, are all common examples of the harm feminists worry will be enacted on non-elite members of marginalized cultural groups if the latter were to receive jurisdiction or other special rights over certain aspects of their members' lives. But for a large number of cultural claims, human rights violations do not inhere within them. Nobody is suffering acute physical pain or emotional trauma if we permit indigenous groups, for example, to assert property rights in their cultural resources. To the contrary, recognizing such claims may be a balm for collective psychic pain. Arguably, the benefit of preventing the hegemonic cultural onslaughts from the state, multinational corporations, and other elites is greater than the harm that misrepresentation through essentialism represents.

In reply, a postcolonial "culture-skeptic" would likely respond that what is at stake is not just a question of misrepresentation. The harm in cultural claims rests not just with misrepresentation qua misrepresentation, but also in the remaking of social reality, as people perceive it, and the attendant injuries that misrepresentation will entail on the individuals of cultural groups bound by these misrepresentations. Martin Chanock's (2000) work linking the articulation of cultural claims to the process of branding within advertising is especially instructive in drawing out the contours of the harms inherent in the manipulation of social reality.[12]

Chanock is a culture-skeptic for typical postcolonialist reasons. He uses a different tactic, though, to alert us to the ephemeral nature of culture and the dangers of trying to "pin it down." Chanock invites us to think of the efforts of cultural protectionists – those who believe in a right to culture, the integrity of cultures, and the state's duty to help preserve "distinct" and "unique" cultures in its midst from the onslaught of hegemonic norms sustained by the polity's majority culture – to assert cultural claims as a type of branding similar to the marketing strategies that advertising agencies carry out. Branding refers to the process by which advertising agencies attach cultural meaning to a particular product (Gautier 1999, 141-42). They want a product to hold a particular meaning for the consumer, whether functional, emotional, or otherwise, and this meaning is commonly generated through an essentialized cultural identity that is attached to the brand. Think of the Marlboro Man and cigarettes, the Gerber Baby and baby food, or the Ivory Girl and bath soap. Increasingly, branding is about forming emotional attachments between consumers and products they otherwise may not need, which tempt the consumer with the promise of clarifying an unsettled identity he or she may hold or, frequently, through the projection of fantasy, offer the consumer the promise of a new identity that he or she covets (Chanock 2000, 26).

The success of advertising depends on how well campaigns tap into the consumer's aspirations and create aspirational preferences to associate with the brands. Chanock asks us to consider to what extent the cultural protectionist claim about a unified, discernible identity is an attempt to create brand recognition for a culture or cultural product. In his words, "cultures, like brands, must essentialise, and successful and sustainable cultures are those which brand best" (ibid.), that is, are those which can promote attachments and identities with which their targeted consumers/members may identify and which nonmember consumers of their culture will respect.

To say cultures are like brands is to imbue cultural claims with the deception, manipulation, and preference creation commonly associated with advertising – to imply they are "selling" people something they do not need or that they are trafficking in untruths and fantasy. But one of the problems with branding is the extent to which this manipulation is soon forgotten, and the massaged social identity it has cultivated to sell a particular product is taken to represent actual reality. Chanock gives the example of a particularly successful Bacardi advertisement that associates the alcohol brand with sexy young men and women enjoying themselves in a tropical paradise. The representation of social life presented is that people embodying sex appeal, youth, and relaxation drink Bacardi (and you can be like these beautiful people if you drink Bacardi too), but the social reality of what alcohol does to your body is something else entirely (ibid.). Another example is McDonald's advertisements, with their absence of overweight people or people with cardiovascular disease. The harm lies not just in the fact that culture is essentialized, but in the fact that an ideal and imagined version of culture is being put forth as truth. These truths, then, more than selling products, encourage or even coerce people to behave in a certain way.

When this branding function is performed by cultural protectionists to "sell" the public and the government on the "product" of cultural rights, the distortion of social reality receives the support of the power of law to lend it credibility and quash other interpretations of cultural identity. Hence, the potential harm in cultural claims is not just a matter of misrepresentation, but also a stifling of alternative interpretations by the very members of marginalized cultures in whose name cultural protectionists advance their claims. To the extent that these vulnerable minority cultural members or "hyper Others" are at risk, we may have to refuse the claims of some other Others. Although culture-skeptics are sensitive to claims by marginalized cultural groups, they nevertheless resist cultural claims to avoid these dangers.

But does this fear of the sharing of cultural hegemony between majority cultures and minority cultural elites mean that we can never attend to cultural claims? There is another argument in favour of cultural protectionists that is rarely addressed by culture-skeptics. It proceeds as follows: Are we not singling out the concept of culture for critique when we highlight its unfitness for legal edification because of its instability and fluid character? After all, the law is full of other contested terms that easily portend misrepresentation. Similar destabilizing critiques have been lodged against such concepts, yet these terms are dispersed liberally in statutes, cases, and government policies.

For example, consider the term "women" (Holmes 2000, 3; Ramirez and Rumminger 2000-1).[13] Arguably, over the last decade or so the anti-essentialist critique has constituted the predominant debate in feminist theory (Okin 2000, 36). Many feminists have demonstrated how earlier Western feminist theory used the term "women" in a universal sense, purporting to speak for all women when it really referred only to experiences of middle-class, white, Western, heterosexual, and able-bodied women. The myth of the Universal Woman was as much a myth as the myth of the Universal Man since the experiences of non-elite women were not associated with the term "women," but were subsumed in identity categories dealing with nongender differences such as "blacks," "the poor," "the disabled," and so on. Yet just as "women" invoked only a fraction of female experiences, these nongender categories took male experiences as their referent, which resulted in a discursive slippage that stranded "different" women at the intersections of gender and nongender categories (Crenshaw 1989, 1991; Harris 1990; hooks 1984; Lorde 1984; McClintock 1995, 11; Spelman 1988; Trinh 1989). In addition to noting the marginalization that such discourse effected, many feminists argued that the terms "woman" or "women" were incapable of definition because there was no natural essence of womanhood and thus no generalizable element of being a "woman" since one's experience of "being a woman" was contingent on one's race, age, ability, sexual orientation, religion, and perhaps a host of other factors (Young 1997, 12-37). To claim that "women" meant anyone with female sexual organs was to conflate concepts of gender, race, class, and age, for starters, with sex and to ignore how womanhood was a constitutive rather than a natural process informed by multiple axes of power (ibid.; Walby 1992, 34-35).[14]

Despite the widespread recognition of the instability of the category "women," we do not encounter elegant arguments and passionate pleas to remove this concept from legal discourse as we do with the concept of "culture." Why not? Indeed, the law usually defines "women" as a universal category; that is, it includes all female persons (read "persons having natural female sexual organs"). If law is reductive in this way, why do we permit the concept of women to remain prevalent in legal discourse, *especially* discourse about human rights, where the culture concept is most contested?

One answer to this may lie in the observation that issues of legal justice for gender do not require the law to entertain questions of what being a "woman" or "women" means. In other words, the tortuous problem of adjudicating culture that has been highlighted by postcolonialists does not arise in adjudicating gender. While it may be unclear what cultural sign the signifier "women" is supposed to invoke, legal responses referring to gender only require that we know what a female is as opposed to a male because it is all females who suffer discrimination as "women." So, the argument proceeds, even if there is not a single experience of being a woman and no essence to gender discrimination or injustice, it still makes sense to deploy "women" as a legal term since it captures all the females who are subject to discrimination because they are socially marked as "women." In other words, it is not a problematic activity for the law to use this term because law itself is not suggesting or condoning an essentialist understanding of "women," but merely trying to stop gender discrimination.

This response seems unsatisfactory. Although law could ideally work to equalize gender relations without relying on stable notions of who women are, it rarely does. In fact, law is a significant participant in entrenching the unitary concept of "women" that has proven so problematic for intersectionalists (Jhappan 2002, 187-91). This is the problem that has confounded courts with respect to sex and race discrimination cases. When the cases of women who come to court claiming sex or race discrimination contain aspects that explicitly or implicitly refer to both race and gender differences, courts have a difficult time "seeing" their claims as simply sex or race discrimination because their experiences do not match the contours of the imagined referent for either type of claim (Cornell 1995, 214-15; Crenshaw 1989, 139-52). Courts *are* adjudicating questions of gender when they try to define what sex discrimination is and try to ascertain whether a particular practice amounts to sex-based discrimination. These are the same types of adjudications legal feminists are wary of when "culture," rather than "gender" or "women," is the term at issue.

To be sure, feminists are criticizing the formalistic logic of discrimination laws, but one would be hard-pressed to find anyone calling for the removal of "women" as a category from statutory language or judicial decisions. Yet, as we have seen in the postcolonial approach, these are precisely the calls being made with respect to "culture." It is not easy to think of wording to insert into a statute that would adequately describe what culture is, how it should be measured, and how to evaluate whether someone has a legitimate claim to a cultural right. Unless the law will permit everyone to assert the claim, it will have to enter the messy terrain of deciding whether someone is a "practising" member of his or her culture or, at least, whether someone is rightfully a member of that culture. While it may be true that courts have less essentialist trouble with the term "women" than the term "culture," it is still unclear why the latter is rejected and the former accepted. If we do not "know" what either term means, it still seems arbitrary to normalize the presence of one in legal discourse while stigmatizing the other.

The better critique against the recognition of culture is one that draws our attention to the difference in the nature of the two terms – "women" and "culture" – themselves. "Women," however unstable the term may be, still refers to the material bodies of women, or to "things," and it is easy to see why, in an ethically feminist framework, we would want to recognize these "things" and desire them to flourish. The project for legal feminists has been, and continues to be, to ensure that the law caters to the flourishing of all (human) female bodies. To the extent that the current state of the law does not provide for this, feminist legal theorists are advocating reform. But can the same be said of culture? Under an ethical feminist framework, is it the case that cultures are things that should flourish?

It is not necessary to decide this question definitively because my point is borne out by either an affirmative or a negative answer. If we say "no," that ethical feminism does not require cultivating cultures, then the distinction between "women" and "culture" is made and we have a reason for legal discourse to incorporate the first but not the latter term.

But even if we say "yes," that ethical feminism does require the cultivation of cultures, then we must ask whether this entails recognizing culturally protectionist claims. If we favour the interpretation or "truth" that cultures are fluid and changing, which we would want to do to take care of the "internal dissent" or "vulnerability" concern that most legal feminist scholars writing about cultural claims underscore, then the cultivation of cultures means enabling change and fluidity, the very characteristics that cultural protectionists wish to guard against. What is wrong with the use of culture in legal discourse, then, is not so much that it is a term largely immune to definition, since the law properly incorporates other destabilized terms such as "women" and "sex." Instead, the problem with the inclusion of culture stems more from what it is we are trying to improve by making a legal claim about culture. It is not a single culture itself, like a single woman or groups of women, that we are trying to improve, but rather the ability of individuals to have cultural lives that differ from the norm, whether that norm belongs to the majority culture or cultural elites.

This argument distinguishing the terms "culture and "women" seems convincing. Yet if we are going to avoid the business of adjudicating culture because it would embroil us in tortured determinations of authenticity and problematic suppression of internal dissent, we are still left with the dilemma of what we are to do with the claims of vulnerable cultural groups. If we eliminate cultural claims at this historical moment, many vulnerable groups will be left without any legal right or claim to guard against cultural disintegration, extinction, or exploitation. Indigenous groups seeking to assert intellectual property rights in their culture, for example, have no recourse against the research rights of scientists or copyright claims of those they view as cultural appropriators (Coombe 1995). To the extent our belief in the fluidity of cultures does not entail support of the unmitigated bombardment of marginalized cultures with majoritarian hegemonic norms, we are going to have to respect at least some cultural formations. To the extent we want to provide this relief now and not suspend justice or cultural equality for marginalized cultural groups until an ideal time when legal definitions do not domesticate the concept of culture, we are going to have to tolerate some essentialist cultural claims. It will be a trade-off of means for the ends of a more egalitarian society. Admittedly, protectionist accounts share with universalist accounts the problematic reliance on a fairly static notion of culture and thus expose themselves to the sharp critiques of postcolonial and differentiated accounts relating to inaccurate representations of culture. But what is the use of deconstruction, we should ask, if we deconstruct concepts to the point of political paralysis?

Why a Differentiated Approach Is Preferable

The differentiated approach is better under an ethical feminist framework because it takes the claims of marginalized groups seriously. Intersectionalist feminists should thus favour it. Recall that the differentiated feminist legal view of culture is a slight variation of the postcolonial one. It shares the postcolonial view's skepticism about the truth of arguments resting on totalized and ahistoric understandings of cultural "traditions" and "practices," but it is ultimately more receptive to cultural claims. The differentiated approach seeks to evaluate cultural claims on a case-by-case basis to determine when and where they may be legitimate. This line is exemplified in the writings of feminist legal scholar Leti Volpp (1994, 1996, 2000, 2001). In her writings, Volpp has sought to interrogate both universalizing claims and the potential nihilism that inhabits some deconstructive accounts.

For Volpp, the way to grapple with cultural discourse in law is to permit cultural claims except where such claims would subordinate vulnerable members of that group. Hers is a strategically essentialist approach (1994,

95).[15] Strategic cultural essentialism is appropriate under an ethical feminist framework because it tries to secure political gains for the marginalized cultural group that improve the egalitarian balance of society. But it is this same logic of protecting the vulnerable that leads to Volpp's insistence that not all strategic essentialist claims are defensible under an ethical feminist framework – only those that do not enact violence on the marginalized members of the subculture (1994, 96-100). This requirement, however, seems to be too utopian in its simple formulation. If we applied this requirement to the civil rights struggle in the United States, for example, most of the gains may not have been realized, given that racial justice was privileged over gender justice (Crenshaw 2001). Indeed, it is difficult to name a political gain made by any marginalized group in the last century in Canada or other Western liberal polities that was completely inclusive in terms of its non-essentialism in discourse and practice.

If we were to apply a differentiated approach that permits only those claims that do not require any subordination of others, we may have to be more particular about what counts as "subordination" unless we are prepared to dispense with all essentialist claims, no matter how politically path-breaking, and revert essentially to an immobile postcolonial position. Ideally, we would imbue the term "subordination" with as generous and expansive a meaning as possible in order not to exclude any marginalized groups, taking care, of course, to craft a definition of "marginalized group" that excludes the claims of cultural elites (Young 1990).[16] But to do that in the realm of multicultural accommodation would eliminate even those cultural claims that do not themselves advance arguments against other cultural dissenters, but may only privilege certain non-elite voices without *actually* or *foreseeably* marginalizing others. Given the improbability that a claim articulated by a marginalized culture in its encounter with the state will reflect the views of all cultural subalterns within that culture, let alone reflect them in equal degree, to constitute an inclusive rather than exclusionary discourse, we may wish to maintain a distinction between cultural claims that actually or foreseeably marginalize other cultural dissenters and those that do not (D. Réaume, pers. comm.).

This nuanced understanding of what counts as subordination would probably permit cultural claims in support of, for example, affirmative action, land redistribution, ownership in cultural resources, and other general claims for tangible benefits from the state that accrue universally to all group members and are not meant to stifle dissent. This view of "subordination" would not, however, support cultural claims demanding exemptions from certain laws or the enactment of special protectionist laws without examining how the exemption or enactment at issue would affect vulnerable members of the marginalized cultural group. Thus, a cultural claim that, for example, proposed a cultural defence for criminal acts that advanced gendered stereotypes would be impermissible. However, a claim that did not sanction violence or advance such stereotypes or grand generalizations, but that also did not refer to the gendered nature of its own terms and so was merely discursively essentialist, might be permissible if it was presented as contingent and particularized. To put it another way, the differentiated approach I am advocating would not permit this statement: "Wife-beating is a cultural practice in my culture and thus I should be exonerated of criminal charges if this multicultural state respects cultural equality." It would, however, tolerate this very different statement: "Marriage between first cousins is a common current practice among a significant portion of members of a certain class from my culture, so any proposed criminal prohibition against marriage between first cousins should not apply to me if this multicultural state respects cultural equality."[17]

I want to stress at this point that while my proposal for feminist engagement with law is relativist in that it encourages the recognition of cultural differences, it does not condone a belief in *reified* or *totalizing* cultural differences or the naturalization or presumption of neatly separated distinct cultures (Narayan 2000, 96). It accordingly does not rely on the classic colonial logic of irreconcilable cultural differences (94-95). As Uma Narayan has conceded, amid her impressive critique of cultural essentialism, "it would be foolish to deny that there are practices in certain contexts that are absent in others, and values that are endorsed in some quarters that are not endorsed in others" (96). Put simply, culture matters. Humans are cultural beings. The proposal I advance recognizes this "acceptable" universal to affirm poststructural insights against grand generalizations or generalizations that expressly subordinate some members of the group being generalized about to sustain the power of others. Narayan, in discussing the problematic parallels between gender and cultural essentialism, puts the point well when she writes: "I believe that antiessentialism about gender and culture does not entail a simple-minded opposition to all generalizations, but entails instead a commitment to examine both their empirical accuracy and their political utility or risk. It is seldom possible to articulate effective political agendas, such as those pertaining to human rights, without resorting to a certain degree of abstraction, which enables the articulation of salient similarities suffered by various individuals and groups" (97-98).

Narayan's criteria of empirical accuracy and political utility accord with the differentiated approach I am advancing. The major risk that an individual or group must assess, when it contemplates pursuing legal action based on a cultural claim under the differentiated approach, is the subordinating potential of the claim. Indeed, rare will be the political strategy that is discursively innocent; the goal of the differentiated approach is to permit feminists to try to find strategies that are nominally, instead of centrally, invested in power hierarchies.

Why Bother with "Cultural Equality" At All
If It Is "Justice" We're After?

To this, the critic might reply, "Why bother with cultural claims at all, even when they do not subordinate vulnerable subcultural members? If what we are really concerned about is undoing the effects of past injustice against cultural minorities, why do we not simply effect redistribution based on a sense of compensatory justice?" For example, in the case of increasing the presence of a particular marginalized cultural group in the public service of the government, is it really necessary to resort to culture to argue for the justice in establishing affirmative action for this cultural minority? Would it not be more accurate to state that the reason we have chosen to implement a particular affirmative action measure is not because of a group's culture per se, but because of the discrimination the group has experienced on the basis of this culture? Thus, the argument for affirmative action would be seen not as an argument about *cultural* recognition, but as one of *discrimination* recognition. Instead of respecting the cultural claims of minorities for their cultural authenticity, the claims could be respected for their articulation by a group that has suffered adverse consequences because of its marginalized status.

So, for example, states do not have to ground exceptions to hunting and fishing laws for indigenous groups in some problematic account of that indigenous culture, but could ground them in the discrimination experienced by the indigenous cultural group.[18] Thus, the justification for the exemption from the law is not the group's "distinctive culture" vis-à-vis others, but its distinct history of injustices because it was marked and disfavoured as culturally different. The advantage of this approach is that it avoids the first set of problematic inquiries surrounding the definition of a particular culture that cultural claims occasion. Since the right to an exemption is no longer grounded in culture but in justice, one need not be concerned with whether certain practices are culturally authentic. The inquiries into the "nature" of specific cultures, of which anti-essentialists are rightfully wary, then become unnecessary. Hence, one level of essentialist reductionism is removed. To be sure, courts and tribunals asked to adjudicate these claims would still have to inquire into whether a particular claimant is properly a member of the culture that is receiving the benefit. Undoubtedly, such claims will still generate scrutiny of whether someone is an "authentic" member of her or his culture.

Still, if claims can be articulated in a manner that does not invoke categories susceptible to reification, so much the better. Insofar as another principle or a general idea of compensatory justice can rescue our discourse from culturally related essentialist snares, we may deploy it. Whether this switch in discourse is possible would be a matter for the marginalized individual or culture to decide. Yet to the extent such claims do not apply to a

specific cultural claim or cannot dissociate completely from cultural que-
ries, it is necessary and desirable to grapple with culture within the law.

Conclusion

In the "feminism versus multiculturalism" debate among feminist legal scholars, intersectionalist feminists committed to ethical feminism should favour
a differentiated approach to culture. This differentiated approach exhibits
the following traits in its acceptance of "culture talk" within legal discourse:
(1) it rejects a reliance on discourses that would actually or foreseeably subordinate vulnerable minorities along gender or other lines, although an
unintended and unforeseeable subordinating effect may result; and (2) to
the extent possible, it would reframe cultural claims as justice claims where
this is feasible according to the judgment of the cultural actors advancing
the legal claim.

The appeal in this qualification of cultural claims is its ability to respond
to the exigencies of marginalized cultural groups without actually or
foreseeably subordinating their vulnerable members, and without, as much
as possible, promoting an essentialized concept of culture. Invariably, some
essentialism will occur with this approach, but it is defensible under an
ethically feminist framework to trade some essentialism for some political
gain, particularly when other unstable concepts freely circulate within legal discourse. In short, the differentiated approach strikes an appropriate
balance between the postcolonial and the protectionist approaches. It rejects modernist narratives about non-Western women and their hyper-
misogynistic cultures as the rationale for eschewing culture talk within the
law, as implied by universalist accounts. It also rejects the relatively uncritical embrace protectionist accounts accord to a static and unified concept of
culture, which shelters internal differences for the benefit of the group vis-
à-vis the state as a whole. Most importantly, it crafts a way to advance the
postcolonial critique of culture while retaining responsiveness to the concerns of individuals *and* groups with cultural affiliations seeking state recognition. The differentiated approach, properly strategized in a particular
set of circumstances, makes intersectionalist feminist support for subaltern
cultural claims possible, even if these claims are mildly essentialist.

To be sure, the differentiated approach does not remedy all discursive
problems in generating theory or formulating political strategies. Primarily,
it still calls for first-order assessments of what constitutes a practice that
deliberately or foreseeably stifles cultural dissent, is sexist, or subordinates
vulnerable members of the culture. Invariably, even among members of the
majority culture, there will be disagreement as to which marginalized cultural claims raise the risk of in-group subordination. My proposal needs to
be supplemented with theorizations of the appropriate bodies and procedures to settle this type of disagreement, a task that is significant in terms of

developing an ethic of which views to solicit and how to balance them. But since both the universalistic and postcolonial approaches involve this complicated inquiry into how "we" "know" which cultural practices qualify as manifestations of in-group subordination, its presence in my modified differentiated proposal is not a reason to dispense with it. Rather, it is a call for further theorization.

Acknowledgments

This chapter is an earlier extract of Maneesha Deckha's "Is Culture Taboo? Feminism, Intersectionality, and Culture Talk in Law" (2004).

Notes

1 See Cohen et al. (1999); Coombe (1995, 267; 1998); Kapur (2001); Narayan (1997); Shachar (2000, 399; 2001a; 2001b, 259); Sunder (2000); Volpp (1994; 1996, 1575-76; 2000, 103-4; 2001).

2 We can understand the term, "differentiated," made popular by first-wave multiculturalists such as Will Kymlicka and Iris Marion Young, as referring to a concept receptive to multicultural claims.

3 I want to clarify that I am not invoking the original feminist distinction between sex and gender, where "sex" is understood as referring to natural biological differences, while "gender" constitutes the reference for the socially constructed meanings attached to purportedly natural sex differences. More recently, feminists have identified "sex" as a location of social construction as much as "gender," and it is this understanding that I impute to both terms.

4 I am using "respect" here in the sense of Stephen Darwall's articulation of the term "recognition respect" (1977, 38). That is, "respect" is meant to connote the idea of "giving appropriate consideration or recognition to some feature of its object in deliberating about what to do." Thus, in this sense, "respect for culture" would mean referring to an individual's or a group's culture in making a decision.

5 My argument assumes the unavailability of any significant institutional redesign of the kind Ayelet Shachar proposes in her book *Multicultural Jurisdictions* (2001a). Shachar is interested in thinking creatively about multicultural institutional design. She does not wish to sacrifice the interests or rights of vulnerable members to the tyranny of the imagined majority culture, but is searching for fresh ways of structuring rights so that the potential for intra-group violation diminishes if inter-group rights are granted. Shachar advocates a joint governance approach in which competing jurisdictions act as constraints on cultural groups and cultivate motivations for them to eliminate intra-group subordination. It is an approach that "strives for the reduction of injustice between minority groups and the wider society, together with the enhancement of justice within them ... Under this system, both the state and the group can no longer take the old style of jurisdictional monopoly for granted because individuals are given leeway in deciding which substantive legal systems they will be subject to in different social arenas. And since each authority must now earn the individual's continued attachment by deed, this in turn creates a more complex incentive structure, and means that the traditions and conduct of both group and state authorities are held to higher standards" (2001b, 294-95).

6 Theories of ethics, which I am engaging here, are often discussed and analyzed in terms of what they envision the "good" or goal of a society to be and how they envision the "right," or the means by which to attain or maximize the "good."

7 My use of the term "autonomy" draws from Jenny Nedelsky's reconceptualization of this term. Nedelsky (1989) is interested in severing the associations of autonomy from an image of an unencumbered, isolated, and independent political actor unconnected and unaffected by his (deliberate use of the male pronoun intended) relationships with others or his social location. She argues that the state of affairs we invoke when we use the term

"autonomy" is one that is sustained by our relationships with others, both social and personal, who nurture, support, and generally enable us to exercise our human capacities. Thus, Nedelsky encourages us to reconceptualize autonomy as a condition enabled by human interconnectedness rather than social isolation.

8 By "loose reading," I wish to alert the reader to the fact that my use of the term is a simplified version of Cornell's in that I do not discuss its psychoanalytic significance for Cornell.

9 I owe this insight to Katherine Franke in one of our personal discussions about an earlier version of this research. In this regard, one may recall John Stuart Mill's classic formulation of liberty as the right to be free of impediments or constraints.

10 For example, Cornell (1995) wants to recognize the claims of black women who braid their hair and then are penalized at their workplaces for doing so as claims of sex-based and race-based discrimination. Such claims have typically been met with the liberal reply that braiding is not a racial or gender marker. Since it is a choice and not a physical characteristic, it is not about "race"; and since it is not a practice that all women do, it is not about "sex." Cornell criticizes the legal dispositions of the braiding cases because they fail to recognize that for black women hair-braiding is an affirmation of "national, racial, and sexual pride" in the context of a society that devalues black women's national, racial, and sexual difference. Cornell asks, "What does it mean to degrade an African-American woman who chooses to braid her hair? What does it mean to fire her? It means that she has been denied her own power to affirm her feminine sexual difference as it is profoundly linked in her affirmation of what it means for her to be an African-American woman. It implicates sexual, national, and racial degradation and devaluation ... An analytical structure unable to analyze the connection between sex, race, and nationality cannot give adequate redress to African-American women. From within what I have called 'ethical feminism,' the hair-braiding of African-American women should be affirmed as exemplary of the feminine within sexual difference in all its diversity and difference" (215-16).

11 One of the most celebrated utilitarians, Jeremy Bentham, was a scholar of the late eighteenth century.

12 I am grateful to Nityanand Deckha for conversations that developed my understanding of branding.

13 A similar point could also be made about the term "race."

14 Several types of theory brought about this destabilization of the term "women" in much of feminist theory. One line came from American women of colour and lesbians focusing on the unstated but adopted whiteness and heterosexism of gender analyses. Another prominent impetus for destabilizing feminism's classic terms stemmed from the adoption of the Foucaultian insight regarding the intense dispersal of power and the popular academic project of deconstruction inspired by the Derridean concept of "difference." Many feminist poststructuralists sought to unearth the plurality of the femininities and masculinities repressed in the broad categories of "men" and "women." The general trend in all this multi-pronged destabilization was to refuse the unqualified "woman" or "women" as a category of social analysis. What is now thought of as intersectionality is most closely associated with the critiques made by women of colour and lesbians, but intersectionalist feminists adhere to many if not all of these theories.

15 Volpp, as she herself points out, is drawing from Gayatri Chakravorty Spivak's concept of "strategic essentialism" as articulated in Spivak (1987, 197, 205).

16 Here we may wish to rely on the definitions of who legitimately counts as an "oppressed group" that Iris Marion Young has charted (1990). That is to say, the cultural claims that an ethical feminism would want to take seriously are those that engage concerns of justice to the extent that they emanate from marginalized groups and not groups seeking to cement privilege.

17 Canada currently permits marriages between first cousins. See *Marriage (Prohibited Degrees) Act*, R.S.C. 1990, c. 36, s. 2(2).

18 This problematic approach is the current approach, established by the Supreme Court of Canada in *R. v. Van der Peet*, [1996] 2 S.C.R. 507, for proving Aboriginal non-title rights under section 35(1) of the *Constitution Act, 1982*, being Schedule B to the *Canada Act 1982* (U.K.), 1982.

References

Berlin, I. 1969. Two Concepts of Liberty. In *Four Essays on Liberty,* 118-72. Oxford: Oxford University Press.

Chanock, M. 2000. "Culture" and Human Rights: Orientalising, Occidentalising and Athenticity. In *Beyond Rights Talk and Culture Talk: Comparative Essays on the Politics of Rights and Culture,* ed. M. Mamdani, 15-36. New York: St. Martin's Press.

Cohen, J., Mathew Howard, and Martha C. Nussbaum, ed. 1999. *Is Multiculturalism Bad for Women?* Princeton, NJ: Princeton University Press.

Coombe, R. 1995. The Properties of Culture and the Politics of Possessing Identity: Native Claims in the Cultural Appropriation Controversy. In *After Identity: A Reader in Law and Culture,* ed. D. Danielsen and K. Engle, 251-76. New York: Routledge.

–. 1998. Contingent Articulations: A Critical Cultural Studies of Law. In *Law in the Domains of Culture,* ed. A. Sarat and T.R. Kearns, 21-64. Ann Arbor, MI: University of Michigan Press.

Cornell, D. 1990. The Doubly-Prized World: Myth, Allegory and the Feminine. *Cornell Law Review* 75:644-98.

–. 1991. *Beyond Accommodation: Ethical Feminism, Deconstruction and the Law.* New York: Routledge.

–. 1995. *The Imaginary Domain: Abortion, Pornography and Sexual Harassment.* New York: Routledge.

Crenshaw, K. 1989. Demarginalizing the Intersection of Race and Sex: A Black Feminist Critique of Antidiscrimination Doctrine, Feminist Theory and Antiracist Politics. *University of Chicago Legal Forum* 189:139-68.

–. 1991. Mapping the Margins: Intersectionality, Identity Politics and Violence against Women of Color. *Stanford Law Review* 43:1241-99.

–. 2001. Intersectionalities: Race and Gender. Lecture at Columbia Law School, New York.

Darwall, S. 1977. Two Kinds of Respect. *Ethics* 88(1):36-49.

Deckha, M. 2004. Is Culture Taboo? Feminism, Intersectionality, and Culture Talk in Law. *Canadian Journal of Women and the Law* 16(1):14-53.

Gautier, K. 1999. Electronic Commerce: Confronting the Legal Challenge of Building E-dentities in Cyberspace. *Mississippi College Law Review* 20:117-64.

Gilman, S.L. 1999. "Barbaric" Rituals? In *Is Multiculturalism Bad for Women?* ed. J. Cohen, Matthew Howard, and Martha C. Nussbaum, 53-58. Princeton, NJ: Princeton University Press.

Harris, A.P. 1990. Race and Essentialism in Feminist Legal Theory. *Stanford Law Review* 42: 581-616.

al-Hibri, A.Y. 1999. Is Western Patriarchal Feminism Good for Third World/Minority Women? In *Is Multiculturalism Bad for Women?* ed. J. Cohen, Matthew Howard, and Martha C. Nussbaum, 41-46. Princeton, NJ: Princeton University Press.

Holmes, S.A. 2000. The Politics of Race and the Census. *New York Times,* 19 March.

Honig, B. 1999. "My Culture Made Me Do It." In *Is Multiculturalism Bad for Women?* ed. J. Cohen, Matthew Howard, and Martha C. Nussbaum, 35-40. Princeton, NJ: Princeton University Press.

hooks, b. 1984. *Feminist Theory: From Margin to Center.* Boston: Beacon Press.

Jhappan, R. 2002. The Equality Pit or the Rehabilitation of Justice. In *Women's Legal Strategies in Canada,* ed. R. Jhappan, 175-236. Oxford: Oxford University Press.

Kapur, R. 2001. Postcolonial Erotic Disruptions: Legal Narratives of Culture, Sex, and Nation in India. *Columbia Journal of Gender and Law* 10:333-85.

Lacey, N. 1998. *Unspeakable Subjects: Feminist Essays in Legal and Social Theory.* Oxford: Hart Publishing.

Lorde, A. 1984. *Sister/Outsider: Essays and Speeches.* Trumansburg, NY: Crossing Press.

McClintock, A. 1995. *Imperial Leather: Race, Gender and Sexuality in the Colonial Contest.* New York: Routledge.

Mill, J.S. 1859. *On Liberty.* London: J.W. Parker and Son.

Narayan, U. 1997. *Dislocating Cultures: Identities, Traditions, and Third-World Feminism.* New York: Routledge.

–. 2000. Essence of Culture and a Sense of History: A Feminist Critique of Cultural Essentialism. In *Decentering the Center: Philosophy for a Multicultural, Postcolonial, and Feminist World,* ed. S. Harding and U. Narayan, 80-100. Bloomington: Indiana University Press.

Nedelsky, J. 1989. Reconceiving Autonomy: Sources, Thoughts and Possibilities. *Yale Journal of Law and Feminism* 1:7-36.

Okin, S.M. 1999. Is Multiculturalism Bad for Women? In *Is Multiculturalism Bad for Women?* ed. J. Cohen, Matthew Howard, and Martha C. Nussbaum, 7-26. Princeton, NJ: Princeton University Press.

–. 2000. Feminism, Women's Human Rights, and Cultural Differences. In *Decentering the Center: Philosophy for a Multicultural, Postcolonial, and Feminist World,* ed. S. Harding and U. Narayan, 26-46. Bloomington: Indiana University Press.

Post, R. 1999. Between Norms and Choices. In *Is Multiculturalism Bad for Women?* ed. J. Cohen, Matthew Howard, and Martha C. Nussbaum, 65-68. Princeton, NJ: Princeton University Press.

Ramirez, D., and J. Rumminger. 2000-1. Race, Culture, and the New Diversity in the New Millennium. *Cumberland Law Review* 31:481-522.

Rawls, J. 1971. *A Theory of Justice.* Cambridge, MA: Harvard University Press.

Scheffler, S., ed. 1988. *Consequentialism and Its Critics.* Oxford: Oxford University Press.

Shachar, A. 2000. The Puzzle of Interlocking Power Hierarchies: Sharing the Pieces of Jurisdictional Authority. *Harvard Civil Rights-Civil Liberties Law Review* 35:385-426.

–. 2001a. *Multicultural Jurisdictions: Cultural Differences and Women's Rights.* Oxford: Oxford University Press.

–. 2001b. Two Critiques of Multiculturalism. *Cardozo Law Review* 23:253-98.

Spelman, E.V. 1988. *Inessential Woman: Problems of Exclusion in Feminist Thought.* Boston: Beacon Press.

Spivak, G.C. 1987. Subaltern Studies: Deconstructing Historiography. In *In Other Worlds: Essays in Cultural Politics,* 197-221. New York: Routledge.

Sunder, M. 2000. Intellectual Property and Identity Politics: Playing with Fire. *Journal of Gender, Race and Justice* 4:69-98.

Thurschwell, A. 1994. On the Threshold of Ethics: Review of *Beyond Accommodation* and *The Philosophy of the Limit,* by D. Cornell. *Cardozo Law Review* 15:1607-55.

Trinh, T.M. 1989. *Woman, Native, Other: Writing Postcoloniality and Feminism.* Bloomington: Indiana University Press.

Volpp, L. 1994. (Mis)Identifying Culture: Asian Women and the "Cultural Defense." *Harvard Women's Law Journal* 17:57-102.

–. 1996. Talking "Culture": Gender, Race, Nation, and the Politics of Multiculturalism. *Columbia Law Review* 96:1573-617.

–. 2000. Blaming Culture for Bad Behavior. *Yale Journal of Law and the Humanities* 12:89-116.

–. 2001. Feminism versus Multiculturalism. *Columbia Law Review* 101:1181-1218.

Walby, S. 1992. Post-Post-Modernism? Theorizing Social Complexity. In *Destabilizing Theory: Contemporary Feminist Debates,* ed. M. Barrett and A. Phillips, 31-52. Oxford: Oxford University Press.

Waldron, J., ed. 1987. *Nonsense upon Stilts: Bentham, Burke and Marx on the Rights of Man.* London: Methuen.

Young, I.M. 1990. *Justice and the Politics of Difference.* Princeton, NJ: Princeton University Press.

–. 1997. *Intersecting Voices: Dilemmas of Gender, Political Philosophy, and Policy.* Princeton, NJ: Princeton University Press.

7
Interpreting the Identity Claims of Young Children
Colin Macleod

Disputes about the recognition of minority rights often concern the relevance of identity as a basis for vindicating a claim made by a minority group to some form of legal or political accommodation. The general issue is this: To what degree do dimensions of a person's or a group's distinct identity merit explicit recognition and accommodation within just political institutions? Many theorists think that various, often intersecting, dimensions of identity – such as those rooted in nationality, culture, language, ethnicity, sexuality, religion, and race – ground valid identity claims. In this chapter, I shall refer to these commonly appealed dimensions of identity as "identity factors." By "valid identity claims," I mean claims that an identity factor or a set of factors be recognized as a legitimate basis for influencing the allocation of rights, resources, power, and opportunities in social and political institutions, as well as for influencing the jurisdictional boundaries of political authority. Minority rights of the sorts that are designed to protect distinct but potentially fragile linguistic, cultural, or national communities can be viewed as an important variety of identity claims. Discussion of identity claims has focused on the status of claims made by or on behalf of groups who have a (reasonably) determinate sense of their own identity. In effect, discussion has focused on the identity claims of mature adults and the groups to which they belong. Here, as in other areas of political philosophy, the distinct and complex interests of children have been left largely unanalyzed.[1]

This neglect is puzzling for a number of reasons. First, the identity claims of adults are often advanced as grounds for extending to adults special prerogatives to shape the identity of children in particular ways. Many parents seek the authority and resources to educate children in particular languages, as well as in particular cultural and religious traditions. Although these claims are not restricted to minority groups, the identity claims made by minority groups often generate controversies. For instance, some minorities have cited their religious and cultural identity as a basis for controlling the access children have to medical treatment and as a way of legitimizing control over the bodies of children.[2] Similarly, parental identity is cited as grounds for insulating children from cultural materials that parents, in light of their cultural or religious commitments, view as objectionable. Since children can be directly and profoundly affected by the recognition of the identity claims of adults, it seems reasonable to determine the degree to which an appeal to the identity-related interests of adults actually justifies the enormous authority adults claim to wield over children.

Second, important legal and political controversies turn directly on the interpretation of the identity claims of children. In family law, for instance, judgments about the religious, cultural, and racial identity of children can play a pivotal role in resolving child custody and parental access disputes.[3] Similarly, controversies concerning transracial and cross-cultural adoption directly raise questions about the identity claims of children. More generally, legal conventions, such as the United Nations *Convention on the Rights of the Child,* suggest that children have special identity-related entitlements. Despite the invocation of the importance of respecting children's identities in these contexts, there is no clear understanding of the nature or significance of children's identity-related interests.

Third, we cannot address the foregoing issues simply by assimilating the identity claims of adults and children. The sense in which children have a claim to the recognition and protection of their identity is importantly different from the identity claims of adults because many dimensions of children's identities are much less determinate than those of adults. To a large extent, adult identity claims are aimed either at protecting identity factors that the adults in question already display or at protecting the conditions under which adults can explore, construct, and express their own identity as autonomous beings. Thus, adults who seek accommodation of their distinctive religious practices typically have established religious identities. But a young child does not seem to have a religious identity in this sense. Similar remarks apply to the relation of young children to other identity factors. Children can have English as a mother tongue, but that does not mean that we can attribute to them an English-speaking identity. The cultural identity of parents does not necessarily fix the cultural identity of children. This means that we cannot simply assume that the identity claims of children are parallel to or even compatible with those of their parents or the community into which they were born. Similarly, we cannot simply assume that the interests of adult members of minority groups are substantively indistinguishable from the interests of children in these groups.

This chapter develops an analysis that can help us address three general questions concerning the identity claims of children. First, in what sense can we attribute distinct identity claims directly to children? Second, what is the relation of children's identity claims to other claims children have to the protection and promotion of interests that are not grounded in considerations of identity? In effect, this question concerns the relative significance of identity claims and what can be called non-identity claims. Non-identity claims are the entitlements people have to resources and opportunities in virtue of their welfare interests and their interests in developing and exercising basic moral capacities. Third, what is the relation of the identity claims of adults to both the identity and non-identity claims of children? Answering these questions is crucial to the proper resolution of many legal and political controversies about minority rights. However, I will mainly steer clear of engagement with particular cases. Instead, I will focus on the conceptually prior issue of analyzing the factors relevant to the interpretation of the identity claims of children.

Identity is a multifaceted phenomenon, and its normative significance is contested. We cannot properly interpret the identity claims of children until we have a clearer general understanding of the different facets of identity and the senses in which appeals to facts about identity might seem important from a normative point of view. My analysis of identity proceeds in the following way. First, I provide a general taxonomy of different dimensions of identity. Second, I note some important differences between the ways we can attribute identities to adults and children. Third, I examine different kinds of identity-related interests and describe criteria that are relevant to the justification of valid identity claims. Finally, I offer a brief analysis of the kinds of identity claims young children can have.

As children develop emotionally, morally, and cognitively, but before they reach the threshold at which they can be considered fully responsible agents, they may express their own evolving sense of their identity by advancing claims for the recognition of their distinctive identity. At least some of these claims deserve to be taken seriously. They may justify constraints on the efforts of adults in positions of authority over children to shape and direct the lives of children. However, I shall, for the most part, set aside important complexities that are introduced when we consider the evolving character of children's interests and capacities. Instead, I shall concentrate mainly on the identity claims of preschool children.

Dimensions of Identity
In this section I introduce a framework for distinguishing different dimensions of identity. The framework applies to both adults and children. I examine three general dimensions of identity – source, quality, and alterability – and discuss some further distinctions that can be made within these dimensions.

Source
When we characterize ourselves or others as having an identity, it is natural

to inquire into the etiology of identity. Understanding the forces that shape identity can play a role in assessing the way we do or should value our identity. Identities that have been heavily shaped by oppressive forces are likely to be evaluated differently than those that have developed in virtue of the free and reflective choices of people. Similarly, we are apt to respond differently to aspects of identity that can change and those that cannot. There are various facets of a person's or a group's identity, and each facet can have a different source. Moreover, any given aspect of identity can have more than one source. Nonetheless, we can distinguish four general sources of identity. First, some elements of identity are rooted in facts about our biological ancestry and genetic endowment. The fact that I was born a male and inherited certain traits from my parents influences, at least to some degree, my identity. These features of a person's identity can be termed "given."[4] With "given" elements of identity it is next to impossible to make counterfactual judgments about how a person's identity could be or could have been different from what it is. There is a metaphysical sense in which a person's identity as a numerically distinct person is crucially constituted by "given" elements of identity. For example, I could not have been born a female. If my mother had given birth to a female child on the day I was born, that child would not be a female me but would be an entirely different person. We can view "given" elements of identity as furnishing the basic substrate of the person to which other dimensions of identity are added.

Second, some aspects of a person's identity are transmitted to the person through a process of upbringing. "Transmitted" elements of identity can be deliberately cultivated by others or generated unintentionally as a result of the sort of upbringing a person receives. Transmitted dimensions of identity are nonvoluntary in the sense that they are not created through the deliberate choices of the person whose identity they shape nor are they created against the will of that person. In effect, the process of transmitted identity formation involves a kind of passivity on the part of the subject whose identity is shaped. Transmitted aspects of identity are also contingent, unlike "given" aspects of identity. We can meaningfully say that people would have had a different identity if they had been raised differently. Many important features of children's emerging identity and of the identity they subsequently have as adults are the result of transmission. This is most obvious in the case of religious identity. Except in rather implausible metaphysical views, an infant qua infant does not have any religious identity.[5] But children may come to have a particular identity as, for example, a Christian in virtue of the efforts of their parents and other members of their community to transmit Christian commitments to them. To the degree that a Christian identity is transmitted to a child, the transmission, from the point of view of the child, is initially nonvoluntary because the child does not have the capacities to choose or reject the identity that is being conveyed. Of course, even fairly young children are not completely passive subjects, and the character of some aspects of their identity, including aspects of transmitted identity, may be influenced by children's choices, even if their choices are not fully autonomous. For example, the willingness with which children participate in the cultural practices favoured by their families can affect the success parents have in transmitting a particular cultural identity to their children.

Third, some dimensions of identity have their roots in people's choices to develop or assume an identity. This is the "assumed" aspect of identity. In this case, individuals (and groups) play an active role in the construction of their own identity via the choices they make about what commitments to embrace and how to conduct their lives. A Christian may decide to become Jewish or an American may decide to emigrate to Canada and become a Canadian. The precise character of a person's assumed identity can, of course, be affected by the character of the identity they have at the point of choice. Arguably, there is an identity difference between a Jew who decides to become a Christian and a Christian who chooses to remain a Christian. The identity of the former will presumably include a sense of being a convert. Young children cannot have, in a strong sense, assumed elements of identity because they lack the capacities of choice and reflection on which such identity depends. As children mature, however, they can acquire capacities for reflective self-direction in virtue of which they can autonomously shape important aspects of their own identity. And as I noted above, even before they have become autonomous, children can play some active role in shaping their own identity through some of their choices. This suggests that some elements of assumed identity are best treated as semi-voluntary. Child who are given the option of learning a second language and choose to do so arguably play a role in constructing their own identity even if their choice cannot be characterized as an exercise of capacities for reflective self-direction. Assumed identity is contingent and is either voluntary or semi-voluntary.[6]

Fourth, there are some dimensions of a person's identity that are imposed by others and that are, in an important respect, alien to the person's self-conception. Often, people will experience "imposed" aspects of identity as facets of their identity that are foisted on them against their will. Imposed aspects often involve the ascription of negative qualities to persons who display or are thought to display other identity factors.[7] The negative characterization of the identity factor often results in disadvantage, social stigma, and forms of social exclusion for the person on whom it is imposed. Persons with disabilities and members of racial minorities living in racist societies provide examples of imposed identity. Consider common reactions to disability. The majority of able-bodied people may ascribe certain traits to persons with disabilities (e.g., that disabled persons are defective and inferior qua persons). The ascription of these traits to disabled people affects the way they are received in society, but it can also affect how disabled persons see themselves. Disabled persons may reject the identity-related traits that are ascribed to them because those traits are alien to their own self-understanding, but they may also recognize that they will be treated as though they actually had the attributes in question. Thus, they can see that an aspect of their identity, which they would completely repudiate if they could, is constructed for them via the attitudes of others. The desire to repudiate an imposed identity, though common, is a contingent feature of imposed identity. People can also internalize aspects of imposed identity in ways that damage self-respect. Imposed identity is typically involuntary and contingent but can be nonvoluntary. In many cases, imposed identity is objectionable because it depends on falsely ascribing negative traits to persons.

The first three sources of identity – "given" identity, transmitted identity, and assumed identity – typically share a characteristic that is not generally a feature of imposed identity. The contrast here is between what might be called "see oneself as" aspects of identity and "seen by others as" aspects of identity. A woman from a Christian household who has decided, as an adult, to abandon her faith may see her identity comprising a complex constellation of "given," transmitted, and assumed identity factors. She sees herself as a former Christian, et cetera. But if she is also disabled and is, on that account, treated as having diminished status as a person, then even though she does not view her identity as importantly constituted by her disability and does not accept the demeaning construal of disability, she can recognize that she is seen by others as importantly constituted by a disability that is evaluated negatively.

Qualitative Dimensions: Thick versus Thin Aspects of Identity

In addition to considering the possible sources of identity, we should consider ways in which identity factors can vary qualitatively. Some features of identity strike us as profoundly important. They may pervade almost all aspects of our lives, and they may thereby affect the way we conduct or seek to conduct an enormous variety of activities in our lives. Other features of our identity may strike us as fairly trivial or unimportant. They are not thereby disqualified as components of our identity, but they do not strongly resonate with our sense of self, and typically the impact they have on our lives is fairly inconsequential. Unimportant facets of identity are unlikely to be invoked as the basis of asserting a putatively valid identity claim. I shall call those facets of a person's identity that exhibit a pervasive influence on a person's sense of identity "thick" aspects of identity. In contrast, "thin" aspects of identity contribute only weakly to a person's sense of identity.[8]

The fact that an identity factor plays a pervasive role in shaping a person's sense of identity need not mean that the facet of identity is, in fact, valuable or even that it is viewed as valuable by the person who assigns it importance. Some thick aspects of identity can be unwelcome encumbrances. For instance, people may find themselves irrevocably tied to religious commitments that they do not value but which nonetheless pervade their sense of self. We can regret aspects of our identity that are very important to us. An ambitious academic whose pursuit of academic success pervades his life may view academic success as crucially important to his sense of self, yet regret that he is deeply consumed with professional goals and cannot, consequently, adequately meet his commitments to his family and friends. Even though thick aspects of identity need not be positively valued, they frequently are highly valued by persons.

Alterability

A final dimension of identity concerns the degree to which an aspect of a person's identity can be altered or revised. Here we encounter a continuum that ranges from "highly fixed" to "readily revisable" aspects of identity. Some elements of identity cannot, even in principle, be altered. For instance, virtually all aspects of "given" identity are beyond possible revision. Thus there is no way of changing the fact that I am the son of Alistair and Ruth. But other elements of identity can be amenable to revision. I can fairly readily shed my identity as an aspiring blues guitarist. We often care about having some substantial control over aspects of our identity, and this typically carries with it an interest in being able to contemplate facets of our current identity. We value the opportunity to consider ways in which we might alter our identity. And we would like to be able to change those features that we judge worthy of amendment. We can, however, stunt or subvert persons' capacities for identity revision. This occurs most dramatically in cases of indoctrination and brainwashing.

Although the degree of identity alterability is affected by the source of identity, it is not wholly determined by it. "Given" aspects of identity are fixed, but the degree to which other sources of identity are subsequently revisable can vary tremendously. For instance, parents can transmit contingent aspects of identity to their children in ways that render it all but impossible for children to revise these aspects later in life. Indeed, the nurturing strategies of some parents and communities are expressly aimed at permanently fixing dimensions of children's identity. The possibility of decisively determining contingent elements of children's identity at an early age is nicely reflected in the Jesuit saying "Give me the first six years of a child's life and you can have the rest." Even assumed elements of identity can become more or less fixed features of identity. A person can voluntarily embrace a religious faith in a manner that renders subsequent abandonment of the faith extremely difficult.

Similarly, degree of alterability is quite independent from the quality of identity. Thick aspects of identity can be either revisable or fixed, and the same applies to thin aspects of identity. We should not conflate depth of commitment with fixity of commitment. It is a mistake to think that the dimensions of identity that we value most are least susceptible to possible revision. A commitment need not be important or valuable because it is fixed.[9] And a valuable commitment is not made more valuable by its being beyond possible reflective revision. The profundity of a commitment is not diminished by the fact that it could be revised.

Attributing Identities to Children and Adults

The foregoing framework is useful because it helps us understand some salient similarities and differences in the way it is appropriate to attribute identities to adults and children respectively. In particular, it alerts us to construals of the identities of children that are potentially distorting.

Casual attributions of identity to children often imply that there is no significant difference in the sense in which children and adults respectively are bearers of identity factors. Thus, we categorize both adults and even very young children as having a common or shared identity – for example, as Jewish or Christian, Canadian or American, black or white, French or English. Frequently, the attribution of an identity to children flows from assumptions about the identity of children's parents. Children born to Jewish parents are Jewish, those born to anglophones are anglophones, and so on. In many contexts there is nothing particularly problematic about such attributions, providing they are understood mainly as forecasts as to the probable identity factors children will come to have as they mature. But they can be misleading insofar as they are taken to signal the idea that the identities of children are effectively structurally isomorphic to those of adults. The danger here is that the identity claims of children will simply be assumed to be identical or reducible to those of their parents or communities on the grounds that there is no real difference between the identities of children and their parents. For instance, if we assume that the child of Amish parents necessarily has a thick Amish identity, then we may assume that the identity-related interests of the child are more or less identical with interests that the Amish parents have in protecting and accommodating their Amish identity. And on this basis we may be inclined to treat the identity claims of Amish children as virtually continuous with those of their parents. This tendency is exhibited in the ruling of the U.S. Supreme Court in *Wisconsin v. Yoder*. In this case, the court interpreted the interests of the children of Amish parents by assuming, in large measure, that the children were Amish and thus their interests in education extended only as far as receiving sufficient schooling to prepare them for life in the Amish community. We have reason to guard against the conflation of identity interests and the associated conflation of adults' and children's identity claims.[10] This does not mean, of course, that we should make the opposite mistake of supposing that there is some inevitable antagonism between the identity claims of adults and children.

In addition to this point, the foregoing framework allows us to capture some other ways in which the attribution of identity factors to children is different from the attribution of identity to adults. We can attribute to both children and adults "given" identity factors. But whereas we can attribute both transmitted and assumed identity factors to adults, infants and very young children display neither of these factors. Infants and very young children lack the capacities necessary to embrace, reject, or even appreciate assumed or transmitted identity factors. Some imposed identity factors can be shared by adults and young children, but strictly speaking it is only in the case of adults and older children that imposed identity factors are involuntary.[11] Young children, unlike adults, do not display "seeing oneself as" dimensions of identity, at least not in any robust way. But they can still experience the ill effects of having a "seen by others" aspect of identity. Qualitative dimensions of identity do not really exhibit themselves in young children, but whether a "given" identity factor will become a "thick" or "thin" dimension of identity can depend crucially on how children are raised.

Similar observations apply to the fixity of children's identity. Aside from "given" identity factors, children's identities are initially extremely open, but, once again, adults can make efforts to strongly fix certain identity factors in maturing children. Except with respect to "given" identity factors, children qua children begin life without an identity. Moreover, the identity factors that often assume the most importance in discussions of identity claims – namely, religion, culture, and language – are precisely the identity factors that we cannot directly attribute to young children. So in these respects there are fundamental differences between the identities of children and adults. We must now turn to the issue of the normative significance of these differences.

Justifying Identity Claims

I shall now address some matters concerning the valuation of identity factors and, in particular, the relation between identity factors and the justification of valid identity claims. As I noted above, we need not assume that all dimensions of a person's identity merit positive valuation. We can be encumbered by identity factors that for one reason or another inhibit the leading of a good life. The homosexual who identifies himself and is identified by others as a corrupt sinner is likely to lead a worse life, other things being equal, than the homosexual whose identity is not characterized by self-loathing. So in assessing the soundness of identity claims advanced by or on behalf of various individuals and groups, we should resist the temptation to suppose that all dimensions of a person's identity can serve as the basis for a valid identity claim. In the case of children, this means we should not suppose that any identity parents or communities might wish to transmit to their children will actually serve their interests. There are constraints on the efforts that parents and others can make in the attempt to mould the identity of their children (Macleod 1997). In order to understand these constraints and to interpret the identity claims of children, we need first to consider what is involved in justifying an identity claim.

Three conditions must be satisfied for the justification of a valid identity claim. I shall call these the value condition, the vulnerability condition, and the fairness condition.

According to the value condition, the identity factors for which some form of political recognition, accommodation, or protection is sought must contribute, in some nontrivial way, to the value of the lives of the people the identity claim is meant to serve. In effect, this means that the identity factors must be valuable. There are at least two ways in which the value condition can be satisfied. First, having some kind of determinate, though not necessarily fixed, identity may be a precondition of leading a good life. Second, a particular identity factor (or some particular constellation of identity factors) may augment the goodness of a person's life by contributing something that is worthwhile in itself.

The vulnerability condition holds that in the circumstances in which an identity claim is advanced, the valuable identity factors of a person or a group are vulnerable in the sense that in the absence of institutional recognition, accommodation, or protection of the identity factors, the people for whom they are valuable cannot securely realize their value. The vulnerability condition implies that the validity of identity claims can vary from circumstance to circumstance and over time. A valuable identity factor that is vulnerable now and consequently merits consideration for some form of political recognition may not be vulnerable in the future.

Finally, the fairness condition holds that recognition, accommodation, or protection of identity factors for some people should be compatible with fair treatment of the interests of other parties that are potentially affected by political acceptance of an identity claim. I assume that the fairness condition can be violated in a variety of ways. But a crucial dimension of the fairness condition involves determining whether a particular way of accommodating identity confers arbitrary or disproportionate benefits or burdens on some members of the community at the expense of others.

Many controversies concerning the legitimacy of identity claims, especially those concerning minority rights, can be interpreted as turning on whether one or another of these conditions is satisfied. For example, some opponents of the recognition of gay marriage doubt that the recognition of gay marriages confers significant value on the gay couples who wish to have the prerogative to marry legally. Such skeptics about gay marriage question, in effect, whether the value condition is met. Language laws in Quebec aimed at protecting French as a societal language seem predicated, at least in part, on the assumption that the French language is threatened. And, of course, it is often contended that the recognition of minority rights is unfair either because the establishment of such rights confers special and unfair benefits on the minority that are not enjoyed by the majority, or because such rights permit minority groups to impose unfair burdens on their members.

We can also use these criteria to interpret disagreements concerning the identity claims of children. Controversies about transcultural adoption often involve debates about the value, vulnerability, and fairness conditions. Disagreements as to whether children's best interests are served when they are raised in the culture of their biological parents concern the value condition. Disagreements as to whether the integrity of minority cultures is threatened by transcultural adoption implicate the vulnerability condition. And there are disagreements about the fairness of the procedures governing adoption to various interested parties, such as prospective adoptive parents, children, and minority communities.

Valuing Identity: Constitutive Identity Interests and Instrumental Identity Interests

Although justification of an identity claim depends on its satisfying all three conditions, I shall focus mainly on how we should understand the value condition in connection with the interests of children. In order to determine what the valid identity claims of children are, we need to know the kind of value identity factors can have for children. We can approach this issue by first considering what it means to say that people have an interest in identity factors. This will allow us to discern significant differences between the "identity interests" of children and those of adults.

We can begin by drawing a contrast between "constitutive identity interests" and "instrumental identity interests." Constitutive identity interests are located in the value of being who we are. This may initially sound a bit cryptic, but further reflection will illuminate what is actually quite a familiar idea. There are limits to how we can conceive people as distinct from the constellation of identity factors that they display at any given time. Although we can imagine a person shedding or adopting an identity factor without becoming a different person, we cannot imagine a person who is entirely bereft of identity factors. For adults, there is an important sense in which our selves are largely constituted by particular configurations of identity factors. Moreover, it is the self so conceived that is the bearer of many important interests and that defines the very person to whom we attribute other, even basic welfare, interests. An adult who has an interest in securing food, medical attention, or shelter always has these welfare interests as a self who is constituted by a certain constellation of identity factors (e.g., as a male Canadian anglophone atheist). This is not to say that the person needs the food and other welfare interests, just as a male Canadian anglophone atheist, but rather that the person who has the needs is partly constituted by certain identity factors.

There is a sense in which we value ourselves and others as persons constituted by particular identity factors per se. In this sense, the value of our identity is not fully reducible to the contribution it makes to facilitating well-being. Of course, as adults we cannot experience well-being in the absence of some kind of constitutive identity, but the value of our constitutive identity need not be understood solely in connection to its role in facilitating well-being. We can also value our identity in its own right. We can value being who we are for its own sake. To the degree that constitutive identity is valuable in this way, we can say that persons have an interest both in having and in maintaining a reasonably stable sense of self as constituted by various particular identity factors.[12] I shall call this a "constitutive identity interest." It is, in effect, the interest one has in having a secure sense of oneself as a person with a reasonably stable and continuous, though not necessarily fixed, identity. Once people have acquired a reasonably robust constitutive identity, they typically have an interest in protecting the conditions that nourish the identity and that permit them to express, explore, and perhaps even challenge aspects of their identity in the conduct of their everyday life. Constitutive identity interests are interests in preserving who we already are (or perhaps in restoring us to an identity that has been eroded). The constitutive identity interests of any specific person will be a function of the particular identity factors that currently constitute that person's self. For example, a francophone, because she is already a French speaker, has a constitutive identity interest in being able to conduct her life in French.

The identity interests of adults usually have an important constitutive dimension. When we say an adult has an interest in protecting some identity factor, we frequently assume that the identity factor has some *sui generis* importance qua a constitutive element of the person's identity. Moreover, we suppose that the identity factor in question is a fairly thick identity factor: it plays a substantial role in constituting the person's identity. But identity factors can also have instrumental value. A person can have an interest in protecting or acquiring an identity factor because of its instrumental value in advancing or facilitating other interests. For example, a prospective immigrant can have an instrumental identity interest in adopting a new nationality or becoming fluent in a new language just because, and insofar as, such changes in identity improve the person's well-being (e.g., by improving economic opportunities). We can value an identity factor for the contribution it makes to the realization of other goods rather than for the role it plays in making us who we are.

Establishing that a person has an "instrumental identity interest" involves showing that there is a connection between the protection of an identity factor and the advancement of the person's non-identity interests. Human beings typically have many interests that can be identified independently of their identity. A full specification of such non-identity interests is not possible here, but two broad categories of non-identity interests are worth mentioning. First, there are basic welfare interests. These are interests in having access to resources, social structures, and human relationships of the sort conducive to physical and psychological health, to the normal development of cognitive powers, and to the leading of a safe, comfortable and pleasant life. Second, there are interests that persons have with respect to development and exercise of moral powers, namely a sense of justice and a capacity for a conception of the good (Rawls 1993, 19). The sense of justice is the moral power in virtue of which persons can identify the legitimate claims of others and regulate their behaviour in light of recognition of these claims. A capacity for a conception of the good is the moral power in virtue of which persons can reflectively pursue, shape, and, if necessary, revise their life plans and commitments.

There is a close connection between identity factors and both welfare interests and moral powers. Our connection with others via a common culture, nationality, or language often facilitates reliable and mutually beneficial forms of cooperation that advance our welfare interests. More directly, our well-being is often interwoven with our participation in the practices, traditions, and rituals of various identity groups, whether religious, cultural, or ethnic. Similarly, the development and exercise of our moral powers depends on our access to a secure "context of choice" (Kymlicka 1989) that is itself a manifestation of various identity factors. We learn about ourselves and reflect on how to conduct our lives in a particular language and against the backdrop of options provided and made salient by the cultural, historical, and national communities to which we belong. Even our sense of self-respect – our sense that our lives are meaningful and worth pursuing – is closely linked to identity. In sum, we have instrumental identity interests because realization of our non-identity interests occurs partly through the vehicle of identity factors. To live well and flourish as an autonomous person we need a language, a culture, and perhaps even a nationality.

Two further observations about instrumental identity interests are in order. First, unlike constitutive identity interests, instrumental identity interests are not linked, as such, to any particular identity factors that persons display antecedently. From the point of view of instrumental identity interests, persons have an interest in *a* language, *a* culture, or *a* nationality but not to any particular language, culture, or nationality. For instance, although I need to acquire fluency in some language in order to engage in meaningful deliberation about my life, my instrumental identity interests are just as well served, other things being equal, by learning French as by learning English. By contrast, a francophone – that is, someone who has already acquired fluency in French – arguably has a constitutive identity interest in ensuring the survival of the French language. Second, the degree to which a non-identity interest is advanced by the protection of identity factors can vary. Some identity factors can be more closely tied to the promotion of welfare or the facilitation of moral powers than others. For example, the development and exercise of moral powers depends more crucially on fluency in a living language than on having a national identity. It is possible, moreover, for some identity factors to function as an impediment to the achievement of non-identity interests. For example, certain kinds of religious identity can operate in ways that are hostile to the development and exercise of moral powers. Consider fundamentalist varieties of Christianity that are misogynistic. A woman who identifies herself as a fundamentalist Christian and participates in the associated community may view herself as subservient to her husband and will face obstacles in pursuing rewarding activities that conflict with her perceived duties to her husband. In this sort of case, a person's self-respect and opportunities for welfare are diminished by an aspect of her identity. This suggests that there can be tensions between individuals' constitutive identity interests and their instrumental identity interests. To the degree that the fundamentalist Christian woman views herself as a fundamentalist Christian, she can be said to have a constitutive identity interest in living in the sort of community in which the sexist variety of Christianity can flourish. Yet the realization of some of her non-identity interests is frustrated by the continued success of fundamentalism. From this perspective, she would be better served by either fairly radical revision of fundamentalist doctrines concerning women or by abandoning the fundamentalist community altogether.

The Identity Interests of Adults and Children

The foregoing discussion about identity interests suggests contrasts between the identity interests of adults and young children. First, children, unlike adults, do not have many, if any, constitutive identity interests. This is because the existence of such interests depends on our being able to attribute identity factors to persons, and, as we have seen, the main identity factors we can attribute to children are "given" identity factors. Such factors are a fairly insignificant source of identity and hence there can only be weak constitutive identity interests grounded in "given" identity factors. Second, although both children and adults have crucial instrumental identity interests, there is a difference in the respective character of these interests. Children's instrumental identity interests have a more "open" character than those of adults in the sense that there is a wider range of identity factors that can feasibly serve children's non-identity interests than can serve the non-identity interests of adults. Language is the most obvious example of the difference between the relatively open and relatively closed character of the respective instrumental identity interests of children and adults. Children need to acquire literacy in some language, but from the perspective of their welfare interests it does not matter which language they learn. By contrast, adults' welfare interests are typically better served by becoming literate in a language in which they already have some competency. For adults, there are typically significant transition costs associated with changing aspects of one's identity, such as in learning a new language, integrating into a new culture, or changing one's religious commitments. It can be difficult and costly to shed an identity factor or to adapt to a new one. Since children do not have an identity to shed, the direct transition costs associated with changing significant facets of identity are typically much lower for children than they are for adults.

The difference between the identity interests of children and adults allows us to make parallel distinctions between the identity claims of children and adults. I have suggested that a necessary condition of a valid identity claim advanced by or on behalf of a person is that the claim serve a nontrivial interest of the person. If this is correct, we can conclude that children cannot have valid identity claims that are grounded in constitutive identity interests. They can have valid identity claims that are grounded in instrumental identity interests. If their welfare and moral power interests are to be adequately served, children arguably need to be raised in a viable culture and community that permit them to develop a secure sense of self. However, children's identity claims will typically be much more open-ended than those of adults because children do not have antecedent links to particular cultures that affect the degree to which their non-identity interests can be served by a particular culture. In effect, children have no inherent identity claim to be raised in any given culture or to be raised in ways that make it more likely they will display one set of identity factors than another. For example, a young child who has not yet acquired a meaningful constitutive identity has no more inherent claim to be raised in an atheist, American, anglophone household than to be raised in a Catholic, Canadian, francophone household.

Children's Identity Claims in Relation to Adult Identity Claims

The analysis thus far suggests that respecting the identity-related interests of children is mainly a matter of ensuring that the processes through which children come to acquire a constitutive identity and that the constitutive identity they actually acquire serve children's welfare interests and their interests in development of moral powers. For any given child, there will be, in principle, a very broad range of child-rearing environments that can adequately advance these interests. This does not mean that children cannot have what might be called valid indexed identity claims. These are claims to be raised in ways that privilege particular cultural, religious, or linguistic environments that are conducive to the creation of specific identities. In this sense, the identity claims are indexed to specific identity factors, such as a particular language, rather than to generic identity factors, such as language per se.

There are two ways in which children can have valid indexed identity claims. The first route to establishing an indexed identity claim depends on the contingent connections between particular cultural, religious, or linguistic environments and particular children. In some cases, the connections may be sufficiently close for children to have a right either to be raised in a particular cultural, religious, or linguistic context or to be raised in ways that give special attention to certain kinds of identity over others. An orphaned child whose biological parents were black has no inherent claim to be to be raised by black parents or in ways that give special emphasis to black history and culture. However, if the society in which the child will be raised is racist, and this means that in all probability a potentially damaging racial identity will be imposed on the child, there will be reasons for supposing that the child does have a claim to be raised in a context that places special emphasis on black culture. For instance, it may be that combating and resisting the damaging effects of racism on the child's self-esteem is best effected by raising him or her with a special understanding of black history and culture. If this is so, then we can say that the child has a strong instrumental identity claim that he or she participate in distinct elements of black culture. It is in virtue of these instrumental considerations that the child has an indexed identity claim to be raised in ways conducive to forming a secure identity as a black person. In this sort of case, the substantive identity claim of the child is predicated on what are, in effect, instrumental identity interests, not constitutive identity interests.

The second way of attributing indexed identity claims to children is indirect. It appeals not to the interests of children per se, but rather to the identity-related interests of adults. The idea here is that adults typically have what might be called "identity aspirations." Some important identity aspirations implicate children directly. Adult identity aspirations consist in preferences that valued and important facets of one's identity flourish, are protected from erosion, and are perpetuated. Children are obvious, and in some cases unique, vehicles for the realization of such identity aspirations. It is unsurprising that parents and identity groups seek to use various strategies to transmit particular identity factors to children. Moreover, it seems reasonable to suppose that communities, but especially parents, have some *prima facie* claim to shape the identities of their children in particular ways. The constitutive and instrumental identity interests of adults can be secured partly through passing identity factors onto children. Moreover, the cross-generational transmission of identity factors from parents to children provides a natural way through which the identity-related interests of children can be realized. The natural bonds of affection that obtain between parents and children typically serve the welfare interests of children well. Children are loved and cared for by their parents, and parents express their concern for children partly by introducing them to various facets of identity. There will often be harmony between parental expressions of identity interests – whether constitutive or instrumental – and the advancement of children's instrumental identity interests.

There is an important caveat here. I noted above that persons can encounter tensions between their constitutive identity interests and their instrumental identity interests. Since children do not have constitutive identity interests, these tensions cannot initially manifest themselves in the lives of young children. However, children can be raised in ways that involve the transmission or imposition of a constitutive identity that is, in important respects, in conflict with their instrumental identity interests. Identities can be shaped through indoctrination that stunts development of moral powers. Similarly, basic welfare interests such as those concerning health and normal human functioning can be set back by methods of transmitting identities to children. Children have a vested interest in avoiding such a conflict. Assuming there is a variety of constitutive identities that can be transmitted to children and that are compatible with their instrumental identity interests, we have reason to favour childraising strategies that privilege the creation of constitutive identities conducive to children's non-identity interests. In other words, as much as possible we should raise children so that their constitutive identity interests can be in harmony with their instrumental identity interests. This means, however, there are likely to be significant constraints on the expressions of certain kinds of parental identity interests. In order to recognize the valid identity claims of children, adults may need to modify or limit pursuit of their own identity claims. Most importantly, parents cannot cite their interest in transmitting an identity to their children either as a grounds for denying children access to the social and educational conditions that are conducive to the development of the moral powers or as a grounds for compromising the basic welfare interests of children.

Conclusion

If the analysis in this chapter is sound, then the identity-related interests of children are importantly different from those of adults. These differences are likely to affect our understanding of the scope and content of some minority rights. In particular, we should be cautious about assuming that the kinds of minority rights that are most compatible with accommodation of the identity-related interests of adults are appropriately sensitive to the distinct interests of children.

Notes

1 But see Allen (1996), Archard (2002), and Van Praagh (1997).
2 See, for instance, *B. (R.) v. Children's Aid Society of Metropolitan Toronto.*
3 See, for instance, *Young v. Young* and *A. v. A.*
4 Some nonbiological facts about a person's ancestry, such as where and when they were born, may also function as "given" elements of identity.
5 Depictions of cultural identity as predicated directly on biological relations are sometimes mistakenly endorsed by courts. See, for instance, the Ontario case of *A. v. A.*, in which the court held, simply in virtue of the fact that a woman had converted to Judaism just prior to the birth of her son, that the child "was born a Jew and will remain such all his life no matter what religious training he receives during his life." In this case, the mother, who had been awarded custody, abandoned her commitment to Judaism shortly after the birth of the child and re-embraced her Christian faith.
6 Assumed identity that is the product of fully voluntary – i.e., genuinely autonomous – choice could be labelled "strong assumed identity." Assumed identity that is the product of semi-voluntary choice could be labelled "weak assumed identity." In my view, young children can only have weak assumed identity.
7 Imposed aspects of identity do not necessarily involve the ascription of negative qualities to persons. The key feature is that there is a lack of fit between the imposed identity and other salient features of the person's identity. This lack of fit can take at least two forms. First, individuals' own understanding of their own identity may conflict with the identity trait that others attribute to them. Second, there can be a lack of fit between some actual trait of a person and the traits that are attributed to that person. In this sort of case, the person need not have a developed self-conception. Children who don't have a conception of themselves as either virtuous or vicious can nonetheless have an identity imposed on them. Others may treat them, perhaps because of racist assumptions, as morally inferior even though they are not. It is lack of fit in either of these senses that makes the imposed identity alien. Of course, alien characterizations of a person's identity will often be negative.
8 The way in which imposed elements of identity resonate with a person's sense of self is arguably somewhat different from the way other elements of identity resonate. People who are disabled may not view their disabilities as an important aspect of their identity, but the fact others will impose on them an identity of being disabled can have a profound impact on their lives. In this case, the identity of being a disabled person pervades many important aspects of the person's life and is a thick dimension of identity even though the person views the identity as alien.
9 One can, of course, try to express one's commitment to an identity factor by binding oneself to it in ways that make it difficult to change the commitment.
10 See Arneson and Shapiro (1996) and Macleod (1997).
11 This does not mean that the interests of children are not adversely affected by imposed dimensions of identity. A child who, on the basis of race, is characterized as morally inferior will suffer unjust deprivations – e.g., of access to suitable medical care. But the imposition of a racist identity does not occur against the will of the child because the child is not yet a being with an autonomous will.

12   To be clear, the interest is not an interest in preserving a static self. Rather, it is a matter of securing sufficient support for enough of the identity factors that constitute the self at any given time to permit there to be a continuous and reasonably coherent underlying sense of self. This self can undergo changes, even radical changes. But too much disruption of the identity factors at any one time results in the dissolution of the self. Nonetheless, we should not suppose that circumstances conducive to the protection of constitutive identity are necessarily antagonistic to changes in constitutive identity.

References

Books and Articles

Allen, Anita L. 1996. Does a Child Have a Right to a Certain Identity? In *Children's Rights Re-Visioned: Philosophical Readings,* ed. Rosalind Ekman Ladd, 98-106. Belmont, CA: Wadsworth.

Archard, David. 2002. Children, Multiculturalism, and Education. In *The Moral and Political Status of Children,* ed. David Archard and Colin M. Macleod, 142-59. Oxford: Oxford University Press.

Arneson, Richard, and Ian Shapiro. 1996. Democratic Authority and Religious Freedom. In *NOMOS XXXVIII: Political Order,* ed. Ian Shapiro and Russell Hardin, 365-411. New York: New York University Press.

Kymlicka, Will. 1989. *Liberalism, Community, and Culture.* Oxford: Oxford University Press.

Macleod, Colin. 1997. Conceptions of Parental Autonomy. *Politics and Society* 25(1): 117-41.

Rawls, John. 1993. *Political Liberalism.* New York: Columbia University Press.

Van Praagh, Shauna. 1997. Religion, Custody, and a Child's Identities. *Osgoode Hall Law Journal* 35:309-78.

Cases

A. v. A. (1992), O.J. No. 50.

B. (R.) v. Children's Aid Society of Metropolitan Toronto, [1995] 1 S.C.R. 315.

Wisconsin v. Yoder, 406 U.S. 205 (1972).

Young v. Young, [1993] 4 S.C.R. 3.

8
Protecting Confessions of Faith and Securing Equality of Treatment for Religious Minorities in Education
John McLaren

> While certain aspects [of the right to religious freedom] may clearly be said to belong to the citizen's Caesar and others to the believer's God, there is a vast area of overlap and interpenetration between the two. It is in this area that balancing becomes doubly difficult, first because of the problems of weighing considerations of faith against those of reason, and secondly because of the problems of separating out what aspects of an activity are religious and protected by the Bill of Rights and what are secular and open to regulation in the ordinary way.
>
> – *Christian Education South Africa v. Minister of Education,*
>   para. 34.

During the years of the Second World War, when the Jehovah's Witnesses was a banned organization in Canada, children from the sect in some communities were victimized by both court action and removal from their families for failing to participate in patriotic exercises at school assemblies (Kaplan 1989). The City of Hamilton school board seems to have been particularly distressed by this resistance to obeisance to icons of the state, and it committed to securing unconditional compliance with its regulations on the matter (127-46, 158-64). In two cases arising from the actions of the Hamilton school board, decisions favourable to the board were either quashed or overturned on appeal.[1] Similarly, a decision of the Alberta Court of Queen's Bench, Trial Division, upholding the right of the Lethbridge school board to demand compliance with patriotic exercises, was effectively overturned by the provincial legislature's amendment to the *School Act,* which allowed an exception for conscientious objection *(Ruman v. Board of Trustees of Lethbridge School District).*[2] That it was possible for school boards to discriminate against the members of dissenting religious minorities and for lower courts, at least, to validate the discrimination says a great deal about the structure of religious belief, mainstream anxieties about "disloyalty," and the lack or limited character of religious tolerance that existed during that era. Although a right to freedom of religion was said to exist, presumably in the interstices of the common law, it could prove highly elusive for religious groups, especially those such as the Jehovah's Witnesses, for whom theology and life were indistinguishable, who openly rejected Mammon and were widely suspected of being subversive.

It is a sizeable jump from that earlier mindset to the decisions of the Ontario Court of Appeal in *Re Zylberberg et al. and the Director of the Sudbury Board Education* [*Zylberberg*] and *Re Corporation of the Canadian Civil Liberties Association and the Minister of Education* [*Elgin County*]. In these two decisions the court banned, respectively, public school religious exercises and religion courses that were Christian in inspiration and content and that attempted to impose particular interpretations of faith on non-Christian believers or nonbelievers. Both of these elements of the public school program were required by a regulation under the provincial education act (section 50(1); the regulation in question was section 28 of Regulation 262). There was, said the court, a clear infringement of the right to freedom of religion and conscience under section 2(a) of the *Charter of Rights and Freedoms*. According to the court, any profession of faith in public education that offends the faith beliefs of others is both offensive and unconstitutional.

Here is at work a very different attitude of mind to that which triggered the prosecution of Jehovah's Witness children and their parents in the early 1940s. It reflects acceptance of a community that is pluralistic in terms of its religious and cultural composition, and acceptance of the belief that there must be respect for religious and secular diversity even to the extent of limiting the claims of what has been the dominant religious tradition. Unlike those of the earlier period, Canadian courts are now bound by the Charter to recognize and protect a diversity of religious traditions when an adherent's freedom of religion is compromised by state action. At the same time, the decisions in *Zylberberg* and *Elgin County* demonstrate that issues of freedom of religion and religious conscience are as alive today in Canada as they have been in the past, despite the changes in mindset noted above. Under Charter law as it evolves further, we can expect the litigation of more such cases than before as the contours of religious freedom are explored and tested. Within the new constitutional order the members of religious minorities are not only resisting discriminatory laws and conduct by which they are penalized or their beliefs are marginalized, but are also making proactive claims to be accorded particular rights to state support for the exercise of their religious beliefs, most notably in education.

The contrast between these sets of cases from the 1940s and the 1990s suggests that we live in a different and more enlightened era than was true of earlier generations. Accordingly, it may be supposed, religious minorities can rest content that they are constitutionally protected from discrimination and can enjoy equality before and under the law. As I shall suggest in this chapter, Canada as a liberal democratic state continues to have problems in dealing with legal constraints on religious belief and practice. This is especially true in those instances when a religious minority is claiming state accommodation for its beliefs in the context of law or activities thought to be secular in nature. The judicial instinct seems to be to limit and understate the domain of the sacred and religious in the public life of the secular state. Moreover, there is even today on occasion a tendency for judges to distinguish between respectable and nonrespectable religion. Recently, several commentators have vigorously argued that the trend in the Supreme Court of Canada's jurisprudence in cases of claims for accommodation of religious belief and practice is to diminish the place of religion, if not to exclude it entirely from discourse about and debate on public policy – in short, to confine the concerns of those arguing from a religious point of view to the purely private realm (Benson 2000; D.M. Brown 2000; Buckingham 2001). Although I touch upon the broader context of freedom of religion in Canadian law and the constitution, my particular concern is to expose the often tense relationship between law and religion in the matter of education. I conclude with some thoughts on how clashes between freedom of religion and secular values may be better mediated in the future.

History

First to the history that helps explain the treatment of religion in Canada in the past and the roots of some of the problems we continue to have with taking particular religious beliefs and practices seriously. In the United States the constitution was designed to protect individual freedom of religion and conscience by denying any faith tradition special status as a state church or as part of a broader religious establishment.[3] This has resulted in case law that has denied the elevation of any faith or set of beliefs in public schools and denied financial support for denominational schools. At the same time, the constitution has been used to shield the faith and confessions of individuals from discrimination in the school system. For example, in the early 1940s the United States Supreme Court upheld the right of Jehovah's Witnesses children to refuse to engage in patriotic exercises (*West Virginia State Board of Education v. Barnette*). For its part, Canada sought to accommodate and recognize dominant Christian religious traditions in various provinces while seeking to ensure protection for the religious minority, Protestant or Catholic, as the case might be. This was achieved constitutionally by the inclusion of section 93 in the *British North America (BNA) Act* of 1867.[4] Religious rights, where they were recognized, were not attached to individuals but to membership in religious groups or communities. The lack of constitutional protection for freedom of religion more generally, however, meant that repressive state action against unpopular religious groups, such as the Witnesses, went unchallenged for a long time (Kaplan 1989).

There was in Canada, then, some recognition of religious rights, especially relating to denominational education.[5] However, before we begin to feel smug about what seems like toleration, at least, of other Christian denominations in the matter of education, we need to understand some realities about our history.[6] Neither the constitution nor the law proved very effective at preserving the rights accorded by section 93 of the *BNA Act*. Denominational schools were abolished in New Brunswick by 1871 (Morton 1964, 159, 169).[7] Bilingual denominational schools accommodating Franco-Ontarian Catholics were legislated out of existence in the 1910s (Brown and Cook 1974, 252-62). In Manitoba, denominational schools, which were theoretically constitutionally protected by the *Manitoba Act* of 1871,[8] fell to the legislative axe of an anglophone government in 1890 (Waite 1971, 215, 246-47). In each of these instances, appeals by the minority religious group to the courts proved unavailing; the law was interpreted to trump their interest in preserving their religious beliefs, culture, and language (Brown and Cook 1974, 262; Waite 1971, 247-50; *City of Winnipeg v. Barrett and Logan; Trustees of the Ottawa Separate School Board v. Mackell*).

Canada was also faced with the challenge of granting exemptions from the normal application of the general law to religious communities that claimed their faith and consciences prevented them from complying with it. The relations between pacifist communal Christians, especially the German-speaking Hutterites and Strict Order Menonnites and the Russian-speaking Doukhobors, and the state in Canada during the twentieth century were marked by episodic periods of tension (Janzen 1990). This extended to education law and policy. Despite apparent protections for an individual's right to practise religion and to follow the dictates of conscience, or for the confessions of religious collectivities, very real mental and structural constraints existed when it came to the actual practice of tolerance.

In the early twentieth century, when immigration to Canada reached a peak and cultural and religious demographics were changing, what had amounted to Protestant Christian dominance outside Quebec seemed to those who were part of it to be in jeopardy (McLaren 1999, 122). Educated to believe in the inherent superiority in cultural and intellectual terms of the Anglo-American "race" and its institutions, the dominant community felt a strong impulse to ensure the continued strength and welfare of this country by dictating conformity among and assimilation of non-English-speaking immigrants (Sutherland 1976; Woodsworth 1972). This was especially true of those whose social and cultural practices were to one degree or another seen as exotic, inferior, or irresponsible. The solution, the dominant community argued, was the early inculcation of the English language and education in the values of the dominant society, which reflected, in fact if not in law, mainstream Protestant Christianity. There was little or no time or effort dedicated to understanding, let alone approving, the cultural and religious traditions of non-English-speaking newcomers. A telling example of this mindset is the 1918 book *Educating the New Canadian* by John Anderson, a school inspector from Yorkton, Saskatchewan. In this work Anderson advocated education as the major vehicle for assimilation of non-British immigrants. Moreover, he openly criticized the Doukhobor leader Peter V. Verigin, the Lordly, for encouraging communalism and seeking to preserve Russian language and culture among his people (33-34).

This obsession with inducing conformity and "playing by the rules" was to weigh heavily on those groups, such as the Mennonites, Hutterites, and Doukhobors, for whom life and the practice of faith were indivisible. Their members professed a primary and unwavering obligation to God working among them over any responsibility to human governments or ecclesiastical authority. These immigrant groups, whose communal existence was both culturally encoded and divinely inspired, found change most difficult. It was they who thus incurred most readily the impatience, if not the hostility, of the dominant population and its political representatives. Responsibility for education was to become a source of conflict between Canadian governments and these religious communities (Janzen 1990). In one instance, state action forcing public education on a community led to further migration. Many Strict Order Mennonites took part in an exodus from the Canadian prairies to South America in the early 1920s in the face of imprisonment for failing to send their children to public schools (Enns 1980, 73). With both radical and orthodox Doukhobors, state intervention demanding compulsory school attendance produced resistance, civil disobedience, and property destruction (Woodcock and Avakumovic, 1968). Where tensions intensified, as they did with the Doukhobors, the evidence is that several Canadian governments, both federal and provincial, became committed to more activist policies of breaking this form of religious communal tradition (McLaren 1995a, 1999).

It was in British Columbia that the tension between the Doukhobors, the state, and the dominant community was most intense and durable. Education became a major bone of contention as Doukhobor resistance to or skepticism about state-sponsored education clashed with strong and nativist impulses to conformity and "nation-building" among Anglo-Canadian settlers and their politicians. A spiral of misunderstanding, ill will, and periodic recrimination developed. Doukhobors refused to send their children to school or withdrew them, and the province sought to force compliance by introducing communal responsibility and prescribing the seizure of community assets in cases of truancy (McLaren 1995b). Traditionalists among the Doukhobors, the Sons of Freedom, reacted in the 1920s by burning schools because, they argued, public education made children "slaves of Satan." In its turn, the provincial government in Victoria responded to these depredations and other forms of protest by introducing two resocialization experiments: in the 1930s and 1950s, Freedomite children were taken from their parents in calculated experiments to reeducate them to accept Canadian ways and values (McLaren 2002).

Whatever the pretensions to enshrining a degree of religious tolerance within the constitutional order in Canada, legislatures, administrators, and courts historically made clear distinctions between what was "acceptable" and "unacceptable" religious belief and practice. Moreover, as these governing institutions reserved to themselves the characterization of where the line between what was sacred and what was secular lay, they had and exercised the capacity to shrink the realm of religious belief and conscience and expand the reach of the general law to suit the context of conflict with the state.

This mindset, as it applied to the field of education, is well illustrated by the words of Justice Sydney Smith of the British Columbia Court of Appeal as late as 1956 *(Perepelkin v. Superintendent of Child Welfare (No. 2))*. The context was an action by radical Doukhobor (Sons of Freedom) parents to have their son Bill, who had been seized by the province under the truancy and child protection laws, returned to them. Mr. and Mrs. Perepelkin argued that how and where their children were educated was for them to decide according to the dictates of religious conscience. Smith gave short shrift to the claim:

> I, for my part cannot feel that in this case there is any religious element involved in the true legal sense ... I absolutely reject the contention that any group of tenets that some sect decides to proclaim form part of its religion thereby necessarily takes on a religious colour ...
>
> [Treating education as a matter of faith and conscience] involves the claim that a religious sect may make rules for the conduct of any part of human activity and that these rules thereby become for all the world a part of that sect's religion. This cannot be so. *(Perepelkin, 599-600)*

Even if within the constitutional order there was recognition of freedom of religion, opined Smith and his colleagues, it had no application in this case, which involved a purely secular matter – education.

If the dominant political and legal system in Canada historically found it difficult to accommodate the religious beliefs and practices of groups who were radical practitioners of "primitive" Christianity, it usually had even less empathy for those who were non-Christian. This was particularly true if the non-Christians held out for special treatment or exemptions, or were viewed as dangerous proselytizers. In the case of the Jews, as long as they were considered respectable, worshipped in private, seemed to have assimilated, and assumed a relatively low profile, they were tolerated, although they were by no means free from social discrimination and professional exclusion (Speisman 1992, 113-16). Greater hostility, and therefore discrimination at all levels, was demonstrated towards working-class Jewish immigrants from Eastern Europe after 1880. These people were seen as less-desirable migrants and unassimilable by the dominant Christian population (Anctil 1992, 135; M. Brown 1992, 114-22). More marginal was the position of those Hindus, Sikhs, Muslims, and Buddhists who settled in Canada. Their religious beliefs were often openly treated as positively heathen and as another reason for discriminating against them (Roy 1989, 27-29, 231). In matters of education, non-Christian children were normally forced to lap up whatever was served to them by public schools, with their Protestant trappings, or by Roman Catholic schools, where that interpretation of the Christian faith infused programs of instruction more extensively and openly.

The traditional religious practices and spirituality of Aboriginal peoples were often the targets of vigorous attempts at suppression and conversion (Youngblood Henderson 1999, 168). This policy of cultural colonialism towards tribal peoples, with its regime of "tutelage," achieved in Canada its most destructive results in the system of residential schools (Miller 1996; Milloy 1999). Ottawa paid for these institutions, although the churches ran them. Thousands of Aboriginal children were taken or sent to them, cut off from their families and cultural roots, to be "Canadianized," a process that effectively undermined the language and culture, not to mention the life skills, of several generations of First Nations communities.

Ironically, it was the Jehovah's Witnesses, a small millenarian Christian sect whose members put God first and foremost in their lives and rejected obligations to Mammon, that experienced the most overt and intense discrimination for its religious convictions during the middle third of the twentieth century in North America. Especially during the years of the Second World War and, most notably in Quebec, for a decade thereafter, the Witnesses were subject to both legal disabilities and harassment for their beliefs (Kaplan 1989, 224-53). As we have seen, Witness children were victimized by the education system for their resistance to engaging in patriotic exercises. The recognition by the sect that the law might have something to offer in the way of protection led them, despite their beliefs, to challenge state action in court. These contested prosecutions were to contribute significantly in Canada, as they had earlier in the United States, to some judicial recognition of freedom of religion and conscience. Litigation involving the Witnesses in the 1950s provided the Supreme Court of Canada with the opportunity to move closer to the recognition of a hazily defined but inherent constitutional right to religious freedom.[9]

The Charter and Freedom of Religion and Conscience

It is in the decades since the Second World War and its tragic lessons in wholesale denial of human rights and the conscious implementation of genocide that the most decisive steps have been taken in the Western world to give meaning to rights of freedom of religion and conscience. Constitutional challenges to state interference with minority religious beliefs and practices have been mounted in countries such as the United States and Canada, providing the courts with an opportunity to mark out, and in some instances expand, the legal ambit of tolerance of religious diversity. In Canada, constitutional changes secured in 1982 in section 2(a) of the Charter have provided express protection for freedom of religion and conscience where there was, at best, vague and inarticulate commitment before.

What then of the status of rights protecting religious belief and practice since 1982 and the enactment of the Charter? The record of the courts in Canada, led by the Supreme Court, has been inconsistent. Several critics representing various faith traditions have noted that despite Justice Dickson's broad statements about the need to protect religious freedom, including both belief and practice, in the seminal case of *R. v. Big M Drug Mart*, he narrowed potential protection by characterizing the right to religious freedom as an individual right instead of a right shared with and by a group or collectivity. As a result, the critics suggest, there has been in Canada a judicial tendency to emphasize the primacy of secular values when assessing claims of religious freedom and to recoil from active engagement with claims made in the name of religion by faith communities (D.M. Brown 2000, 564-71; Buckingham 2001, 468-73, 477-89). These critics concede that the court has shown an enlightened approach to the protection of the religious rights of employees whose religious beliefs clash with the demands of their work (D.M. Brown 2000, 572-75). Moreover, the court has scrupulously avoided interfering with the employment policies of church groups or organizations that demand commitment to the religious principles of the church or church-run institutions, including schools, even though they discriminate against nonadherents (575-78). In recent Canadian jurisprudence there is also evidence of recognition of the right of members of religious groups to conform to the requirements of their faith in terms of dress, even in work situations (ibid.). One commentator has described these cases, in which Canadian courts have had no compunction about applying section 2(a) of the Charter to protect religious beliefs and practices, as demonstrating strong support for "freedom *for* religion" (571-72).

The jurisprudence of the courts on protection of religion in the context of education, with the Supreme Court of Canada in the lead, is much more equivocal (Shilton 1999, 206). This is partly the result of judicial reluctance to extend traditional constitutional protections afforded to particular religious groups in education to other religious minorities in an increasingly multi-religious, multicultural society. It is also partly because the courts have backed themselves into an increasingly secular corner on the place and role of religion in public schools. The approach has tempted the same critic to describe this set of decisions as reflecting a "freedom *from* religion" cast of mind (D.M. Brown 2000, 571-72).

As we have already observed, the First Amendment to the American *Bill of Rights* established the jealously guarded "wall of separation" in the cause of preventing an alliance of state and ecclesiastical power or a preference being given to particular faith traditions *(Everson v. Board of Education)*. In educational terms this has meant the insulation of public education from the propagation of religious beliefs or practices. In contrast, the Canadian *Constitution Act, 1982,* continues the practice of the state protecting certain religious groups in the matter of education.[10] The wording of section 93 in the act reflects the experience of a country that was a federation of two European linguistic communities that had different political and social cultures and that subscribed to divergent interpretations of the Christian faith. While Canada, like the United States, eschewed the establishment of a state church, since 1867 its constitution has taken explicit account of the historic reality of the dominance of the Roman Catholic or Protestant religions in different parts of the country, embodying, on paper at least, a pragmatic political impulse to protect the minority religious tradition in matters of education in those regions. In this sense the Canadian constitution sought to construct a "bridge" between church and state in the educational sphere *(Zylberberg,* 610, *per* Lacourcière J.A.).

What has happened in recent decades is that Canadian courts have moved closer to the American juridical position in matters of religion and education, not through any overt attempt to emulate United States authority, but through the adoption of an increasingly secular view of the role of the state and of the interpretation of constitutional values. How has this come about?

It might have been supposed that in the event of a clash between section 93 of the *BNA Act* and the Charter, the section might be read down or otherwise interpreted to provide a basis for the broader recognition of religious minority group rights in matters of education. The reverse has happened. The Supreme Court of Canada has determined that the historic accord on the protection of religious rights in matters of education contained in section 93 of the 1867 *BNA Act,* and incorporated in the *Constitution Act, 1982,* continues to qualify and override the commitment to freedom of religion and conscience in section 2(a) of the Charter *(Bill 30 Reference)*. Accordingly, the religious faith groups mentioned in section 93, Roman Catholics or Protestants as the case may be, have now, as previously, a constitutional right to public support and financing for their schools. In the *Bill 30 Reference* the court did allow that it was open to provinces under section 93 to provide support and funding for other denominational and non-Christian schools through legislation, but added that such legislation or its repeal would not be subject to challenge under the Charter.[11] While opening the door, then, to provincial initiatives in matters of minority education, the decision erects a barrier between religious traditions in Canada that are and are not constitutionally protected (Shilton 1999, 208-11).

The position taken by the Supreme Court of Canada in the *Bill 30 Reference* – that the Roman Catholic separate school system in Ontario is entitled to full funding by the province, in accord with the undertakings in section 93 of the constitution – was quickly followed by a further decision that confirmed the court's view that this concession of religious rights is both historic and exceptional. In *Adler v. The Queen,* another Ontario case, a group of Jewish, Muslim, and evangelical Christian parents claimed a constitutional right of state support for religious education of their children according to the tenets of their faith. The province's failure to provide that support would, they argued, amount to an interference with their right to religious freedom under section 2(a) of the Charter. The court rejected the action asserting that section 93 reflected an historic compromise written into the constitution that could have no broader effect. Moreover, the court argued that the reference to freedom of religion in section 2(a) of the Charter did not require the state to provide benefits that were essentially secular in nature to religious groups. The result is that in Ontario and other provinces that have not made legislative provision for the funding of alternative, including religious, schools, parents who want an education for their children that incorporates religious teaching have to seek it privately, while still paying taxes to support the public school system. In contrast, provinces such as Alberta or British Columbia have legislative provision for state financial support of minority religious schools, either, as in Alberta, within the umbrella of the existing school system, or, as in British Columbia, parallel to the public school system. In these provinces parents may be provided with a choice of schooling for their children, in the knowledge that if they select a religious school, tax dollars will support it to some extent (Shilton 1999, 207).

The frustration for parents with strong religious beliefs, who wish their children's education to be related to their religious values and the ethical systems that support their faith, might have been less had the public schools in the relevant provinces provided acceptable courses in religious studies or perhaps even access to religious teaching by members of the children's various religious traditions. What I mean by religious study courses is not mere overviews of religious belief systems, but courses that examine the connections between religious values and ethical systems and life in society, or civic virtue. This possible avenue of accommodation of religious belief has been effectively cut off by a series of decisions that have marked the public school system as secular, with a mandate only to impart secular values to children.

Employing reasoning that looks very similar to that in American jurisprudence, in which the "wall of separation" of church and state in matters of education is an article of faith, the Ontario Court of Appeal in *Zylberberg* and *Elgin County* struck down attempts by boards of education to sustain or introduce religious exercises or courses respectively in public schools in their districts. The court reasoned in both cases that the exercises and courses in question, which were Christian in content or flavour, constituted an attempt to impose particular interpretations of faith on others, whether non-Christian believers or nonbelievers in religion. These actions by the school boards, said the court, represented a clear infringement of the right to freedom of religion and conscience under section 2(a) of the Charter.

On the surface, these decisions of the Ontario Court of Appeal seem to reflect the view that protection is afforded "for" religion in the sense that the court is insulating the children of minority faiths from exposure to majoritarian religious beliefs and practices. The court was of the view that the choice given to parents to request that their children not be subjected to the exercises or courses in question did not rob the policies of their discriminatory character. What the decisions lack is any clear notion of what public schools can or might do to meet the concerns of parents who do not want the views and values of another religion foisted on their children, but do want their education to be related to their own religious beliefs. As Elizabeth Shilton notes, in *Zylberberg* "the court hinted that a more inclusive and multicultural approach to religious exercises might be acceptable, but stopped short of making a finding to that effect" (1999, 212).[12] The apparent vacuum on the place of religion in the public schools of Ontario that resulted has been further complicated by subsequent decisions in which the courts have sought to navigate the combined effects of the *Bill 30 Reference* and *Adler* cases on the one hand, and *Zylberberg* and *Elgin County* on the other. In Ontario the situation became particularly fraught because the government amended the offending regulation on religious exercises and religious education in public schools – regulation 262, section 28, under the *Ontario Education Act* – to remove the requirement for opening and closing exercises entirely and prohibited any sort of doctrinal religious education in the curriculum (213).[13]

Members of religious minorities in Ontario and other provinces that have not provided legislative support for alternative or minority religious schools now find themselves in a constitutional bind – some would argue limbo – as they seek accommodation of their religious beliefs and practices in public school systems. This is so, it seems, whether they are seeking to put their beliefs and practices on a par with the dominant religious tradition or are arguing for a public school system that allows and encourages their children to relate their studies to their faith. The nature of the problem is evident in two recent decisions in Ontario. In *Islamic Schools Federation of Ontario v. Ottawa Board of Education,* Muslim parents were told that their request for the Ottawa public school system to recognize two Muslim holy days, if the number of students warranted it, because Christian holidays are observed was not sustainable. The court determined that the latter are purely secular days off. In a decision inconsistent with the position of the Ontario Court of Appeal in *Zylberberg* and *Elgin County,* this court indicated that the parents could claim exemptions for their children's nonattendance on holy days, as for any other legitimate reason for absence from school. No embarrassment or alienation should be anticipated. The second case, *Bal v. Attorney General of Ontario,* involved children of Sikh, Hindu, Muslim, Mennonite, and Christian Reformed parents who formerly received sectarian religious education in several publicly funded alternative schools in Ontario. The funding had been pulled from those schools in the wake of the findings in *Zylberberg* and *Elgin County* that faith-specific religious exercises or courses in religion offended section 2(a) of the Charter. The parents challenged the new regulation that proscribed any teaching of religion in public schools.[14] They argued that they were forced to send their children to public schools because of financial constraints that made it impossible for them to afford fees in private religious schools. The Ontario Court of Appeal, noting the Supreme Court in *Adler* had denied the right of minority parents to claim accommodation and funding of their children's faith needs in the public school system, refused to strike down the regulation. The parents' problem was one of funding, said the judges, not of interference with religion. The court delivered the *coup de grâce* to the possibility of entertaining an accommodation of religions more generally in the public school system in the following assertion: "The public school system is now secular. Its goal is to educate, not to indoctrinate. This is very different from the goal in place at the time that *Zylberberg* and *Elgin County* were decided. Secularism is not coercive, it is neutral ... As stated the public school system is secular. No one religion is favoured. Fundamental to the education system is teaching without religious doctrine" (*Bal,* 706, 713).

The net effect of these judicial contortions is that in provinces where there is no legislative basis for recognizing and supporting financially independent religious schools, public school systems are now able to purge their programs of any religious content. Outside the specific constitutional rights granted to parents from the appropriate minority religious groups (Protestant and Catholic) in such a province, the effective choice is to send their children to private religious schools, where they are available, paying fees as well as contributing tax dollars to the public school system, or, if they cannot afford the fees, to send their children to a public school where there will be no mention, let alone evaluation, of religious values and religiously inspired ethical systems.

Over and above this judicial secularization of public education in general terms, there are also decisions in which Canadian courts have been challenged to address the claims of particular religious groups to exemption from the generic requirements of education law and policy. It is in this context that one observes the difficulty courts still sometimes have accommodating, let alone engaging with, the views of marginal religious groups, especially those that believe firmly that the believer's obligations to his or her God have primacy over any contrary obligation to the state. We have already seen how the judgmentalism of the past, which was often based on belief in the superiority of mainline Christian thought and practice, unfairly affected radical or traditionalist groups, including those with communalist tendencies. The decisions of Canadian courts now no longer proceed from those earlier feelings of religious superiority. Today, the gauge of the claims of such groups is the strong belief in secularity, observed earlier.

In Canada, the exercise of section 1 of the Charter legitimates "reasonable" limitations by the state on basic rights and freedoms. As Quebec scholar Pauline Coté (1991) has persuasively argued, this provision endows the courts with the mantle of the "Master of Good Purposes." In cases involving claims to exemptions from the general law for religious reasons, the courts are endowed with considerable power. First, "they are asked to decide which purposes are good, religious or secular, and who is to be regarded as the agent of public good" (8). At a second level, Coté argues, the tribunals "are placed in a position so as to determine which religions are constitutionally protected and which ones are not" (ibid.). In other words, the courts have the power to determine what is "respectable" or "less than respectable" in terms of religious belief. Third, courts are endowed with the power of distinguishing between what are secular as opposed to religious issues (ibid.). At each level, Coté asserts, the system can assess who succeeds in qualifying for religious freedom and who does not.

The tendency of courts in Canada today to think in purely secular and liberal terms and to steer clear of religious and theological argument and disputation – in other words, to ignore or gloss over the religious dimension to issues – seems to jibe with Coté's critique. Post-Charter jurisprudence in Canada has produced worrying indicators that the capacity for judgmentalism on religious belief or its marginalization continues to exist among the judiciary. As we have observed, Canadian courts, led by the Supreme Court, have shown respect for the importance of religion and religious conscience in cases in which there have been negative threats to religious freedom. However, they have consciously fought shy of becoming embroiled in theological disputations *within* faith traditions, such as those that have emerged occasionally in Hutterite colonies, opting instead for the safe and familiar ground of natural justice or formal due process (Esau 1999).[15]

Although it may well be a desirable stance for outsiders not to judge differences of interpretation within a particular faith group, this attitude has perhaps encouraged the view that the court's predominant commitment is to uphold formal, secular values and not to assess carefully the claims made for religious exemptions from the general law and the evidence adduced to support the demands of religious freedom and conscience.

In those cases where the values or aspirations of a religious community clash with, or are not thought worthy of accommodation by, the state, Canadian courts have tended both to avoid engagement with the religious belief system and to hew to secular assumptions, in the process marginalizing the religious belief, practice, or claim in question.[16] Charter protection for freedom of religion did not protect a Baptist pastor, who believes that God is the final authority in matters of education, from the application of Alberta schools legislation that required him to seek government approval for his decision to educate his children in a church basement outside the public school system. In *Jones v. The Queen* a majority of the Supreme Court of Canada was of the view that a province is required to make a "reasonable accommodation" in its education system for those wishing to educate children at home or in independent schools. Requiring certification of the instruction in an independent school as efficient, as the Alberta Department of Education did, was a minimal requirement that did not offend or compromise the religious beliefs of Pastor Jones. The court thought that regulations relating to how he carried out his educational mission would need closer scrutiny lest they trench upon the religious convictions of parents. However, while it recognized that the religious and civic dimensions might both be important in resolving a clash between freedom of religion and state supervision of education, the court concluded that in this instance the civic obligation trumped the pastor's religious sensibilities. The conviction entered against Mr. Jones in the Alberta Court of Appeal was affirmed.

The criticism here of the courts' treatment of the claims made in these cases for accommodation of religious beliefs and practices (for example, in education), respect for religious tradition, and exemption from the general law is not necessarily that they are wrong in their legal conclusions, although in some instances they may be. The concern is that dressing up the issue as secular or primarily secular often means that insufficient consideration is given to the religious dimensions of the claim and why that dimension is so important to those seeking accommodation, respect, or exemption. Iain Benson has pointed to what he calls "metaphobia" among Canadian judges in religious rights cases – "an undue fear of metaphysics" (2000, 524). By this I understand him to mean the judges' recoiling from dealing openly with philosophical and theological positions on morality and ethics. I believe there are historical, political, social, and cultural explanations that have induced many contemporary Canadians, including judges, to be chary of entertaining religious doctrine and belief in developing the law. This is a country whose political alignments were constructed to cut across and downplay religious divisions. Moreover, one should not forget the judgmentalism, particularly in its more extreme forms, of which religious communities of various types have been guilty historically and which can still rear its ugly head. It is no surprise, considering the treatment that some religious communities have given them in the past, that many women and gays, lesbians, and transgendered persons worry about the application of restrictive religious beliefs and values in judging their place in Canadian society.

That having been said, it must also be recognized that religion is important to many Canadians. Moreover, we live in a society in which Judeo-Christian ideals and precepts have affected our cultural development and sense of who we are. Religion, while it has been invoked and continues to be invoked in parts of the world in the cause of oppression and violence, also has a capacity for emphasizing divine grace, humaneness, and inclusivity. Furthermore, its ethical systems often provide the basis for seeking a higher sense of virtue in human affairs, and in that sense they are worthy of consideration in both public and jural debate. Where to set the balance between the demands of secular civic virtue and religious virtue is clearly a question that continues to challenge our judges, and it has led to a tendency to stress the secular to the detriment of the religious. One cannot help feeling that, as one Canadian commentator, Paul Horwitz, has observed, we are left with the paradox that while liberal democracy "[cherishes] religious freedom as a valuable part of the freedom of any autonomous individual ... it fails in its inability to fully recognize that religion is (or, at least, may be) more than an individual choice on the individual's part" (1996, 23).

Religion and Public Education in Canada

Where does this discussion leave us in terms of the relationship between religion and public education in Canada, given that parents of a significant number of children wish their offspring to have the benefit of an education that relates to their religious beliefs and values? In the United States the wall of separation has ensured that there is effectively no financial support to denominational schools. Parents who wish to send their children to them must pay or otherwise find the fees (Shilton 1999, 206). As a result of judicial interpretation of section 93 of the *Constitution Act* in relation to the Charter, the present situation with public and religious education in Canada hangs uncomfortably between the American situation on the one hand and full or significant state funding for religious schools on the other. In some provinces – for example, in Alberta – religious and alternative schools are supported significantly by tax dollars and compete with the secular public schools (207). In others, Ontario being the prime example, only the section

93 minority denominational schools receive state funding along with the public system (ibid.). Those from other faith groups have to set up their own private schools while continuing to pay taxes to support public education.

Is the current asymmetrical pattern on funding for schools run by religious minorities inevitable, or is it possible or even desirable to inject some degree of uniformity into the system nationwide? Elizabeth Shilton (1999, 215-17) provides a measured and culturally sensitive response to this question. If uniformity is chosen, the American route is of course one option. Indeed, it may be attractive in some circles because of a desire not to balkanize the public system of education, and because of ostensible similarities between the constitutional systems in terms of religion. This approach, suggests Shilton, would probably be an unacceptable move in Canada, given our particular political and social culture that, like it or not, has attributed a greater civic value to religion in a constitutional sense (216-17). At the same time, maintaining the present constitutional limitations on claims to publicly funded religious education seems increasingly anachronistic to, and resented by, members of those religious faith traditions that lie outside the embrace of the original constitutional compact embodied in section 93. The sense of injustice to which exclusionary accommodations gives rise can be seen in the litigation that led to the decisions in the *Islamic Schools Federation* and *Bal* cases.

A greater degree of accommodation and consistency would be achieved by abolishing historical privileges granted to certain denominational schools, with stress being placed on the desirability of provinces funding other types of religious or alternative schools from the tax base. Shilton indicates that this decision would be in the realm of political rather than judicial creativity, and thus open to public debate and discussion (217). The notion of an education system fragmented along sectarian lines is troubling because it could well be socially divisive. However, the belief of deeply religious Canadians that the public education system is increasingly ineffectual in opening students' minds to the importance of moral sensibilities, to the spiritual dimension of human existence, and to civic responsibility speaks in favour of a more diverse system of fully funded education (216-17). Parents from minority religious cultures are unlikely to be impressed by attempts to come at the issue by teaching comparative religion in public schools, unless perhaps it is done in a vital and engaging way that treats the moral sensibilities of children as worthy of challenge and development (215-16). It is doubtful whether there are many such courses currently offered. The type of cultural pluralism that now exists in Canada, which belies the "melting pot" theories of the past, may require a degree of educational diversity. That is especially the case where the very survival of religious and spiritual traditions is concerned. For instance, it is difficult to deny the desirability of supporting Aboriginal schools in which First Nations students have the opportunity to relate learning to their culture, including its religions and strong sense of spirituality (Canada. Royal Commission on Aboriginal Peoples 1996, 442-44).

If encouraging some degree of diversity is the direction in which we move in this country, we must recognize that there are risks. They include the teaching of attitudes to life and towards other human beings that are narrow-minded and prejudicial. However, secular school systems have not invariably taught tolerance of and respect for diversity. Moreover, it is clear that religion can be a mind-expanding experience, a source of spiritual education, an inspiration in matters of social justice, and a beacon of humanitarianism. If, as on balance I think we need to, we should accept a pluralistic education system in this country, it must be understood by those who choose sectarian education that they cannot insulate themselves automatically from the demands of the secular law and its values. In particular, as consideration is given to their right to inculcate their religious values in their children, so they should respect that others in society may subscribe to different sets of religious values or to broader secular values of tolerance, and that social policy in a plural society should ideally be negotiated rather than dictated. In this context, negotiation means with all interested parties, secular as well as religious.[17]

Altogether apart from a constitutional right to support the education of religious minorities, I would also argue that courts should try to address more openly the religious dimensions of cases before them, showing greater acceptance of the power that religion exercises in the lives of people. Jane Epp Buckingham (2001) has found evidence of greater sensitivity in the Constitutional Court of South Africa's handling of religious belief and practice cases. She claims that that court has avoided tying its flag to religious freedom as a purely individual right, preferring to recognize the importance of religious belief at a communal level.[18] Buckingham suggests that the court led by Justice Albie Sachs has taken the lead in outlining the principles that should animate discussion in the courts about the role of the state in relation to religion. In his decision in *S. v. Lawrence,* Sachs said that South Africa

- is an open and democratic society with a non-sectarian state that guarantees freedom of worship;
- is respectful of and accommodatory towards, rather than hostile to or walled off from religion;
- acknowledges the multi-faith and multi-belief nature of the country;
- does not favour one religious creed or doctrinal truth above another, accepts the intensely personal nature of individual conscience and affirms the intrinsically voluntary and non-coerced character of belief;
- respects the rights of non-believers;

- does not impose orthodoxies of thought or require conformity of conduct in terms of any particular world view. (para. 148)[19]

Buckingham takes the Canadian jurisprudence – which has, she says, chosen not to expatiate on the limits of religious freedom and has suggested worrisome distinctions between religious belief and religious practice (2001, 478-89) – and contrasts it with the decision of the South African Constitutional Court in *Christian Education South Africa v. Minister of Education*. In this case, parents of children at independent Christian schools challenged as unconstitutional the outlawing of corporal punishment at schools under the country's *Schools Act*. The challengers cited biblical authority justifying the disciplining of children by parents. The act, they argued, infringed their constitutional rights to privacy, religious freedom, language and culture, and religious organizations and their right to establish independent schools. The minister argued to the contrary that corporal punishment infringed the childrens' right to equality, human dignity, and security of the person, protected in the constitution. The provision in the *Schools Act* was directed in part at the tradition of institutional violence under apartheid.

In its unanimous decision penned by Justice Sachs, the Constitutional Court recognized that religious freedom has both an individual and collective dimension, reflected in specific sections of the constitution, and that both had to be considered carefully if community identity was not to be compromised. The judge articulated the problem before him as the failure to accommodate the religious beliefs of the independent schools group. The clash of rights in such cases, he noted, was not easy as the competing interests belonged "to completely different conceptual and existential orders" (para. 33). Recognizing that the issue arose "in an open and democratic society based on human dignity, equality and freedom in which conscientious and religious freedom has to be regarded with appropriate seriousness," the problem was "how far such democracy can and must go in allowing members of religious communities to define for themselves which law they obey and which not" (para. 35). Such a society requires acceptance of certain basic norms and standards as binding. Believers could not expect automatic exemption from the law because of their beliefs, while "the state should, wherever reasonably possible, seek to avoid putting believers to extremely painful and intensely burdensome choices of either being true to their faith or else respectful of the law" (para. 35).

With this open and respectful statement of the nature of the balancing process, Justice Sachs examined the claim to religious freedom and the reasons for the statutory ban. He concluded that the prohibition did not infringe the rights of the parents to raise their children as they wished. They were not restrained by the *Schools Act* from using corporal punishment at home. In assessing the reasons for the prohibition, the judge stressed both the demands of the South African constitution and the various obligations of the country under international conventions relating to the rights of the child and the elimination of intolerance and discrimination based on religion. In the end, the claim of Christian Education South Africa was denied as the parents' right to religious freedom was not compromised by legislation that prevented them from delegating to teachers the power of administering corporal punishment.

What is notable about this judgment is the importance Justice Sachs attached to the place of religious belief and experience in the life of believers, and to the need, as far as is reasonably possible, to accommodate those beliefs in the nonsectarian state while at the same time giving full, serious, and equal consideration to the conflicting right, in this case the right of children to be protected from violence. I would agree with Buckingham (2001, 496) that the record of the Canadian courts, led by the Supreme Court of Canada, with its twists and turns particularly in matters of religion and education, albeit over a longer period, is less intellectually open, suggests a basic judicial fear about responding sensitively but frankly to claims of religious freedom, and tends instinctively to look for refuge in secular principles that are not invariably articulated. It is true that the South African constitution is more detailed and extensive in its statement of constitutional rights and is more explicitly committed to the protection of group rights in matters of religion and culture than the Charter, and thus provides a firmer basis for the sort of analysis the Constitutional Court gave to this clash of rights (466-68). Moreover, difficult questions remain over how far the South African courts will go in setting limits to practices that offend other sections of the constitution but are matters of belief for religious communities (497). The Constitutional Court was able to circumvent the more general issue of parental rights of physical chastisement in this case. Nevertheless, in comparison, the Canadian courts have withdrawn, to a significant extent, from the promise contained in that part of Justice Dickson's decision in *Big M Drug Mart* that appeared to take a liberal approach to interpretation of religious belief and practice, and in the process have prevented themselves from exploring the broader dimensions of religious claims being made and their legitimacy, let alone whether the Charter could be interpreted with greater concern for the protection of associational and communal interests (497-99).

What is most significant about the South African cases, and in particular the position taken by Justice Sachs, is Sachs' belief that where religious rights and other rights protected by the constitution conflict, the rights and the interests they protect are important issues for careful and sensitive analysis and, where appropriate, critique. As Buckingham (499) notes, "Justice Sachs elucidated the significance of religion both in the lives of adherents and in broader society. He recognized that there is both a private and a public dimension to religion, demonstrating that religion cannot be privatized without impinging on religious freedom. Religion also has both individual and collective aspects that must be respected. Sachs J. further identified that there is no definitive line between what is religious and what is secular." He was prepared to acknowledge that Christian parents who are members of the applicant organization consider physical discipline of children a religious exercise. Buckingham adds that no Canadian court has "affirmed the nature and content of religion in Canada with this kind of vigour" (499-500).[20]

Is it conceivable that Canadian courts, including the Supreme Court of Canada, could change direction in matters of freedom and religion and adopt a more open and serious approach to claims being made in the name of religious belief and practice? Several of the Supreme Court of Canada decisions, inspired in part by the liberal segments of *Big M Drug Mart* that dealt with protecting religious minorities from discrimination in employment and with employees' claims that they had a right to dress in accordance with their religious beliefs, already point in this direction. That approach is reflected in several lower-court decisions, such as that in the recent *Beauchemin v. Blainville,* which struck down an anti-soliciting bylaw directed at Jehovah's Witness visitations. The judgment demonstrates a remarkably open assessment of the basic beliefs of the Witnesses and how visitations reflect their reading of the mission of the earliest Christians.

An encouraging reconciliatory approach to this issue of conflict between religious freedom and secular values is one taken by Benjamin Berger (2002). Berger accepts that freedom of religion and the articulation of religious beliefs and practices are worthy of serious consideration by courts because of their connection with our culture and the importance of the place of religion in the lives of a sizable number of Canadians (46-48). However, he also considers it important that due consideration be given to important secular values in a pluralistic society like Canada's, which draws together a complex of religious believers, Christian and non-Christian, as well as non-believers. He asserts that the Supreme Court has endeavoured, in a line of decisions beginning with *Big M Drug Mart,* to isolate a modest set of civic values, including human dignity, autonomy, and security, that are necessary to a complex, pluralist society and against which religious beliefs and practices can be judged when they seem to conflict with the rights of individuals or groups that do not share those beliefs and practices (49-62). Drawing on philosopher Charles Taylor's description of value clashes in a pluralist society as involving "a language of perspicuous contrast" (1985, 125-26), Berger argues that the Supreme Court has used this sort of linguistic tension to describe the values in conflict in several of its decisions on religious freedom (2002, 52-53). It has sought, he suggests, to balance against claims made to freedom of religion a clear articulation of the other interests at stake – dignity, autonomy, and security (including public safety, order, and health) – that demand respect in a pluralist democracy. In substance, this is not far removed from the approach taken by Justice Sachs, although it probably understates the communal side of the rights equation. I would also argue that the language used by the Supreme Court of Canada and lower courts in several decisions, especially those related to minority religious education issues, betrays a less than open and frank engagement of the religious side of the argument, a failure to address the reasonable limits of what can be described as religious belief, and a tendency to treat secular values as inherently prescriptive. Courts in what Justice Sachs has felicitously described as "non-sectarian societies" that are also pluralist in makeup are called upon to balance the claims of believers against those of other believers and nonbelievers. This cannot be done in a democratic society simply by giving automatic primacy to one or the other interest. It requires an articulation of the values that are necessary to and that undergird a "civil society," as Berger describes the democratic, pluralist state, and it requires these values be used to evaluate conflicting claims of right, including the religious (51). At the same time, a full canvassing of the character and dimensions of the claim to religious freedom and conscience should be made respectfully, recognizing its strong hold on the minds of believers, and with an impulse to accommodate the belief or practice where that is possible given the plural character of the society.

In the final analysis, I would suggest that the sort of matrix for balancing freedom of religion against competing rights suggested by Justice Sachs and Benjamin Berger embodies the practical considerations that need to animate the litigation process and is openly sensitive to and respectful of the place of religious faith within, rather than outside, the community. This is not to suggest that Canadian judges should become the arbiters of religious belief and practice. In most instances they will not be equipped to take on such a role, and in any event will be chary of it. What I am suggesting, however, is that, subject to the evidence led, the judges treat the religious arguments openly in as respectful and engaged a manner as is possible and appropriate, recognize the importance that religion plays in the life of individuals and communities, endeavour to satisfy themselves that the claims made for the religious belief or practice are warranted, and set those beliefs and practices alongside the secular considerations that infuse the Charter and the constitutional values that underlie it. There is no magic wand that can be waved to remove the tensions between the demands of religion and secular society. What we can hope for is that the tensions will be openly recognized and fairly mediated.

Notes

1 See *R. v. Ellison,* discussed in Kaplan (1989, 131-39); *Donald v. Hamilton Board of Education.*
2 See also *School Act* Amendments, S.A. 1944, c. 46, s. 9.
3 United States *Bill of Rights,* First Amendment.
4 1867, 30 and 31 Vict., c. 3, reprinted in R.S.C. 1985, Append. II, No. 5.
5 By the *Quebec Act* (1774, 14 Geo. III, c. 83), Roman Catholics secured freedom to exercise their religion. The *Religious Freedom Act* (1852, 14 and 15 Vict., c. 175 (Canada)), still in effect (R.S.O. 1990, c. R-22) established freedom of worship.
6 There is a tendency in some contemporary literature on the interface between law and religion to overemphasize the legal dimensions of religious tolerance before 1960, when the *Canadian Bill of Rights* was enacted (S.C. 1960, c. 44). See D.M. Brown (2000, 552-58).
7 See *Common Schools Act,* 1871 S.N.B., c. 21.
8 *Manitoba Act,* S.C. 1870, c. 3, s. 22.
9 See *Boucher v. The King, Saumur v. Quebec, Chaput v. Romain,* and *Roncarelli v. Duplessis.*
10 See s. 93.
11 In the process the court seems to have approved of a much earlier decision of the Judicial Committee of the Privy Council, *Hirsch v. Protestant School Board of Montreal.*
12 See *Zylberberg,* 599. Shilton notes further that in *Elgin County,* as the court had concluded that the regulation allowing religious instruction in schools and the local curricula based on it amounted to indoctrination in the Christian faith, "the more complex issue of whether opportunities for multifaith education within the school curriculum would be unconstitutional therefore did not arise" (1999, 212).
13 R.R.O. 1990, Reg. 298, ss. 28-29.
14 The changes were contained in Policy Memorandum 112, issued 6 December 1990.
15 The *Hofer* case is reported at (1992), 97 D.L.R. (4th) 17 (S.C.C.). In his recent book, Esau (2004) suggests that Canadian courts have in fact become increasingly enmeshed in a series of rancorous Hutterite disputes without any positive effects to show for it.
16 See *Edwards Books and Art v. The Queen.* In this case the Supreme Court of Canada invoked section 1 of the Charter to save the legislation, even though the court determined that Ontario legislation limiting shopping on Sundays interfered with the freedom of religion of people whose Sabbath was another day of the week and who wished to trade on Sundays. The court concluded that the legislation was secular in nature; that is, it was designed to provide for a nonreligious statutory day of rest. If the purpose had been religious and had unfairly affected other religious groups, it would have been open to being struck down under the Charter. However, since its purpose was secular, its unequal burden between religious groups was irrelevant. Furthermore, as the burden to plaintiffs here related to their religious tenets, it provided no basis for inequality with nonreligious persons.
17 Canada has been vigilant in developing law that seeks to penalize those who would preach hatred and ethnic supremacy, including where that is done under a claim of religious belief and is directed against particular faith traditions, in this case Judaism. This law has been successfully deployed, as the decisions of the Supreme Court of Canada in *R. v. Keegstra* and *Ross v. Moncton District School Board* demonstrate, although it might well be ineffectual where the discriminatory messages are more subtle.
18 Buckingham argues that despite the promise for tolerance implied in Justice Dickson's judgment in *R. v. Big M Drug Mart,* he undermined that promise by describing religious freedom in individualistic terms.
19 Buckingham notes that Albie Sachs "was a crusader against apartheid and was the victim of a letter bomb during the apartheid years." He then went off to Harvard and "distinguished himself as a constitutional scholar." She continues: "He wrote two accessible books on human rights in post-apartheid South Africa, both of which are supportive of religion and religious expression" (2001, 489n92; see Sachs 1992, 2000).
20 I find myself in disagreement with Buckingham's conclusion that the judgment "gives full effect to the religious practices of parents as well as complete protection to children" (2001, 495). That is only true if we are talking of institutional corporal punishment. The decision does nothing to limit corporal punishment within the family setting.

References

Books, Articles, and Public Documents

Anctil, Pierre. 1992. Interlude of Hostility: Judeo-Christian Relations in Quebec in the Inter-war Period, 1919-39. In *Anti-Semitism in Canada: History and Interpretation,* ed. Alan Davies, 135-65. Waterloo, ON: Wilfrid Laurier University Press.

Anderson, James. 1918. *The Education of the New Canadian: A Treatise on Canada's Greatest Education Problem.* London: J.M. Dent.

Benson, Iain T. 2000. Notes towards a (Re)definition of the "Secular." *UBC Law Review* 33:519-49.

Berger, Benjamin. 2002. The Limits of Belief: Freedom of Religion, Secularism and the Liberal State. *Canadian Journal of Law and Society* 17:39-68.

Brown, David M. 2000. Freedom from or Freedom for? Religion as a Case Study in Defining the Content of Charter Rights. *UBC Law Review* 33:551-615.

Brown, Michael. 1992. From Stereotype to Scapegoat: Anti-Jewish Sentiment in French Canada from Confederation to World War I. In *Anti-Semitism in Canada: History and Interpretation,* ed. Alan Davies, 39-66. Waterloo, ON: Wilfrid Laurier University Press.

Brown, Robert Craig, and Ramsay Cook. 1974. *Canada 1896-1921: A Nation Transformed.* Toronto: McClelland and Stewart.

Buckingham, Jane Epp. 2001. Caesar and God: Limits to Religious Freedom in Canada and South Africa. *Supreme Court Law Review* 15:461-501.

Canada. Royal Commission on Aboriginal Peoples. 1996. *Gathering Strength.* Vol. 3. Ottawa: Ministry of Supply and Services.

Canadian Charter of Rights and Freedoms, Part I of the *Constitution Act, 1982,* being Schedule B to the *Canada Act 1982* (U.K.), 1982, c. 11.

Constitution Act, 1982, being Schedule B to the *Canada Act 1982* (U.K.), 1982, c. 11.

Coté, Pauline. 1991. *Religious Minorities and the Charter of Rights and Freedoms in Canada: A Case Survey.* Cahier 91-06.

Enns, Adolph. 1980. The Public School Crisis among the Mennonites in Saskatchewan 1916-25. In *Mennonite Images,* ed. Harry Loewen, 73-81. Winnipeg: Hyperion Press.

Esau, Alvin. 1999. Communal Property and Freedom of Religion: *Lakeside Colony of Hutterian Brethren v. Hofer.* In *Religious Conscience, the State and the Law: Historical Contexts and Contemporary Significance,* ed. John McLaren and Harold Coward, 97-116. Albany, NY: SUNY Press.

–. 2004. *The Court and Colonies: The Litigation of Hutterite Church Disputes.* Vancouver: UBC Press.

Horwitz, Paul. 1996. The Sources and Limits of Freedom of Religion in a Liberal Democracy: Section 2(a) and Beyond. *University of Toronto Faculty of Law Review* 54:1-64.

Janzen, William. 1990. *The Limits of Liberty: The Experience of Mennonite, Hutterite and Doukhobor Communities in Canada.* Toronto: University of Toronto Press.

Kaplan, William. 1989. *State and Salvation: The Jehovah's Witnesses and Their Fight for Civil Rights.* Toronto: University of Toronto Press.

McLaren, John. 1995a. The Strange Case of Peter Verigin II. *Canadian Ethnic Studies* 27: 95-130.

–. 1995b. Creating "Slaves of Satan" or "New Canadians"? The Law, Education and the Socialization of Doukhobor Children, 1911-1935. In *Essays in the History of Canadian Law, Vol. 6: British Columbia and the Yukon,* ed. Hamar Foster and John McLaren, 352-85. Toronto: Osgoode Society.

–. 1999. The Doukhobor Belief in Individual Faith and Conscience and the Demands of the Secular State. In *Religious Conscience, the State and the Law: Historical Contexts and Contemporary Significance,* ed. John McLaren and Harold Coward, 117-35. Albany, NY: SUNY Press.

–. 2002. The State, Child Snatching and the Law: The Seizure and Indoctrination of Sons of Freedom Children in British Columbia, 1950-60. In *Regulating Lives: Historical Essays on the State, Society, the Individual and the Law,* ed. John McLaren, Robert Menzies, and Dorothy Chunn, 259-93. Vancouver: UBC Press.

Miller, J.R. 1996. *Shingwauk's Vision: A History of Native Residential Schools.* Toronto: University of Toronto Press.

Milloy, John S. 1999. *A National Crime: The Canadian Government and the Residential School System 1879 to 1986.* Winnipeg: University of Manitoba Press.

Morton, W.L. 1964. *The Critical Years: The Union of British North America, 1857-1873.* Toronto: McClelland and Stewart.

Ontario Education Act, R.R.O. 1980, Reg. 262, s. 28 (am. O. Reg. 617/81, s. 21; O. Reg. 6/89).

Roy, Patricia. 1989. *A Whiteman's Province: British Columbia Politicians and Chinese and Japanese Immigrants, 1858-1914.* Vancouver: UBC Press.

Sachs, A. 1992. *Advancing Human Rights in South Africa.* Capetown: Oxford University Press.

–. 2000. *Protecting Human Rights in a New South Africa.* Capetown: Oxford University Press.

Shilton, Elizabeth J. 1999. Religion and Public Education in Canada after the Charter. In *Religious Conscience, the State and the Law: Historical Contexts and Contemporary Significance,* ed. John McLaren and Harold Coward, 206-23. Albany, NY: SUNY Press.

Speisman, Stephen. 1992. Anti-Semitism in Ontario: The Twentieth Century. In *Anti-Semitism in Canada: History and Interpretation,* ed. Alan Davies, 113-33. Waterloo, ON: Wilfrid Laurier University Press.

Sutherland, Neil. 1976. *Children in Canadian Society: Framing the Twentieth Century Consensus.* Toronto: University of Toronto Press.

Taylor, Charles. 1985. Understanding and Ethnocentricity. In *Philosophy and the Human Sciences: Philosophical Papers 2,* 116-33. Cambridge: Cambridge University Press.

Waite, P.B. 1971. *Canada 1874-1896: Arduous Destiny.* Toronto: McClelland and Stewart.

Woodcock, George, and Ivan Avakumovic. 1968. *The Doukhobors.* London: Faber and Faber.

Woodsworth, James S. 1972. *Strangers at Our Gates.* Toronto: University of Toronto. Reprint of 1909 original.

Youngblood Henderson, James. 1999. The Struggle to Preserve Aboriginal Spiritual Teachings and Practice. In *Religious Conscience, the State and the Law: Historical Contexts and Contemporary Significance,* ed. John McLaren and Harold Coward, 168-88. Albany, NY: SUNY Press.

Cases

Adler v. The Queen (1996), 140 D.L.R. (4th) 385, (SCC) [*Adler*].

Bal v. Attorney General of Ontario (1994), 21 O.R. (3d) 682 (Gen. Div.), affirmed (1997), 101 O.A.C. 219 (C.A.) [*Bal*].

Beauchemin v. Blainville (2001), Q.J. No. 1503 (S.C.) (Q.L.).

Bill 30 Reference, [1987] 1 S.C.R. 1148, upholding (1986), 53 O.R. (2d) 513 (C.A.).

Boucher v. The King, [1951] S.C.R. 265.

Chaput v. Romain (1955), 1 D.L.R. (2d) 241, (SCC).

Christian Education South Africa v. Minister of Education (2000) 4 S.A. 757, 2000 (10) B.C.L.R. 1051 (C.C.).

City of Winnipeg v. Barrett and Logan (1892), A.C. 445 (P.C. Canada).

Donald v. Hamilton Board of Education (1944), 4 D.L.R. 227 (H.C.), rev'd (1945) O.R. 518 (C.A.).

Edwards Books and Art v. The Queen, [1986] 2 S.C.R. 770.

Everson v. Board of Education, 330 U.S. 1 (1947).

Hirsch v. Protestant School Board of Montreal (1928), 1 D.L.R. 1041 (P.C. Canada).

Islamic Schools Federation of Ontario v. Ottawa Board of Education (1997), 145 D.L.R. (4th) 659 (Ont. Gen. Div) [*Islamic Schools Federation*].

Jones v. The Queen, [1986] 2 S.C.R. 284.

Perepelkin v. Superintendent of Child Welfare (No. 2) (1957), 23 W.W.R. 592 (B.C.C.A.) [*Perepelkin*].

R. v. Big M Drug Mart, [1985] 1 S.C.R. 295; (1985), 18 D.L.R. (4th) 321 (SCC) [*Big M Drug Mart*].

R. v. Keegstra, [1995] 2 S.C.R. 381.

Re Corporation of the Canadian Civil Liberties Association and the Minister of Education (1990), 65 D.L.R. (4th) 1 (Ont. C.A.) [*Elgin County*].

Re Zylberberg et al. and the Director of the Sudbury Board Education (1988), 52 D.L.R. (4th) 577 (Ont. C.A.) [*Zylberberg*].

Roncarelli v. Duplessis, [1959] S.C.R. 121.

Ross v. Moncton District School Board, [1996] 1 S.C.R. 825.

S. v. Lawrence (1997), (1) B.C.L.R. 1348 (C.C.).

Saumur v. Quebec, [1953] 2 S.C.R. 299.

Ruman v. Board of Trustees of Lethbridge School District (1944), 1 D.L.R. 360 (Alta S.C.T.D.).

Trustees of the Ottawa Separate School Board v. Mackell (1917), A.C. 62 (P.C. Can).

West Virginia State Board of Education v. Barnette, 319 U.S. 624 (1943).

9
The Irreducibly Religious Content of Freedom of Religion
Jeremy Webber

There has been a tendency, in recent times, to define freedom of religion in terms that do not attach particular value to religious belief – that are neutral, in other words, between religion and irreligion. In this chapter I explore the problems inherent in a secularized definition of freedom of religion. I will not focus on the effects of such a definition on the place of religion in public life, as several recent commentators have done (e.g., Carter 1993; Neuhaus 1986; Perry 1988). Rather, I will focus on the incoherence and instability of such a definition. I argue that if freedom of religion is genuinely concerned with religion's protection rather than its active discouragement (which I will assume rather than argue),[1] and if freedom of religion extends beyond the protection of one's inmost thoughts to include any dimension of religious practice, then the freedom cannot be separated from the affirmative valuing of religious belief. That in turn requires that one consider, in the interpretive process, what one values about religion, an exercise that inevitably requires that one make substantive judgments about the nature and content of religious commitment.

This is what is meant, in the title of this chapter, by the "irreducibly religious content" of freedom of religion. Freedom of religion cannot be secularized so that it is entirely neutral between belief and unbelief. The interpretation and application of the right necessarily involve acknowledging, contemplating, and seeking to protect distinctively religious commitments. Freedom of religion carries with it, then, a much richer set of normative judgments than is often recognized. An idea of neutrality does play an important part in the right. Freedom of religion requires that one seek to eliminate sectarianism from the state and that one preserve the sanctity of conscience exempt from coercion. But one ostensibly easy way of achieving neutrality is foreclosed: the state cannot be indifferent to the value of religious commitment without departing substantially from the very idea of protecting religious freedom. The pursuit of neutrality becomes at once more complex, more difficult – and more interesting.

The argument proceeds in four stages. The first charts, in schematic fashion, three concerns underlying different conceptions of freedom of religion, the development through which explains, to some extent, the historical evolution towards a secularized definition of the right. The second explores the problems inherent in two such definitions of freedom of religion: one that treats that freedom as merely a special case of the freedom to choose one's conception of the good; the other that treats it as a special case of a secular freedom of conscience. The former fails to account sufficiently for the singling out of religion. The latter ignores the extent to which conscientious beliefs are themselves defined by analogy to religious belief; this suggests that freedom of religion is the primary category, conscience the derivative. The third section then describes how the aspiration to neutrality may be reconceived once one takes seriously the irreducibly religious content of freedom of religion. That realization pushes one towards a conception of neutrality that emphasizes process and modesty in the articulation of the right. Freedom of religion takes the form of a work in progress, starting from an historical insight into the significance and individuality of faith and then extending outwards to embrace a broader range of religious and religious-like commitments, as the deepening encounter with those phenomena convinces one of similarities. Finally, in the fourth and concluding section, I will briefly address the potential for secularism in public life.

Secularism and Freedom of Religion

How then did freedom of religion come to be conceived in secular terms, that is, in a manner that avoided any claim that religious belief had intrinsic value? That evolution is best understood by describing a progression through three concerns underlying different conceptions of the freedom.

The first and primordial concern is familiar: the prevention of direct coercion, exercised over individuals, in matters of religious belief. In Canada, Chief Justice Dickson emphasized this concern in *R. v. Big M Drug Mart* (1985) when he said: "The essence of the concept of freedom of religion is the right to entertain such religious beliefs as a person chooses, the right to declare religious beliefs openly and without fear of hindrance or reprisal, and the right to manifest religious belief by worship and practice or by teaching and dissemination ... Freedom can primarily be characterized by the absence of coercion or constraint" (paras. 94-95). A theological justification is sometimes provided for the renunciation of coercion: one preserves the free operation of conscience so that religious conviction can be true conviction, grounded in the individual's willing adherence. But the recognition of freedom of religion does not depend on a theological justification. For many, the right derives simply from the force of religious belief and the desirability of maintaining a modus vivendi among contending religions.

In recent years the primordial concern with coercion has been directed towards indirect, as well as direct, interference with religious belief. This extension is sometimes expressed in terms of a distinction between religious beliefs and religious practices. Only the former are fully protected; the latter are subject to less protection, perhaps none. The distinction is easily overdrawn. The holding of belief blends imperceptibly into its manifestation. The suppression or constriction of the latter is usually the means taken to influence the former. The protection of belief necessarily extends to some aspects of action (Tribe 1988, 1183-85).

The critical issue is not the maintenance of an indistinct line between belief and action, but the extent to which government policies adopted for secular purposes and in secular form, with no religious intent, should nevertheless be modified in order to minimize their impact on religious profession and practice (ibid.). It concerns the right of religious minorities to exemptions from the ordinary application of the law when that law conflicts with religious injunctions. This has been the battleground in many recent debates over religious freedom. Note that its principal rationale remains the avoidance of coercion in matters of faith. Its innovation lies in the extension of protection so that it guards not only against deliberate assaults on religion, but also against inadvertent and indirect effects of government power.[2] That doesn't make this form of protection any less controversial. Given religious diversity, the extensive strictures of some faiths, the patterns of authority in some religious communities, and the desire to pursue purposes, affirm values, and build community at the level of society as a whole, the demand for religious accommodation can give rise to very difficult issues indeed. In fact, the U.S. Supreme Court has recently retreated from the view that the United States' constitutional guarantees protect against the indirect impact of the law on religious practice if the law is neutral and of general application *(City of Boerne v. Flores; Employment Div. v. Smith).*

The desire to eliminate coercion in matters of religious belief has contributed to another focus of the freedom: the disestablishment of religion. But here one begins to see the clear emergence of the second concern driving the freedom: the desire to achieve equality in citizens' adherence to the state, regardless of religion, or, to put it another way, the desire to achieve a more inclusive citizenship in which no religion is given preference. The transition to this second rationale is also reflected in Dickson's reasons in *Big M Drug Mart* (1985): "The theological content of the [*Lord's Day Act*] remains as a subtle and constant reminder to religious minorities within the country of their differences with, and alienation from, the dominant religious culture ... The protection of one religion and the concomitant non-protection of others imports disparate impact destructive of the religious freedom of the collectivity" (paras. 97-98).[3]

This quotation combines the language of citizenship with, in the last sentence, echoes of coercion. The connection between disestablishment and coercion was patent when establishment meant that members of society were compelled to observe the state religion. It has become much less obvious in recent years, as disestablishment has come to mean the exclusion of religious symbols and observances (and arguments?)[4] from state proceedings. Such breadth has little to do with freedom from religious oppression (unless one adopts a very capacious definition of coercion). It is concerned more with achieving equality in individuals' sense of belonging. Its goal is equal citizenship, without distinction in the state's appeal to individuals of different faiths.

Note that both these rationales – freedom from religious coercion and equality of citizenship regardless of religion – need not require the complete exclusion of religious observance from the public sphere. The first is entirely compatible with the presence of religious forms and symbols, as long as professions of faith are not required from those belonging to minority religions. The second is also consistent with the presence of religious forms and symbols, as long as the symbolism is, as a matter of fact, broadly shared in society. There is no principled exclusion of religion; rather, the focus is on avoiding differential or partial recognition. This reminds us that a commitment to religious toleration – even an extensive commitment, including hostility to certain forms of establishment – need not require the complete exclusion of religion from the state.

As a society becomes more diverse, however, it becomes much more difficult to find religious forms around which the population can coalesce. The inclusion of a variety of religious observances may be sufficient to satisfy the second rationale in some societies, but if the demand for equal representation is great – and if citizens are attentive to fine discriminations – such accommodations can be difficult to maintain. They require a finely calibrated ordering of symbols. In an age of mobility, they require frequent adjustment. The most stable accommodation, then – one that ostensibly eliminates all perception of bias on the part of the state – may be a complete renunciation of religious forms. This step is consonant with the tendency now dominant within liberalism to insist that government remain agnostic about ends and allow citizens to define the good as they see fit. This is the third and final concern driving the interpretation of freedom of religion. In this view, the state should remain absolutely neutral with respect to religious belief, for religion is quintessentially about the definition of the good. The state should leave religion to individuals, not tip the scales in anyone's favour. And with this argument, a concern for nonbelievers becomes forcefully conjoined to the concern with religious dissent. Nonbelievers also have a right to the state's neutrality with respect to the good, including neutrality with respect to nonreligious or even anti-religious conceptions of the good. In this view, freedom of religion must include freedom from religion.

The history of freedom of religion therefore reveals the conjunction of three clearly distinguishable values associated with the freedom, leading towards an increasingly secular definition: (1) the primordial value of freedom from religious coercion; (2) a commitment to equality of belonging, equality of citizenship, without regard to religious difference; and (3) a commitment to the state's neutrality with respect to conceptions of the good. Each has its own ramifications. It is not necessary to accept all three. It is possible to have a genuine commitment to freedom of religion that accepts the first value but not the second or third, or that accepts the first and second but not the third.

There has, however, been a tendency under the *Canadian Charter of Rights and Freedoms* to accept all three, including the last. Consequently, freedom of religion comes to require neutrality not only between religions, but also between religion and irreligion. The very framing of the right supports this tendency. In a single phrase, section 2(a) of the Charter couples freedom of religion with the ostensibly secular value of freedom of conscience.[5] Freedom of religion might be seen, then, as simply a special case of that broader freedom of conscience. In this view, there is nothing distinctively religious about freedom of religion. The essential right is freedom of conscience. The reference to religion becomes, at the limit, an historical artefact.

This approach has great appeal, for it promises straightforward and simple neutrality. Such an interpretation sidesteps religious controversy, offers complete immunity from sectarian partiality, negates any suggestion that a particular vision of the good is being advanced, and purports to be open to people of any religious or irreligious persuasion as long as they are willing to keep their religion out of the public sphere. But does it do justice to freedom of religion?

The Irreducibly Religious Nature of Freedom of Religion

The principal candidate for a fully secularized concept of freedom of religion is one founded on freedom of conscience. Before addressing conscience directly, however, it is worth exploring a still more general approach to rights that often lurks within these debates, one that considers the various freedoms in the Charter to be but particular expressions of a comprehensive, generic theory of liberty. In this view, freedoms are about the sovereignty of individual choice. The rights are interpreted, above all, to affirm and preserve that capacity to choose. Taking this approach, freedom of religion is much more about freedom than it is about religion.

That approach exercises a subtle, pervasive, often subterranean influence on the interpretation of rights by some judges and commentators. It has been influential in a number of judgments under the *Canadian Charter of Rights and Freedoms,* although it is not yet a dominating presence. It is especially apparent in some Canadian judges' tendency to interpret Charter rights as including their negatives. Thus, freedom of association might include the freedom not to associate, for it is the freedom, not the association, that is fundamental. Similarly, the right to "life, liberty and security of the person" in section 7 of the Charter might include the right to die. Choice, not the particular values identified, is the critical element. Freedom of religion might be framed in analogous form. The freedom would therefore comprise not merely the right to hold and practise a religion, but the right to be free from religion. The law might protect religious values, but it would do so only on a level equivalent to nonreligious values (see, for example, McConnell and Posner 1989).

The Supreme Court of Canada has yet to embrace this vision squarely as its framework for interpreting Charter rights. In *Rodriguez v. British Columbia (Attorney General)* it rejected the argument that "the right to life, liberty and security of the person" includes the right to die. The court held (by a narrow majority) that section 7 places an affirmative value on life. Similarly, although the court has concluded (by a majority, not unanimously) that freedom of association includes a right not to associate, it also decided that the negative dimension of the freedom – the right to be free from association – is subject to internal limitations. Some forms of forced democratic association are consistent with the right precisely because of the value attached to collaboration, which is seen to be of the essence of the right. Justice L'Heureux-Dubé maintained a still stronger line, arguing that there was no constitutional right to refrain from association precisely because the Charter's freedom is grounded on the affirmative value of association *(Lavigne v. OPSEU; R. v. Advance Cutting and Coring Ltd.)*.

These conclusions – which implicitly or explicitly affirm that the Charter's freedoms are not neutral as to their elements but rather embody substantive moral commitments – are consistent with recent rejections of a purely procedural liberalism (Galston 1991; Gutmann 1999; Macedo 1999; Raz 1982; Taylor 1985a and 1995, especially 249). These critics have demonstrated that liberalism involves richer commitments, and a richer sense of human personality and human good, than the procedural liberals have traditionally acknowledged. They argue that commitments of this kind are inherent in the procedural liberals' own work, even though procedural liberals may be oblivious to them. The critics seek, in short, to recapture liberalism as a fighting creed: liberalism may value individual autonomy; it may defend, fiercely, a protected sphere of individual choice; but that defence is itself justified on the basis of a rich conception of the human person, which shapes the essence of the rights protected. The argument may be extended to freedom of religion, which is only intelligible if it is approached in similar spirit.

One way of making this argument is to note the importance of context to the protection of freedom of choice in any system of constitutional guarantees. Constitutions do not protect any decision, on any grounds, for any ends.[6] They protect particular sets of choices in particular contexts. Constitutions do not protect "freedom" with no adjectives or qualifiers. They protect "freedom of religion," "freedom of association," "freedom of expression," and so on. Why in those contexts and not others? The reason must have something to do with the distinctive values implicated in those contexts. And this means that the right can only be defined by inquiring into those values and acting upon them. An emphasis on the freedom in freedom of religion, without consideration of those distinctive values, is not merely simplistic; it is nonsense.

In freedom of religion, the right must be defined in relation to the distinctive value of religious belief – the value that lies behind the singling out of religion for special protection. This can be seen (despite the authors' best efforts) in an article by Michael W. McConnell and Richard Posner (1989), in which they attempt to apply economic analysis to religious freedom. Their purpose is to define freedom of religion in entirely neutral terms, neutral not only among religions, but also between religious and nonreligious alternatives. They seek to eliminate both incentives and disincentives to religion, expressly treating the "creed of non-belief" as equivalent to religious creeds (5). They want government to have no impact "upon individual choice with respect to religion" and to adopt a standard by which government "treats competing activities that are secular the same way it treats religious activities" (10-12).[7] Adopting such a standard, they suggest, brings the two clauses of the American guarantee of freedom of religion – the "establishment clause" and the "free exercise clause" – into harmony: the former forbids action that favours religion, the latter forbids action that disfavours it (33).[8]

But they are unable to treat secular and religious activities identically and make any sense whatever of the constitutional guarantees. Instead, they implicitly treat religious practice as carrying special value, especially when they discuss particular cases. This is clear when they deal with the free exercise clause – the constitutional prohibition on state action that impairs the free exercise of religion. There, they accept that religious exemptions are necessary from some laws, even laws that have a purely secular purpose. Examples they accept include "regulations prohibiting polygamy, requiring as a condition of receiving unemployment benefits that the unemployed person be willing to work on Saturdays, and prohibiting the covering of one's head while playing interscholastic basketball." In each case, they say, the rule at issue "arbitrarily imposes greater costs on religious than on comparable non-religious activities" (34-35). But those "greater costs" are entirely a function of the value McConnell and Posner attach to religious activities. The greater costs exist because McConnell and Posner believe that a Seventh-Day Adventist's interest in observing his or her Sabbath is more important than the interest of a watcher of college football, of a person for whom Saturday is a day for family, of a person for whom Saturday is the only day on which he or she can visit an elderly relative. Nor can McConnell and Posner argue that they are merely acting on their best estimate of the Seventh-Day Adventist's subjective valuation of his or her preferences, by weighing that person's religiously based preferences and finding them to be more strongly held than secular preferences. There is no serious attempt to inquire into that person's preferences, and, indeed, no opportunity to do so given that the sole constitutional basis for exemption is on religious grounds. There is no argument that secular preferences should prevail if they are held with a vigour comparable to religious belief. There is no protection of choice regardless of its religious or secular content. The super-ordinate value of religious observance is assumed.

Indeed, McConnell and Posner's argument leads them very close to acknowledging this. After noting that only religious reasons for refusing to work are protected, they ultimately concede (in more convoluted language than I will reproduce here, the very convolutions revealing the difficulty the concession poses for their project) that "a religious exemption would not violate the Establishment Clause merely because it protected the exercise of religion more than other choices. Neutrality toward religion need not imply neutrality toward religious freedom" (38).[9] What can this mean but that neutrality does not extend to the value of religious freedom itself when it is compared to other forms of freedom? *Religious* freedom has special value. In the words of Justice Brennan in the United States Supreme Court (*Marsh v. Chambers*, 812), "in one important respect, the Constitution is *not* neutral on the subject of religion: Under the Free Exercise Clause, religiously motivated claims of conscience may give rise to constitutional rights that other strongly held beliefs do not."[10]

This willingness to countenance exemptions has led to strong criticisms of McConnell and Posner on the basis that they are not *sufficiently* neutral, that they covertly favour religion. Critics say that they claim complete neutrality only to advocate a stronger immunization of religious institutions from state regulation (for example, see Eisgruber and Sager 1997, 117-19). There is some justice in these criticisms. Support for religious exemptions only makes sense in the context of a special valuing of religious commitments, and the merits of particular exemptions can only be assessed by expressly considering the religious claim. Take an example McConnell and Posner themselves use: opposition to the construction of a forestry road on the basis that it would severely damage a site sacred to a First Nation. There is no common scale along which religious and secular interests can be arrayed. The only way to resolve the dispute (if one takes religious interests to be at all worthy of accommodation) is to inquire into the spiritual significance of the place for the First Nation, weigh the force of that interest by attempting to understand the interest in its own terms and by attempting to translate that interest into terms more familiar to the decision maker, consider the importance of the governmental interest, and then decide what degree of deference is due to a religious interest that must remain, in great measure, unfathomable. This is a substantive exercise, one that forces the decision maker to consider the nature and significance of religious belief. Any attempt to approach this "neutrally" in the sense that McConnell and Posner purport to use that term – treating religious and secular interests as human wants of equivalent nature and status, the protection of which is merely a protection of a general capacity to choose – misses the point.

But the Charter's guarantee is not simply a guarantee of religious freedom. Its protection extends beyond religion to include conscientious belief. Perhaps, then, the right is indeed about the protection of freedom in a defined context, but that context is secular: freedom of conscientious, not merely religious, belief. Or, to put it in a way that expressly acknowledges the historical development of the right, freedom of religion may have been the context in which the sanctity of the human conscience was first recognized, but haven't we, and the rights we have created, outgrown a concern with gods and demons? This is a compelling argument. It would be particularly compelling if we had outgrown our gods and demons. But the remarkable thing about freedom of conscience is just how parasitic it remains on freedom of religion in all of its most difficult contemporary dimensions.

This is not true of all potential versions of the freedom. There is a narrow but important strand of freedom of conscience that can be specified without relying on religious analogies. That is the freedom to hold one's own beliefs, to think, to determine for oneself what one takes to be true, without state constraint or compulsion. This freedom is not inconsequential. It protects the interior dimension of thought, prior to expression. States have historically tried – some states try now – to police precisely this. Even in Western European societies there are examples of attempted state coercion of religious belief in recent times. Franco's Spain would offer several examples (Cooper 1975; Delpech 1956). In Canada, the Supreme Court found that the original purpose of the *Lord's Day Act* (1970) – still on the books in 1985 – was to coerce religious observance *(Big M Drug Mart)*. Freedom from coerced belief is a substantial freedom.

At this primordial level it is possible to recognize a freedom of conscience that is purely secular. There is no need to probe religious analogies in order to determine what counts as a conscientious belief, as opposed to some other form of belief. Freedom of thought is intelligible for all thought, no matter how mundane or important. At this level, it makes great sense to treat freedom of religion as a subset of the broader freedom of the mind. This was the notion at the heart of Chief Justice Dickson's secular definition of the freedom of conscience and religion: "The values that underlie our political and philosophic traditions demand that every individual be free to hold and to manifest whatever beliefs and opinions his or her conscience dictates, provided *inter alia* only that such manifestations do not injure his or her neighbours or their parallel rights to hold and manifest beliefs and opinions of their own" (*Big M Drug Mart* 1985, para. 123). This idea of conscience is what Amnesty International seeks to protect through its advocacy on behalf of "prisoners of conscience." It condemns any attempt at mind control or brainwashing. It is a more appropriate foundation for freedom from coerced expression than freedom of expression itself (*Lavigne,* 267; *Slaight Communications v. Davidson,* 1080). If this were all there were to the Charter's guarantee of "freedom of conscience and religion," we would be able to evade any concern with articulating the distinctive value of religion.

But the freedom has been interpreted more broadly than this (indeed, in the Canadian constitution there is strong textual warrant for doing so, given that the purely interior dimension of thought – "freedom of thought, belief [and] opinion" – is expressly protected in a separate clause of the Charter, section 2(b), allied to freedom of expression). Freedom of religion has been interpreted not only to forbid direct coercion of belief, but also to offer at least qualified protection to religious practices. It is difficult to see how this could not be the case, given the almost inseparable link between belief and at least some form of manifestation. It is in this latter territory that the distinctive value of religious belief becomes crucial, and where the definition of conscience takes its lead from what we consider to be most valuable about religion, for the moment one recognizes an obligation on the state to adapt its action to the requirements of religion or conscience, one is forced to distinguish what is the distinctively religious or conscientious element. No longer can one simply treat all thought, all belief, as being on a par. There is no protection for all practices, no exemption from state imposition on the basis of mere disagreement. Only certain types of objections are accepted.

In this context, the notion of conscientious belief derives its content primarily by extrapolation from religious belief. What we take to be the determining features of conscience are precisely those elements that we consider most important about religious belief. Often the extrapolation is express. The interpreter begins from religion and then enlarges the scope by analogy so that the guarantee comes to benefit people whose beliefs are not theistic.[11] This mimics the historical usage of the phrase "freedom of conscience" itself, which was first used to refer to religious commitment. But even when the extrapolation is not express, religion serves as the model. The definitions of conscience rely heavily on adjectives: the "fundamental principles" of an individual (*Big M Drug Mart* 1983, 136, *per* Laycraft J.A.); "profound moral and ethical beliefs" (*Roach v. Canada,* para. 45, *per* Linden J.A.); or "profoundly personal beliefs that govern one's perception of oneself, humankind, nature, and, in some cases, a higher or different order of being" (*R. v. Edwards Books and Art Ltd.*, para. 97, *per* Dickson C.J.C.). The adjectives in themselves give little direction and so generate the demand: "Give us examples." Those examples are either explicitly religious or are framed on the basis of their conformity to the religious heartland. A purely materialistic, hedonistic, or even classically utilitarian conception of humanity – even if "profoundly personal," even if it governs "one's perception of oneself," even if it is taken to be "fundamental" – is unlikely to qualify for constitutional protection.

One sees the same phenomenon in the development of conscientious objection to war, the context in which the notion of "conscience" has had the most currency. There, too, the right to refuse military service was first recognized when claimed on religious grounds, and indeed in some countries is still limited to religious grounds (Lippman 1990-91, 37ff.). Only later have secular grounds come to be accepted, and even then the grounds have generally been tested by religious analogy. It is not sufficient that one is strongly committed to maintaining one's own life and perfectly willing to extend the same respect to others; not sufficient that one is scared to the very marrow of one's bones; not sufficient that one is, simply, horrified at the prospect of taking someone's life. Conscientious objection is only available on the basis of some reasonably coherent moral or religious world view, which the claimant believes has peremptory force (see United Nations, Commission on Human Rights 1985).

The best candidates for a definition of "conscience" that is not dependent on a religious analogy are those that focus on obedience to moral injunctions as the object of the guarantee. Thus, freedom of conscience protects "a set of beliefs by which the person feels bound to conduct most, if not all, of his voluntary actions" (*R. v. Videoflicks*, 380, *per* Tarnopolsky J.A.), or it recognizes "strongly held moral ideas of right and wrong, not necessarily founded on any organized religious principles" (*Roach*, para. 45; see also *R. v. Morgentaler*, 178, *per* Wilson J.). Even here, one suspects that the religious analogy continues to play a strong role: these definitions clearly contemplate peremptory standards, not the provisional conclusions that emerge from moral debate in its philosophical sense. In any case, a definition of conscience focused on morality would not be sufficient to subsume freedom of religion, at least not without severely distorting the latter. Moral injunctions are a dimension of many religions, but religion includes elements that are not contained within morality, such as prayer, methods of worship, communal institutions, and what to a believer is knowledge of the divine.

Religion is, then, indispensable to our understanding of freedom of religion. We cannot escape the religious by treating the freedom as a subset of some larger secular value if the freedom is to have anything like its com-

mon meaning. Or, rather, there is only one way to do so: by treating freedom of religion as being nothing more than an aspect of the freedom of our
inmost thoughts. Freedom of belief has indeed been part of freedom of
religion. But the moment one proceeds from belief to manifestations or
practices, the distinction between types of thought, between classes of belief, becomes crucial. Only certain motives command such respect that they
confer immunity (albeit relative) from the general law. That requires us to
define those motives and reflect upon their value, and that, in turn, means
confronting the nature and human significance of religion – not choice,
not conscience, but the experience of religion.

Neutrality under a Religiously Grounded Freedom of Religion

How does this relate to the commitment to neutrality, which has been such
an influential part of discussions of freedom of religion? Is the right trapped
in a contradiction, aspiring to neutrality but necessarily attaching special
value to certain beliefs? If the freedom does involve the substantive valuing
of religious commitments, how can this valuation be separated from one's
commitment to, one's special respect for, concrete elements of religious faith?
Won't the deference due to religious beliefs – even one's sense of what constitutes a religion – be influenced by one's own beliefs? Historically, religious toleration has often been limited to certain faiths – faiths that are like
the tolerators' own. Perhaps that tendency is more deeply rooted than we
think.

There is room for neutrality, although conceived in significantly different
terms from those used by McConnell and Posner. Its scope is more limited
and its pursuit a dynamic process: neutrality is an end towards which one
aims, not a state capable of immediate definition. The process does not
entirely escape the challenges posed in the last paragraph, but it does contemplate a significant broadening of the sphere of protection beyond the
decision maker's personal convictions. What, then, is the scope for neutrality in freedom of religion?

To begin, it is worth reiterating that there is a dimension of the freedom
that is capable of expression without any regard for the content of belief,
one encountered above in the discussion of freedom of conscience. This is
the protection of one's inmost thoughts (but with no protection for the
actions one takes in consequence). This covers the central core of religious
toleration. It prohibits the direct coercion of belief. It would also prohibit
the state from compelling or preventing religious observance *if those constraints were intended as an indirect means of coercing the individual's beliefs*. If,
in contrast, the law merely requires outward conformity – for example, by
requiring that one maintain a day of rest on Sunday or attend an established church – one is no longer dealing with inward thoughts alone, and
an additional premise – some special claim of respect for religious practices,

some sense of their special significance – is required to bring the actions within the sphere of the prohibition. This distinction between inward beliefs and outward observance may seem too strict. There are some forms of outward observance – pronouncing a creed, for example – that generate such direct dissonance with one's inward beliefs that they place even the narrow right at issue. One can imagine an extension of this reasoning to include other forms of observance, such as church attendance. But I suspect that in pursuing these analogies, we would soon find ourselves concerned not merely with protecting the sanctity of thought – all thought – but with the special claims of religion. Our sense of the force of those claims – our sense of the significance of being compelled to engage in actions that contradict our fundamental *religious* convictions – would drive the perception of dissonance. A guarantee truly confined to beliefs is very narrow indeed. This in part explains why a straight beliefs/action dichotomy proves so unsatisfactory in freedom of religion.

The narrow right ends up looking very different from the scope often associated with freedom of religion – so different, in fact, that it is best considered to be a separate right. It attains complete neutrality precisely because it is no longer concerned with religiosity or conscientiousness at all. It simply protects the sanctity of an individual's thought. That protection is as applicable to individuals' opinion of the government, their opinion of their in-laws, or their preference in ice cream, as it is to matters of faith. And its protection is both narrow and remarkably absolute. It covers only the inward belief, not even its expression (which may be worthy of protection, but on grounds that require additional argument). Within that compass it is virtually complete: because it covers only the mind, prior to any externalization, any state interference has an almost insurmountable hurdle to cross.[12] The narrow right may cover freedom of religion's traditional concern with the sanctity of belief. Its extension to all thought may have, as one of its foundations, the respect due to the individual's conscience in some religious traditions. But its coverage stops short of what the most restrictive interpreters of the right would include within freedom of religion, failing even to protect against forced religious observance (if compulsion is confined to the maintenance of outward conformity and makes no pretence of changing people's minds).

The restrictive interpreters may not realize this. Some clearly oppose religious exemptions from secular laws on the basis that providing exemptions requires that one attach special weight to religious practice, thereby entangling the state in religious judgments. They seek to pare the right back to the protection of belief alone, thereby permitting the state to maintain truly complete neutrality (see, for example, Eisgruber and Sager 1997; *City of Boerne*, concurring opinion of Stevens J.). But note just how far freedom of religion has to be reduced to achieve that. The restrictive interpreters may respond that their theories include a broader sphere of conduct than I have sketched above because, in addition to protecting the autonomy of belief, they are concerned independently with maintaining the neutrality of the state in matters of religion. The state would still be prohibited from requiring the outward forms of religious observance on those grounds. But does this avoid the difficulty? Why should the state be compelled to remain neutral in religious matters when it need not be neutral about anything else? Again, the answer can only lie in there being something about religion that demands special respect. The restrictive interpreters cannot achieve complete neutrality in the pared-down version of the freedom without reducing the constraints on government to a level beyond any interpreter's contemplation.

We find ourselves pulled, then, beyond the pared-down version to at least some recognition of religion's special claim, so that religious observance cannot be prohibited without special justification, and observance cannot be compelled even in the service of secular ends. And once this is acknowledged, it is a short step to the recognition of at least some religious exemptions. Perhaps paradoxically, true neutrality requires greater, not less, attention to exemptions. Special respect for religion is in the law already, in the constitutional commitment to freedom of religion itself and in the respect for already-accepted religious traditions within the detail of existing regulation (for example, in the toleration of male circumcision or in the rules of marriage). The question is whether that same respect will be extended to unfamiliar forms of religion.

The extension of respect is the essence of the dynamic conception of neutrality proposed in this chapter. It is not easy to achieve, in part because the nature and value of religious commitment are not susceptible to easy definition, even among co-religionists. What are we seeking to protect? Religions involve a wide range of phenomena. Within Christian denominations one sees moral injunctions, rites and ceremonies, mystic ecstasies, structures of authority, solitary prayer and contemplation, theological inquiry, bodily mortification, and self-denial. Denominations disagree on the catalogue; some treat some of these phenomena as perversions, not expressions, of religion. Not only do they disagree about the forms of religious experience; they also disagree (sometimes fiercely) about the kind of reality to which these experiences attest. And in the nature of religious belief, they tend to treat their own views as true, those of their opponents as false.

Yet at the level of society (at least in some societies), we have come to show some respect for the beliefs of others, even though we may not share, understand, or accept them. The initial impulse might well have been to secure peace. We recognized that diversity of belief was ineradicable, and if we were to live together with people of different belief, a modicum of tolerance was necessary.[13] But it was then necessary to define the degree of tolerance, and that required some acknowledgment of the normative force of religious belief. That recognition might not have been a function of the perceived merit of the beliefs. The beliefs might well have been considered dangerously erroneous. But acceptance of the individuals holding the beliefs as members of society required that one acquiesce in the beliefs' importance for those individuals. Thus, the value of the beliefs came to be acknowledged not necessarily for the beliefs' sake but for the sake of the people holding them. This set in motion the first generic respect for religious conviction, but without any clear definition of religion or the value of religious belief. That value was assumed by refraction through the respect extended to the individuals holding the beliefs. A reticence to judge was built into the very foundation of toleration.

But the reticence could not be total, for one still had to determine what one was tolerating and what was subject to prohibition. And because toleration could not be absolute, one had to attach some weight to the force of religious belief. Thus began the attempt to understand what individuals saw as valuable in religious belief in terms that achieved some independence from the detail of their own convictions. One's own commitments formed an inevitable starting point in these inquiries, but this was conjoined with a realization that similar qualities might be reflected in others' quite different experience. The admission of people with whom one disagreed to full membership in the society required that religious commitments be understood in terms that aspired to be generic. This involved more than the mere abstention from judgment commonly associated with secularism. One also had to grasp, even if tentatively and schematically, what was common to religious conviction in an inquiry more akin to ecumenicalism than to secularism.[14]

There began a series of attempts to articulate, in a manner that was not framed in terms exclusive to one tradition, the nature of religious belief. We see many expressions along that line, such as "the feelings, acts, and experiences of individual men in their solicitude, so far as they apprehend themselves to stand in relation to whatever they may consider the divine" (*United States v. Sun Myung Moon*, 1227, quoting James 1936, 31-32; emphasis removed); "belief in a supernatural Being, Thing or Principle," together with codes of conduct flowing from that belief (*Church of the New Faith v. Commissioner of Pay Roll Tax*, 136, *per* Mason A.C.J. and Brennan J.); or Chief Justice Dickson's "profoundly personal beliefs that govern one's perception of oneself, humankind, nature, and, in some cases, a higher or different order of being" (*Edwards Books*, para. 97). These are necessary and useful, for they suggest how people have looked beyond themselves for meaning in a manner that transcends sheer empiricism. But the heterogeneity of religious experience is such that none of the generic formulations is particularly adequate. The more detailed they are, the less complete they seem; the more abstract they become, the more empty. It sometimes seems that it is simply the primordial drive to look beyond the normal course of existence that is common; but then the methods for "looking beyond" and the injunctions consequent on that vision are various (and even that drive is not shared by the nonreligious). Consequently, we keep reaching back to the historical elements, the concrete elements, of our own religious traditions – sometimes elements that we had largely forgotten – in order to obtain some purchase in understanding others' faiths.

The struggle to define the nature and force of religious experience therefore stands as a paradigmatic example of the hermeneutic circle: we listen to what others have to say about their traditions, attempting to place ourselves as much as possible within their structure of belief, to understand its significance for them; we probe our own religious traditions for analogies and explanations, looking to see if we too have treated as valuable features that others derive from their beliefs; and through that process we come up with preliminary and partial conclusions as to whether or not something is religious – conclusions that are always subject to future reconsideration, rejection, and refinement.

In its reflection on a reality characterized by disagreement and progressive attempts at extrapolation/generalization from that reality, theorization about freedom of religion is not profoundly different from that on other rights. Those rights also involve reflection upon prior but necessarily provisional hypotheses, the testing of those hypotheses against competing accounts and accumulated experience, and the revision of the hypotheses in consequence, more than they rely on the application of a fixed formula. Moreover, the hypotheses are, like the varieties of religious experience, often linked to deeper judgments about human good, judgments that are themselves formed in history. One might say of moral reasoning generally that we start, provisionally, with a set of premises that are shaped by our personal histories: we are raised within particular religious or philosophical traditions; we encounter other views and revise our positions in consequence. In defining principles appropriate for a diverse society, we seek to work outwards, attempting to take into account a broader range of phenomena; seeking to give due consideration to the diversity of human conceptions of the good; subjecting our premises to scrutiny, revision, and, at times, rejection (see Slattery 1991). Rights, like other moral principles, are not so much universal as universalizing.

Freedom of religion is, however, especially elusive, for the core phenomenon itself is mysterious, the claimed reality ineffable, inaccessible to unbelievers and embedded with broader cultural phenomena. Hence, freedom of religion involves a curious blend of hypothesizing on the nature and significance of religious belief on the one hand, and abstention from judgment on the other. This drawing back from judgment is apparent throughout the literature.[15] Commentators argue that believers should not be interrogated too intensively about their beliefs. There are cautions about requiring a close analogy to familiar religious forms, about requiring logical coherence in beliefs, about basing respect for beliefs simply on the beliefs' age. All too frequently one finds the question of religious character effectively being replaced by an inquiry into sincerity. Surely the latter is important, but given the need to set some scope to the freedom, the question of sincerity cannot entirely displace judgments about religious character and force. One suspects that sincerity looms so large not merely for its own sake, but because it is self-limiting, posing the issues in a way that involves both judgment and abstention. The search for a generic understanding of religious experience is continually arrested at an early stage.

But there is still evaluation, at least at the level of the definition of religion and, to some degree, the determination of its force. There must be if freedom of religion is to be recognized and protected. That evaluation may occur with restraint because of the pitfalls of defining something so elusive and prone to partiality. Indeed, freedom of religion provides a fascinating example of how we can accommodate profound differences of perspective without full definition or even full comprehension, simply because of respect for a religion's adherents and the realization of religion's deep importance for them. But the accommodation cannot be absolute and unquestioning, for the boundary between the freedom and the general law must still be determined in particular cases. And those decisions can only be made in a manner that acknowledges, at least for the purpose of the decision, the value of religious belief.

Conclusion

Freedom of religion does not require, then, that the state remain indifferent to religion. Two motives drive the right: (1) an acknowledgment of the importance of religion, and (2) a realization of religion's diversity, ultimately resulting in an attempt to generalize respect for religion so that all members benefit from equivalent protection, no matter what their beliefs.

This is far from secularism. McConnell and Posner's idea of neutrality as obliviousness to religion is a misguided hope, one that misunderstands the very essence of the protection and leaves one unprepared to say when we should make room for religion and when not. Rather, the only viable neutrality requires active engagement, consciously seeking to understand how and why minority religions claim to be "religions" and comparing those claims to familiar dimensions of religious belief and practice. The only effective approach follows the hermeneutic method sketched above. It is entirely compatible with – indeed it requires, at least provisionally – the acknowledgment of religion's importance.

This chapter's argument provides additional reason for concluding that the attempt to exclude religiously based arguments from public discourse is wrong-headed. The strongest grounds for permitting religious arguments have to do with the impossibility of separating the moral views of believing individuals from their religious convictions, and with the advantages one gains in political participation, integrity, and honesty if individuals are permitted to be frank about those convictions (see Perry 1988, 181-82). But this chapter provides another ground for allowing such reasons, based on the inability to separate protection of religion from respect for religious conviction. If religion is to be protected at all, it has to be actively engaged.

This is especially true when dealing with the issue of religious exemptions. This chapter should not be interpreted as arguing for extensive exemptions. It has certainly argued that exemptions engage the core concerns of freedom of religion, but that is merely the first step in the inquiry. Questions of exemption are difficult to resolve precisely because they require the balancing of general social objectives (which may themselves reflect strong imperatives) against religious beliefs and practices (which may vary in their significance to the religion's adherents, which may cut across others' cherished beliefs, and in respect of which nonbelievers are poorly placed to judge). A simple injunction to defer does not resolve the difficulty, for one must still determine to what, precisely, one should defer. The challenge is inescapable and necessarily requires some degree of judgment by those standing outside the particular religious tradition, including some weighing of distinctively religious values: religion's meaning, its value, its mystery. This chapter has, to this point, ignored issues of institutional role: who should make these decisions. A full discussion of those issues lies outside the scope of this chapter. But there is a strong argument that when dealing with exemptions from secularly motivated legislation, where a difficult weighing of incommensurates is required, exemptions should be defined either by the legislature itself or under legislative guidance as to how the weights should be affixed.[16] If constitutional guarantees are (as I have argued in Webber 2000) to be treated merely as minimum standards, so that one maintains room for democratic debate over complex issues even when they engage profoundly important rights concerns, it may be wise to restrict the constitutionally entrenched guarantees to intentional interference with religious belief. This does not mean that exemptions from secularly motivated legislation should be eliminated; merely that they should be shaped through democratic deliberation. Far from being excluded from political discussion, questions of religious exemption (and therefore the weighing of the force of religious belief) belong in the most participatory realm.

This chapter has also argued that there is good reason for restraint in the manner in which religion is judged. Sometimes this restraint looks something like secularism. It is constantly striving for a generic and inclusive sense of religious conviction, even though that conception has to be constantly reconstructed from the detail of actual traditions. In freedom of religion, one is accommodating a phenomenon that, almost by definition, escapes full comprehension. Evaluation should draw back, then, from too demanding a judgment. But again this attitude is not based on indifference. Quite the opposite: it is driven by respect for the ineffable quality of religious conviction.

There is yet another way in which the conduct of state actors might approach a secular ideal. Certain of those actors (perhaps all of them in different ways) fulfill a representative role that extends beyond the representation of the particular individuals who elected or appointed them. They act (in the case of the executive) in the name of all members of the society or (in the case of legislators) all their constituents. That representative role requires discretion in the actor's identification with particular religious views in order to fulfill the second aim identified above as underlying freedom of religion (the requirement that citizens of all religions feel equally attached to the state). That aim pulls members of the executive and legislature towards an inclusive vision and away from the deliberate favouring of a particular religious interest. This generally means that the actors' personal commitments should be kept in the background. But again, discretion does not amount to renunciation. Citizens surely understand that their representatives have commitments. They also understand that the representatives' character, their moral stances, and even their political opinions are to some extent a function of their convictions. All that citizens can demand is that their representatives reach for an inclusive vision in their public argumentation and refrain from strident identification with particular religious views in the ceremonial dimensions of their roles. Again the restraint is relative, not absolute.

But, finally, what about those individuals who reject all religious belief? Can the aspiration to neutrality in freedom of religion extend to them? It is clear from this chapter that there is an implicit acknowledgment, at least presumptive, of the value of religious conviction in the decision to protect the freedom. It is not surprising, then, that a strong commitment to freedom of religion can coexist with, for example, special tax concessions enjoyed by religious institutions. The guarantee does not treat religious and secular beliefs identically. On the other hand, the constraints of the representative role do apply with equal force to the nonreligious and the religious, and they provide additional reason state actors should refrain from the display of their religious convictions in their public actions.

The nonreligious also share, at least potentially, in the drive for breadth of inclusion in the protection of religious, and religious-like, convictions. The extrapolation from religion to a freedom of secular conscience exemplifies that phenomenon. At the end of the day, the *generic* respect for religion, to which all guarantees of freedom of religion must aspire, may be more an acknowledgment of the central importance of a set of questions –

about meaning, about a purpose beyond ourselves, about the mystery of the world's and our own existence – than it is about answers, even expressed in general terms. It is about the importance of maintaining some space for those questions to be asked and for a range of answers to be given. Those questions are shared by many nonbelievers, who therefore participate in the aspirations underlying the right; paradoxically, they are rejected by some religious believers who are all too convinced of the answers and therefore have little respect for the questions. Perhaps it is that surprising inclusion and exclusion, of nonbelievers and believers, that is the ultimate form of neutrality in freedom of religion.

Acknowledgments
My thanks to Kate Devlin and Chad Vandermolen for their valuable research assistance, and to Marcia Barry, Avigail Eisenberg, Arthur Glass, Rebecca Johnson, Hester Lessard, Jennifer Nedelsky, Patrick Parkinson, Brian Slattery, and Chad Vandermolen for their trenchant comments on previous versions.

Notes

1 The assumption is necessary, for some forms of liberalism have been actively hostile to religion, seeing it as a species of irrational obscurantism. One suspects that such views are not entirely dead but continue to colour some of the recent opposition to a reliance on religious arguments in public life.

2 In *R. v. Big M Drug Mart* (1985), Chief Justice Dickson reflected this extension in his definition of the freedom: "Freedom means that, subject to such limitations as are necessary to protect public safety, order, health, or morals or the fundamental rights and freedoms of others, no one is to be forced to act in a way contrary to his beliefs or his conscience" (para. 95).

3 See also *Lynch v. Donnelly*, 688, *per* O'Connor J., concurring.

4 Rawls' arguments against allowing religious reasons in public debate might be seen as an extension of the "second concern" identified in the text: one excludes religious reasons from public deliberation in order to minimize sectarian divisions and provide a common language of right, which all citizens can embrace no matter what their personal beliefs. It could be seen as aiming, then, at a far-reaching "disestablishment," separating religious commitments not only from state action, but also from the process of deliberation leading to that action (see Rawls 1993, 1999).

5 Section 2(a) of the *Canadian Charter of Rights and Freedoms* reads: "Everyone has the following fundamental freedoms: ... freedom of conscience and religion."

6 Taylor (1985b, 218) makes a similar point in relation to the very idea of "freedom." He notes that we don't treat the erection of a traffic light as a constraint on our liberty, whereas we do treat a law restricting the forms in which we may worship as one. The reason for the difference lies in the differential significance of the two situations for one's sense of personhood.

7 McConnell (2000) has since moved away from this position and now emphasizes that religion is properly subject to special protection.

8 In the United States, the guarantee of freedom of religion is found in the First Amendment to the constitution and reads as follows: "Congress shall make no law respecting an establishment of religion, or prohibiting the free exercise thereof." This is generally read as containing two guarantees: one prohibiting Congress from establishing a religion; the other prohibiting Congress from restricting the free exercise of religion.

9 McConnell and Posner (1989) have difficulty maintaining complete neutrality between religious and secular activities even when dealing with issues of the establishment of religion. They find that government cannot favour one religion over others, even if government

finds that one is preferable to another purely on the basis of those religions' secular effects. There are, of course, no such constraints on government's ability to favour secular activities (9-10). Second, when making comparisons for the purpose of achieving neutrality of treatment, McConnell and Posner treat religious activities as charitable, analogous to education or hospitals. Why? Surely only because they consider religion to be intrinsically more beneficial to society, to be more other-regarding, to carry more positive externalities than activities they class as commercial. But doesn't that judgment depend upon an assessment of religion's value that takes us well beyond objective utility (which in any case McConnell and Posner say government should not judge) or the preferences of individuals? Once again, its value is assumed, not left to subjective valuation and choice.

Eisgruber and Sager (1994, 1997) are more thoroughgoing than McConnell and Posner, but their arguments also depend upon an implicit attribution of special value to religious belief and practice. They argue for a freedom of religion based solely on the special vulnerability of religious adherents to discrimination, not on any special value for religious belief, jettisoning in the process the first rationale for the freedom articulated in the early part of this chapter and retaining only the second. But why should detrimental consequences flowing from religious belief call for "protection," especially when, in Eisgruber and Sager's view, protection is justified when the disadvantage applies to the beliefs, not persons; when the disadvantage may flow merely from indifference and not from antagonism; and when it is "particularly subtle and complex"? Other beliefs (not persons) don't benefit from equivalent protection. The special value attached to religion is also manifest in Eisgruber and Sager's repeated use of the adjective "deep" (e.g., 1994, 1283 and 1285). Eisgruber and Sager's insistence on "protection" merely serves to decrease the level of protection provided to religion while continuing to attribute special value to it.

10 In this case, Justice Brennan was speaking in dissent, but see, to the same effect, the opinion of the court in *Thomas v. Review Board*, 713.

11 See, for example, *Big M Drug Mart* (1985), para. 123, and *R. v. Morgentaler*, para. 251, *per* Wilson J.: freedom of conscience protects "conscientious beliefs which are not religiously motivated" and "personal morality which is not founded on religion."

12 One example that may cross the hurdle is the forced medication of those with severe and destructive mental illnesses.

13 See, for example, Stout (1988, 79-81). I explore a similar transition from a modus vivendi to normative obligation, again in a case of parties who initially share few normative premises in common (Webber 1995).

14 Compare Michael Perry's (1991) concept of "ecumenical political dialogue," which he uses to capture the key component of a politics that is "neither neutral/impartial nor sectarian/authoritarian" in its approach to religion. I am grateful to Adam Czarnota for urging me to consider the implications of ecumenicalism.

15 See, for example, Tribe (1988, 1181-82 and 1243-51), where he gives examples of all the cautions and constraints indicated in the text. Tribe even cautions that inquiries into sincerity can lead one into inappropriate territory (1245-46). Indeed, he ends by arguing that it is valuable to interpret rights other than freedom of religion as broadly as possible in order to obviate the need to address religion at all (1249-51).

16 This is the ultimate effect – and apparently the intention – of the U.S. Supreme Court's decision in *Employment Div. v. Smith*, especially 886-90: religious exemptions from generally applicable laws are permitted, but not constitutionally required. See also the concurring reasons of Justice Scalia in *City of Boerne*.

References

Books, Articles, and Public Documents

Canadian Charter of Rights and Freedoms, Part I of the *Constitution Act, 1982*, being Schedule B to the *Canada Act 1982* (U.K.), 1982, c. 11.

Carter, S.L. 1993. *The Culture of Disbelief: How American Law and Politics Trivialize Religious Devotion*. New York: Basic Books.

Cooper, Norman B. 1975. *Catholicism and the Franco Regime*. Beverly Hills, CA: Sage.

Delpech, Jacques. 1956. *The Oppression of the Protestants in Spain*. Trans. Tom Johnson and Dolores Johnson. London: Lutterworth Press.

Eisgruber, C.L., and L.G. Sager. 1994. The Vulnerability of Conscience: The Constitutional Basis for Protecting Religious Conduct. *University of Chicago Law Review* 61:1245-315.

—. 1997. Congressional Power and Religious Liberty after *City of Boerne v. Flores*. *Supreme Court Review* 1997:79-139.

Galston, William A. 1991. *Liberal Purposes: Goods, Virtues, and Diversity in the Liberal State*. Cambridge: Cambridge University Press.

Gutmann, Amy. 1999. Liberty and Pluralism in Pursuit of the Non-Ideal. *Social Research* 66(4):1039-62.

James, William. 1936. *The Varieties of Religious Experience: A Study in Human Nature*. New York: The Modern Library.

Lippman, Matthew. 1990-91. The Recognition of Conscientious Objection to Military Service as an International Human Right. *California Western International Law Journal* 21: 31-66.

Lord's Day Act, R.S.C. 1970, c. L-13.

Macedo, Stephen. 1999. *Liberal Virtues: Citizenship, Virtue, and Community in Liberal Constitutionalism*. Oxford: Clarendon Press.

McConnell, Michael W. 2000. The Problem of Singling out Religion. *DePaul Law Review* 50:1-47.

McConnell, Michael W., and Richard Posner. 1989. An Economic Approach to Issues of Religious Freedom. *University of Chicago Law Review* 56:1-60.

Neuhaus, Richard John. 1986. *The Naked Public Square: Religion and Democracy in America*. 2nd ed. Grand Rapids, MI: William B. Eerdmans.

Perry, Michael J. 1988. *Morality, Politics, and Law: A Bicentennial Essay*. New York: Oxford University Press.

—. 1991. *Love and Power: The Role of Religion and Morality in American Politics*. New York: Oxford University Press.

Rawls, John. 1993. *Political Liberalism*. New York: Columbia University Press.

—. 1999. The Idea of Public Reason Revisited. In *The Law of Peoples with "The Idea of Public Reason Revisited,"* 129-80. Cambridge, MA: Harvard University Press.

Raz, Joseph. 1982. Liberalism, Autonomy and the Politics of Neutral Concern. *Midwest Studies in Philosophy* 7:89-102.

Slattery, Brian. 1991. Rights, Communities and Tradition. *University of Toronto Law Journal* 41:447-67.

Stout, Jeffrey. 1988. *Ethics after Babel: The Languages of Morals and Their Discontents*. Boston: Beacon Press.

Taylor, Charles. 1985a. Atomism. In *Philosophy and the Human Sciences: Philosophical Papers 2*, 187-210. Cambridge: Cambridge University Press.

—. 1985b. What's Wrong with Negative Liberty. In *Philosophy and the Human Sciences: Philosophical Papers 2*, 211-29. Cambridge: Cambridge University Press.

—. 1995. The Politics of Recognition. In *Philosophical Arguments*, 225-56. Cambridge, MA: Harvard University Press.

Tribe, L.H. 1988. *American Constitutional Law*. 2nd ed. Mineola, NY: Foundation Press.

United Nations, Commission on Human Rights. 1985. *Conscientious Objection to Military Service: Report Prepared in Pursuance of Resolutions 14 (XXXIV) and 1982/30 of the Sub-Commission on Prevention of Discrimination and Protection of Minorities by Mr. Asbjørn and Mr. Chama Mubanga-Chipoya, members of the Sub-Commission*. E/CN.4/Sub.2/1983/30/Rev.1.

Webber, Jeremy. 1995. Relations of Force and Relations of Justice: The Emergence of Normative Community between Colonists and Aboriginal Peoples. *Osgoode Hall Law Journal* 33:623-60.

—. 2000. Constitutional Reticence. *Australian Journal of Legal Philosophy* 25:125-55.

Cases

Church of the New Faith v. Commissioner of Pay Roll Tax (Vic) (1983), 154 C.L.R. 120 (High Court of Australia).

City of Boerne v. Flores, 521 U.S. 507 (1997) [*City of Boerne*].

Employment Div., Dept. of Human Resources of Ore. v. Smith, 494 U.S. 872 (1990) [*Employment Div. v. Smith*].

Lavigne v. Ontario Public Service Employees Union, [1991] 2 S.C.R. 211 [*Lavigne*].

Lynch v. Donnelly, 465 US 668 (1984).

Marsh v. Chambers, 463 U.S. 783 (1983).

R. v. Advance Cutting and Coring Ltd., [2001] 3 S.C.R. 209.

R. v. Big M Drug Mart Ltd. (1983), 5 D.L.R. (4th) 121 (Alta.C.A.) [*Big M Drug Mart (1983)*].

R. v. Big M Drug Mart Ltd., [1985] 1 S.C.R. 295 [*Big M Drug Mart (1985)*].

R. v. Edwards Books and Art Ltd., [1986] 2 S.C.R. 713 [*Edwards Books*].

R. v. Morgentaler, [1988] 1 S.C.R. 30.

R. v. Videoflicks (1984), 15 C.C.C. (3d) 353 (Ont. C.A.).

Roach v. Canada (Minister of State for Multiculturalism and Citizenship) (1994), 2 F.C. 406 (F.C.A.) [*Roach*].

Rodriguez v. British Columbia (Attorney General), [1993] 3 S.C.R. 519.

Slaight Communications Inc. v. Davidson, [1989] 1 S.C.R. 1038.

Thomas v. Review Board, 450 U.S. 707 (1981).

United States v. Sun Myung Moon, 718 F.2d 1210 (2nd Cir. 1983).

Contributors

Maneesha Deckha joined the Faculty of Law at the University of Victoria in 2002. She is a graduate of Columbia Law School, where she received her LLM. Her research interests include feminist legal theories, law and culture, bioethics, and animal rights. She has published in the *Canadian Journal of Women and the Law*, *Osgoode Hall Law Journal*, *Manushi*, and the *International Relations Journal* of SFSU.

Avigail Eisenberg writes on political pluralism and minority rights. She is author of *Reconstructing Political Pluralism* and co-editor of *Minorities within Minorities* and *Painting the Maple*. She has published articles in several journals, including the *Canadian Journal of Political Science*, *Ethnicities*, and *Journal of Political Philosophy*.

Cindy Holder joined the Department of Philosophy at the University of Victoria in 2001. She received her PhD from the University of Arizona and works on issues related to self-determination and international human rights. She has written several articles on group rights and international law, the most recent of which appeared in *Human Rights Review*.

John McLaren is Lansdowne Professor of Law at the University of Victoria. He is a leading expert in legal history and the treatment of minorities in Canadian law. He has published articles in many scholarly journals and is co-editor of and contributor to *Religious Conscience, the State and the Law* and *Regulating Lives: Historical Essays on the State, Society, the Individual, and the Law*.

Colin Macleod is a member of the Department of Philosophy and the Faculty of Law at the University of Victoria. He is an expert on liberalism as well as on the rights, interests, and claims of children. He is author of *Liberalism, Justice and Markets*, co-editor of *The Moral and Political Status of Children*, and has published articles in several journals in philosophy, law, and politics.

Shauna McRanor is an interdisciplinary PhD student in indigenous governance, political science, and anthropology at the University of Victoria. She holds a BA in archaeology and a Master's degree in archival studies. She has published her work in *Archivaria* and *American Archivist*. Her current research is focused on indigenous-settler relations, the politics of difference, and theories of culture.

James Tully is Distinguished Professor of Political Science, Law, Indigenous Governance and Philosophy at the University of Victoria. He works in the area of contemporary legal and political theory and its history. His publications include, among others, *Multinational Democracies* (co-editor) and "Exclusion and Assimilation: Two Forms of Domination," in M. Williams and S. Macedo, ed., *Domination and Exclusion*.

Neil Vallance practiced law for twenty-three years before embarking on graduate studies in anthropology at the University of Victoria, when he also began working as a joint researcher for First Nations and Indian Affairs on Specific Claims for hunting and fishing rights under the Douglas Treaties. He now practices both law and applied anthropology. He has published in *The Advocate*.

Jeremy Webber is Canada Research Chair in Law and Society at the University of Victoria, Director of the Consortium on Democratic Constitutionalism, and Visiting Professor at the University of New South Wales. Before coming to Victoria, Professor Webber was Dean of Law at University of Sydney and, before that, a member of the Faculty of Law at McGill University. He is author of *Reimagining Canada: Language, Culture, Community and the Canadian Constitution*.

Index

A v. A, 151n5
Aboriginal claims, 1-2, 10
 distinctive culture test, 34, 35-36, 37,
  48-49, 67, 99-102, 107, 109
  pre-contact requirement, 49, 51n9,
   67-68
 European reference points, 64, 65-71
 R. v. Sparrow, 100, 107
 R. v. Van der Peet, 35, 37, 45, 48-49,
  51n9, 67, 68, 97, 107, 108
 Sandra Lovelace v. Canada, 43-44, 51n10,
  78
 title test, 68, 74n25
Aboriginal peoples
 Constitution Act, 1982, 35, 50n1, 67,
  111n2
 suppression of religious practices, 159
 See also Aboriginal claims
Additional Protocol to the American
  Convention on Human Rights in the in
  the Area of Economic, Social and
  Cultural Rights, 82-83, 89
Adler v. The Queen, 162, 163
Alberta
 freedom of religion, 153, 156
Anderson, John, 157
Area of Economic, Social and Cultural Rights,
  82-83, 89
Arsenault-Cameron v. Prince Edward Island,
  104
autonomy, 60
 views of Jennifer Nedelsky, 130n7
 See also self-determination

Baker Lake, 68, 74n25
Bal v. Attorney General of Ontario, 164
Ballantyne/Davidson/MacIntyre v. Canada,
  78, 93-94

Barsh, Russel L., 101-2
Baxter et al. v. The Attorney General of
  Canada et al., 110
Beauchemin v. Blainville, 172
Berger, Benjamin, 172-73
Berger, Thomas
 Fragile Freedoms, 1
bilingualism, 105
 constitutional protection of language
  rights, 25, 108, 110n1
Bill 30 Reference, 161-62, 163
branding, 120-22
Brazil, 83
British Columbia
 freedom of religion, 157-58
British North America Act, 1867, 155-56,
  161, 162

Canadian Charter of Rights and Freedoms,
  2, 3-4, 182-84
 section 1, 165
 section 23, 97, 103-6, 108-9
  text, 110n1
  See also Mahe v. Alberta
 section 2(a), 154, 160, 161, 163, 164,
  182
  text, 197n5
  See also freedom of religion
 section 2(b), 187
Chanock, Martin, 120-21
children, 7, 11
 identity claims, 7, 134-35, 144, 149-51,
  151n5
  compared to adults, 141-42, 147-48
 protection, 170-71
 See also education
Christian Education South Africa v. Minister
  of Education, 170-71

Colombia, 82-83
colonial reasoning, 8, 56-58, 64, 67-72
  accommodation of differences and,
      49-50, 55, 65-71
  constitutional protections
    language rights, 23, 108, 110n1
    religious rights, 155-56, 161, 162,
        167-68
conscientious objection, 153, 188
Constitution Act, 1982, 2-3
  section 35, 67, 108
    text, 50n1, 111n2
    See also R. v. Van der Peet
  section 93, 161, 162, 167-68
  *See also Canadian Charter of Rights and
      Freedoms*
Cornell, Drucilla, 116-17, 131n10
cultural rights, 9-11
  equality v. justice, 128-29
  international human rights norms and,
      36, 78-83, 85-86, 89-91
  joint governance and, 130n5
  liberal culturalism, 54-55, 58-67
  views on/definitions of, 78-79, 81-94
culture (concept), 58-59, 62
  colonial rationalities and, 56-57, 72
  definitions of, 8, 10-11, 63-64, 87-89,
      94, 97-99, 109, 110, 123-25
  feminist scholarship and
    differentiated approach, 114, 115, 116,
        125-27, 129-30, 130n2
    intersectionalist approach, 115-16,
        125-27, 129-30
    postcolonial approach, 114, 115,
        119-25
    universalist approach, 114, 117-19
  relations of power and, 61-63, 65-66
  views of W. Kymlicka, 59-61

Delgamuukw v. British Columbia, 68
democratic practice
  struggles over recognition and, 20, 21,
      27-30
dialogical civic freedom, 16, 27-30
Dickson, Chief Justice, 103-6, 107, 108
  freedom of religion, 160, 174n18, 179,
      180, 186-87, 197n2
difference, 6, 58-59, 62-63
  indigenous freedoms and colonial
      rationalities, 63-72
  See also cultural rights
distinctive culture test, 34, 35-36, 37,
      48-49, 51n9, 67-68, 99-102, 107, 109
Donald v. Hamilton Board of Education, 153
Doukhobors, 157-58

education
  faith-based curriculum content, 154,
      163, 164, 168-69
  faith-based educational rights, 156-59,
      160-65, 167-73
  independent schooling, 166
  minority language rights, 97, 103-6,
      107-10
  patriotic requirements, 153-54, 155, 159
Edwards Books and Art v. The Queen,
      174n16
Eisenberg, Avigail, 55
Eisgruber, C.L., 198n9
Elgin County, 154, 163, 164, 174n12
essentialism, 119-22, 128, 129
ethnic groups. *See* minority groups

feminist theory, 7, 11
  ethical feminism, 116-17
    approaches to culture, 117-30
Finland, 36, 82
Ford v. Quebec (Attorney General), 104
francophone schoolboards
  Mahe v. Alberta, 97, 103-6, 107-10
freedom of religion, 11
  Charter law and, 154
  constitutional protection of Protestant
      and Roman Catholic faiths, 155-56,
      161, 162, 167-68
  hate laws, 174n17
  historical contexts, 153-54, 155-59,
      167-68, 179-82, 191-93
  judgmentalism and, 153-60, 165-67
  v. secular values, 155, 160, 162-63, 164,
      165, 166-69, 178-82, 195-97
    distinctive nature of religious beliefs,
        184-89, 197n9
    reconciliatory possibilities, 169-73,
        189-97
freedoms, 9-11, 182-84, 193, 197n6
  freedom of association, 183
  freedom of conscience, 182, 186-88
  See also freedom of religion; indigenous
      freedoms; rights

gender. *See* feminist theory; women
governmentality, 56-57
Guesdon v. France, 36

*Hamlet of Baker Lake v. Minister of Indian
      Affairs and Northern Development*, 68,
      74n25
hate laws, 174n17
Henderson, James Youngblood, 101-2
Hopu v. France, 36, 83

Hutterites, 157, 165

ICCPR. *See* United Nations. *International Covenant on Civil and Political Rights*
identity
autonomy and, 60
freedoms and, 197n6
role of dialog in formation of, 22
identity claims, 134-35
benefits of assessment of, 46-48
children, 7, 134-35, 144, 149-51, 151n5
compared to adults, 141-42, 147-48
criteria for assessment of, 10, 46-48, 50
dimensions of identity, 136-42, 15lnn5-8
international institutions, 36
justification of, 142-144
problems in assessment of, 34-35, 36-37, 46
essentialism, 34, 35, 37, 41-44, 46, 106-7
evidentiary, 34, 35, 36, 37, 39, 40-41, 48
inscrutability, 36, 37, 38-40, 46
social conflict, 34, 35, 37, 44-46
indigenous freedoms
liberal culturalism and, 55, 56-58, 71-72
See also Aboriginal claims
Inter-American Commission on Human Rights, 82-83
international human rights, 36, 78-83, 85-86, 89-91
Protocol of San Salvador, 82-83, 89
See also headings beginning United Nations
Islamic Schools Federation of Ontario v. Ottawa Board of Education, 163-64

Jehovah's Witnesses, 153-54, 155, 159, 172
Jews, 158-59
Jones v. The Queen, 166

Kitok v. Sweden, 44, 85
Kymlicka, Will, 5-6, 8
definition of culture, 60-61, 87
liberal culturalism, 54-55, 57, 58-61, 63, 71-72, 73n4
minority rights taxonomy, 59, 64-67, 88

Lamer, Chief Justice, 100-2, 104
See also R. v. Van der Peet
language rights, 23, 36, 102-10, 110n1
Mahe v. Alberta, 97, 103-6, 107-10
Länsman v. Finland, 36, 82

legal tests, 50
distinctive culture test, 34, 35-36, 37, 48-49, 51n9, 67-68, 99-102, 107, 109
sliding scale test, 103, 107-8
title test, 68, 74n25
L'Heureux-Dubé, Justice, 101, 183
liberal-democratic states. *See* settler states
liberal multiculturalism, 54, 73n4
liberal nationalism, 54, 73n4
linguistic groups. *See* language rights
Lovelace v. Canada, 43-44, 51n10, 78

McConnell, Michael W., 184-86, 197n7, 197n9
McLachlin, Justice, 100, 101, 102
Mahe v. Alberta, 97, 103-6, 107-10
Manitoba
freedom of religion, 156, 157
Mennonites, 156, 157
minority groups, 1
group interests v. individual rights, 3, 6-75, 55
national v. non-national, 59, 64-67
oppression of individuals within, 43-44, 46, 51n10
See also language rights; struggles over recognition
Mitchell v. M.N.R., 69-70, 102
multiculturalism, 5-6
religious freedom and, 156-59, 168-69
See also cultural rights; minority groups

Narayan, Uma, 127
Nedelsky, Jennifer, 130n7
New Brunswick
freedom of religion, 156
norms of mutual recognition, 17-19, 21-23, 27, 30, 51n6
See also struggles over recognition

OAS. *See* Organization of American States
Okin, Susan Moller, 117-19
Ominayak v. Canada, 36, 78, 82
Ontario
freedom of religion, 153, 163-64
See also Elgin County; Zylberberg
Organization of American States
Protocol of San Salvador, 82-83, 89

Perepelkin v. Superintendent of Child Welfare (No.2), 158
political rationality. *See* governmentality
Posner, Richard, 184-86, 197n9
power, 62
concept of culture and, 61-63, 65-66

minority inequality and, 23, 29, 30
  See also colonial reasoning
Protocol of San Salvador, 82-83, 89

Quebec
  Ballantyne/Davidson/MacIntyre v. Canada,
    78, 93-94

R. *v. Big M Drug Mart,* 160, 172, 174n18,
    179, 180, 186-87, 197n2
R. v. Sparrow, 100, 107
R. v. Van der Peet, 35, 37, 45, 48-49, 51n9,
    67, 68, 97, 107, 108
Re Corporation of the Canadian Civil
    Liberties Association and the Minister of
    Education, 154, 163, 164, 174n12
Re Southern Rhodesia, 68-69
Re Zylberberg et al. and the Director of the
    Sudbury Board Education, 154, 163,
    164
recognition
  norms of mutual recognition, 17-19,
    21-23, 27, 30, 51n6
  politics of recognition, 5, 8
  See also struggles over recognition
reindeer husbandry, 43, 44, 82
religious beliefs and practices, 45-46
  distinctive nature, 184-89, 197n9
  role in people's lives
    views of Benjamin Berger, 172-73
    views of Justice Albie Sachs, 169-72
  See also freedom of religion
rights, 1-2, 9-11, 193
  international human rights, 36, 78-83,
    85-86, 89-91
  See also Canadian Charter of Rights and
    Freedoms; cultural rights; freedoms;
    language rights
Rodriguez v. British Columbia (Attorney
    General), 183
Ruman v. Board of Trustees of Lethbridge
    School District, 153

S. *v. Lawrence,* 169
Sachs, Albie (Justice), 169-72, 174n19
Sager, L.G., 198n9
salmon trading. *See R. v. Van der Peet*
Sami, 36, 43, 44, 82, 85
Saskatchewan
  freedom of religion, 157
school boards. *See* education
self-determination, 49, 65-67
settler states
  absence of culture, 63-64
  legitimacy, 55-56

relationships with indigenous peoples,
    55, 56, 61
  See also colonial reasoning; indigenous
    freedoms
Shachar, Ayelet, 130n5
Sikhs, 45
sliding scale test, 103, 107-8
South Africa, 169-72
Sto:lo First Nation
  R. v. Van der Peet, 35, 37, 45, 48-49, 51n9
struggles over recognition, 10, 27
  definition, 15, 16-17
  dialogical orientation, 10, 20-23
    civic freedom and, 16, 27-30
    reasonable dissent and, 24-26
  equality and, 22-23
  future trends in analyses, 30-31
  history of theoretical analyses, 15-16,
    19-26
  minority claims and, 22-23
  monological/finality orientation, 19-20,
    23-24, 26, 27, 28
  role of norms, 17-19, 21-23, 27
Sunday store openings. *See R. v. Big M*
    Drug Mart
Supreme Court of Canada, 183
  aboriginal rights and, 69-70
    distinctive culture test, 34, 35-36, 37,
    48-49, 51n9, 67-68, 99-102, 107, 109
    R. v. Van der Peet, 35, 37, 45, 48-49,
    51n9, 67, 68, 97, 107, 108
    title test, 68, 74n25
  Chief Justice Lamer, 100-2, 104
  freedom of religion, 160-61, 172
  inconsistent use of concept of culture,
    97, 99, 107-10
  Justice L'Heureux-Dubé, 101, 183
  Justice McLachlin, 100, 101, 102
  views on dissent, 25, 27
  See also Dickson, Chief Justice; *Mahe v.*
    Alberta
Sweden, 44, 85

Taylor, Charles, 5, 6, 7-8, 59
terra nullius hypothesis, 70-71, 75n27

UNESCO. *Declaration on the Principles*
    Governing International Cultural
    Cooperation, 89-90
United Nations
  Charter of the United Nations, 64-65
  Convention on the Rights of the Child, 135
  Declaration on the Human Rights of
    Individuals Who Are Not Nationals of
    the Country in Which They Live, 81

Declaration on the Rights of Persons Belonging to National or Ethnic, Religious or Linguistic Minorities, 90
Human Rights Committee, 82-83, 89, 93-94
International Covenant on Civil and Political Rights, 36, 49, 50n3, 64-65, 78, 82, 83, 89
United States
  freedom of religion, 155, 161, 167, 180, 185, 197n8

Van der Peet, Dorothy. *See R. v. Van der Peet*

Volpp, Leti, 125-26

Waldron, Jeremy
  views on identity claim issues, 38-41
Wisconsin v. Yoder, 141-42
women
  African-American women, 131n10
  as a category, 122-25, 131n14
  Lovelace v. Canada, 43-44, 51n10, 78

Zylberberg, 154, 163, 164

Gerald Baier
Courts and Federalism: Judicial Doctrine in the United States, Australia, and Canada (2006)

Randy K. Lippert
Sanctuary, Sovereignty, Sacrifice: Canadian Sanctuary Incidents, Power, and Law (2005)

James B. Kelly
Governing with the Charter: Legislative and Judicial Activism and Framers' Intent (2005)

Dianne Pothier and Richard Devlin (eds.)
Critical Disability Theory: Essays in Philosophy, Politics, Policy, and Law (2005)

Susan G. Drummond
Mapping Marriage Law in Spanish Gitano Communities (2005)

Louis A. Knafla and Jonathan Swainger (eds.)
Laws and Societies in the Canadian Prairie West, 1670-1940 (2005)

Ikechi Mgbeoji
Global Biopiracy: Patents, Plants, and Indigenous Knowledge (2005)

Florian Sauvageau, David Schneiderman, and David Taras,
with Ruth Klinkhammer and Pierre Trudel
The Last Word: Media Coverage of the Supreme Court of Canada (2005)

Gerald Kernerman
Multicultural Nationalism: Civilizing Difference, Constituting Community (2005)

Pamela A. Jordan
Defending Rights in Russia: Lawyers, the State, and Legal Reform in the Post-Soviet Era (2005)

Anna Pratt
Securing Borders: Detention and Deportation in Canada (2005)

Kirsten Johnson Kramar
Unwilling Mothers, Unwanted Babies: Infanticide in Canada (2005)

W.A. Bogart
Good Government? Good Citizens? Courts, Politics, and Markets in a Changing Canada (2005)

Catherine Dauvergne
Humanitarianism, Identity, and Nation: Migration Laws in Canada and Australia (2005)

Michael Lee Ross
First Nations Sacred Sites in Canada's Courts (2005)

Andrew Woolford
Between Justice and Certainty: Treaty Making in British Columbia (2005)

John McLaren, Andrew Buck, and Nancy Wright (eds.)
Despotic Dominion: Property Rights in British Settler Societies (2004)

Georges Campeau
From UI to EI: Waging War on the Welfare State (2004)

Alvin J. Esau
The Courts and the Colonies: The Litigation of Hutterite Church Disputes (2004)

Christopher N. Kendall
Gay Male Pornography: An Issue of Sex Discrimination (2004)

Roy B. Flemming
Tournament of Appeals: Granting Judicial Review in Canada (2004)

Constance Backhouse and Nancy L. Backhouse
The Heiress vs the Establishment: Mrs. Campbell's Campaign for Legal Justice (2004)

Christopher P. Manfredi
Feminist Activism in the Supreme Court: Legal Mobilization and the Women's Legal Education and Action Fund (2004)

Annalise Acorn
Compulsory Compassion: A Critique of Restorative Justice (2004)

Jonathan Swainger and Constance Backhouse (eds.)
People and Place: Historical Influences on Legal Culture (2003)

Jim Phillips and Rosemary Gartner
Murdering Holiness: The Trials of Franz Creffield and George Mitchell (2003)

David R. Boyd
Unnatural Law: Rethinking Canadian Environmental Law and Policy (2003)

Ikechi Mgbeoji
Collective Insecurity: The Liberian Crisis, Unilateralism, and Global Order (2003)

Rebecca Johnson
Taxing Choices: The Intersection of Class, Gender, Parenthood, and the Law (2002)

John McLaren, Robert Menzies, and Dorothy E. Chunn (eds.)
Regulating Lives: Historical Essays on the State, Society, the Individual, and the Law (2002)

Joan Brockman
Gender in the Legal Profession: Fitting or Breaking the Mould (2001)

Printed and bound in Canada by Friesens

Set in Stone by Artegraphica Design Co. Ltd.

Copy editor: Audrey McClellan

Proofreader: Stephanie VanderMeulen

Indexer: Christine Jacobs